"You should read this book with an ope[...] knows pastoral leadership. He took a team o[...] bus, Ohio, area and planted New Life Cor[...] averaging 2,000 in attendance. Dave knew how to involve his team of pastors, as well as hundreds of lay people, in reaching their part of the community for Christ; therefore, he understands pastoral leadership and will help you achieve that goal."

Dr. Elmer L. Towns, Cofounder, Liberty University
Dean, Liberty University School of Religion Liberty Baptist
Theological Seminary and Graduate School

"Dave Earley loves God, people, and pastoring. He has spent a lifetime praying, preaching, and planting churches. He can really help you get a grip on what it means to be a pastor and a leader. Don't miss his newest book. God will speak to you on every page."

Dr. Ed Hindson
Distinguished Professor, Liberty University
Host of *The King Is Coming*

"In his introduction Dave Earley clearly establishes his agenda—to redefine success in the life of a pastoral leader—moving us from a more traditional chaplaincy role to becoming spiritual warriors, missional leaders, and multiplying mentors. This book could not have been written at a better time! North America needs an army of pastoral leaders who embrace prayer, who teach the Word of God, and who lead and mentor leaders. Thanks, Dave, for another great, biblically based resource!"

Dr. John M. Bailey
North American Mission Board

"Sensing God's call to pastor? And what does that mean? Is *pastor* a verb or a noun? Where can I find the tools and information to discharge this calling faithfully and effectively? Dave Earley's book, *Pastoral Leadership*, is a simple yet thorough exposure to the knowledge and wisdom necessary for today's pastorate. Learning to be the pastor God wants you to be takes a lifetime—but it ought to start with this book."

Dr. Russ Barksdale
Pastor, The Church on Russ Creek, Arlington, Texas

"Here he goes again. His new book for equipping the next generation of church planters and pastors is something I have dreamed of attempting but lacked both the resources and resolve. The materials give a thorough overview of both the essential character traits and tasks associated with effective ministry. A unique feature of his writing is a spiritual depth that challenges the most mature believer coupled with a razor-sharp understanding of the most current church growth strategies. This book will become required reading for every minister called out from our Fellowship at Jersey."

John Hays
Senior Pastor, Jersey Baptist Church, Columbus, Ohio

"It seems like only yesterday that Dave and I were both planting churches on the east side of metro Columbus, Ohio. The two growing congregations enjoyed friendly competition that provided some motivation for our people to be more intentional in outreach. I believe this made us better pastors and our churches more effective in the work of the kingdom. Though I must admit I always felt Dave possessed 'intellectual properties' that gave him an advantage and he was always one step ahead of me!

"Satan is launching 'weapons of mass distraction' at today's pastors. Pastors need clarity and conviction about the core biblical priorities for the call to lead the church. Combining his extraordinary experience and excellent insight, Dave Earley delivers 31 chapters of practical wisdom that offer vital focus, spiritual fuel, and long-term fulfillment to those desiring to serve Christ and His church with integrity and impact."

Daniel Henderson
President, Strategic Renewal
National Director, The 6:4 Fellowship

"Whether you are preparing or currently serving in a pastoral role, Dave Earley's book is for you. His experiences as a church planter, pastor, mentor, and seminary professor make this a personal must read for the ministry leader. You will find it to be an incredible blend of both the practical and the spiritual. Earley describes the essentials—both the role and the being of the leader. Keep it close by, as you'll refer to it again and again."

Dr. Brad Hoffmann
Coauthor, *Preventing Ministry Failure*
Pastor, Cool Spring Baptist Church, Mechanicsville, Virginia

"Dr. Dave Earley provides fresh, practical insight for seasoned pastors and students training for ministry from what must be our primary source of information—the *Bible!* How often pastors get busy doing the work of ministry and neglect investing time alone with God in prayer and pouring over His Word as we fulfill the call to preach. All pastors need periodic priority adjustments. This book leads us to our knees with hope and grace. I appreciate Dave reminding me to continue developing my integrity intentionally. Not only are his words accurate and convicting; his clear honest approach to his own character development is a process I, as a pastor, can adapt for my own personal growth. I would encourage every pastor to get alone with God and slowly and honestly see if he can 'pass the test of me.' Being an authentic communicator, Dave encourages pastors to trust God's equipping and shaping for ministry. And, yet again, he gives the reader clear, practical, biblical information on the 'how to' of doing what God has called us to do. Pastors, read this book!"

Dr. Drew Landry
Senior Pastor, Spotswood Baptist Church, Fredericksburg, Virginia

"Dr. Dave Earley has become one of the most trusted authors and teachers for those of us on the front lines of daily ministry. From his wealth of experience in planting, growing and leading a successful church to his years of service as a seminary professor, Dr. Earley is uniquely qualified to write about pastoral leadership. With the profundity of simplicity Dr. Earley gives sound biblical guidance for those in ministry, as well as for those preparing for their vocational calling to God's work."

David Lemming
Pastor, Lewis Memorial Baptist Church, Huntington, West Virginia

"Our culture encourages and sometimes demands that pastors assume too many responsibilities. What was true in Acts is no different today—ministry can be all consuming. *Pastoral Leadership Is . . .* points us to the biblical perspective of narrowing our focus so we can lead and feed our congregations."

Ken Nienke
Pastor, Fellowship Community Church, Salem, Virginia

"Every once in a while you meet someone who doesn't fit the mold and challenges you in ways that inspire you to love Jesus more and be more passionate about His kingdom. Dave Earley is one of those individuals. I thank God for his impact on the kingdom and his investment in the next generation of leaders."

Vance Pitman
Senior Pastor, Hope Church, Las Vegas, Nevada

"This is truly a unique book because the author first determined to walk the walk before he decided to talk the talk! It is a book on pastoral leadership written by a very successful seminary professor. However, his insights did not proceed as much from an academic classroom as from a very busy pastor's study. You see, long before he was respectfully addressed as 'Dr. Earley' in Virginia, he was affectionately known as 'Pastor Dave' in Ohio, where he built a megachurch that is still flourishing since his departure. Thus, the fruit of his ministry as a scholar can be readily traced back to its root, namely, that of a faithful shepherd! Every pastor should secure this book!"

Dr. Harold Wilmington
Dean of the Wilmington School of the Bible for Liberty University
Best-selling author of *Wilmington's Guide to the Bible*

Pastoral
Leadership Is...

How to Shepherd God's People with Passion and Confidence

DAVE EARLEY

ACADEMIC
NASHVILLE, TENNESSEE

ISBN: 978-1-4336-7384-9

Published by B&H Publishing Group
Nashville, Tennessee

Dewey Decimal Classification: 253
Subject Heading: PASTORAL THEOLOGY \ LEADERSHIP \ CHURCH

Printed in the United States of America

4 5 6 7 8 9 10 • 22 21 20 19 18
VP

Contents

Part 3 Teaching the Word of God

Pastoral Leadership Is . . .

Part 4 Equipping and Leading Others

Pastoral Leadership Is . . .

Part 5 Shepherding God's Flock

Pastoral Leadership Is . . .

Foreword

What's going on?

At a time when 90 percent of American pastors surveyed feel inadequately trained to cope with ministry demands, we need some tools that will help them be prepared. In a day and age when 1,500 pastors leave the ministry permanently every month in America and surveys reveal that many more would leave if they could afford it, we need to give them all the help that we can.

Too often pastors and churches are becoming endangered species in the twenty-first century. Yet, that need not be the case. A return to the biblical priorities makes all the difference.

Yes, Jesus is still the hope of the world. Yes, the church is still the body of Jesus on earth. Yes, it is still true that as goes the church, so goes everything else, and as goes the pastor, so goes the church. When pastors return to biblical priorities, it still makes all the difference.

Godly integrity, passionate prayer, sound biblical teaching, and mentoring leadership are still the biblical priorities for pastors. We need more tools that focus on those priorities. Beyond that, those tools need to have been developed by ministry veterans who use them and use them well.

The book you hold in your hands is such a tool. *Pastoral Leadership Is . . .* is not a typical manual for pastoral students. It is ferociously biblical and passionately practical. While including traditionally important staples of pastoral books such as the pastor's character, the call to ministry, and how to perform a wedding, it contains so much more. Earley's approach centers on the biblical pastoral mandates to prioritize prayer, teach the Word, and develop leaders. Even though he has thirty years of pastoral ministry under his belt,

Earley does not think or act like an out-of-date old man. He is appreciated by students and colleagues alike for his knowledge of Scripture, his keen ability to convey deep truths in an understandable manner, and his contagious passion to glorify God in and through His church.

Dave Earley is a pastor who loves pastors. He has served as a collegiate campus pastor, a church planter, and a mega-church pastor, and he trains pastors. Two weekends a month he ministers in churches, encouraging pastors. He also trains pastors as a professor. His Pastoral Duties class is a popular staple our students rave about. He loves the church so much he is assuming the role of missionary church planter in launching a new church in Las Vegas, Nevada.

If you are investigating pastoral ministry, or are a young pastor or a seasoned veteran, I highly recommend *Pastoral Leadership Is . . . .* It will powerfully impact your life and ministry.

Your colaborer in Christ,

Ben Gutierrez, PhD
Associate Dean, Liberty University

Introduction: Read This First!

So you want to be a pastor.

Or at least you think God wants you to be a pastor.

Or somebody told you that you should be a pastor.

Or maybe you already are a pastor.

Great!

That is stellar. Being a pastor is a huge privilege and an immense joy.

But let me warn you right out of the gate. This is not going to be your ordinary book on pastoral ministry. I am not going to tell you as much about how to run a deacons meeting as I will about how to mentor men to make disciples. I strongly believe in the Western world that we have adopted an unbiblical model of pastoral leadership, and it is killing our churches and harming our people. Eighty-five percent of the churches in America are declining, and the percentage of people who are unchurched is doubling with every new generation.

Simply put, we have weakened pastors and undermined their calling by making them chaplains instead of releasing them to be the spiritual warriors, missional leaders, and multiplying mentors God calls pastors to be. This must change! You can be a part of the revolution.

Instead of falling into this prevalent practice in Western churches, let us return to what God has to say in the Bible about being a pastor. Be that person!

The goal of this book is just that. I am seeking to be intensely biblical as we strive together to understand what the Bible says about pastoral leadership.

Let me tell you where I am coming from. I have been a committed Christ follower for the last thirty-five years. As a twenty-two-year-old seminary student, I served a dysfunctional church as the associate and interim pastor. What a mess—not just in the way the church operated but in its ministry vision and impact!

Then I became the director of disciple-making and the campus pastor at a large Christian university. In that role I read everything written at the time on discipleship and grew as a leader. Cathy and I moved from there with some friends to start a church from scratch.

We moved on Saturday and started the church on Sunday in the basement of our apartment. It was a unique experiment, which amazingly grew into a megachurch. We started as a cell church. Wonderfully, 70 percent of our members did ministry. While there, we learned to launch our members out as church planters. We did contemporary worship before it was cool or common (thanks, Don Moen).

The last few years God has had me serving at the world's largest seminary responsible for training pastors and church planters. One summer I was assigned to teach an undergrad course on pastoral leadership. With only six weeks to prepare to teach, I went to the library and started reading all of the popular textbooks on the subject. Some were more biblical than others, but most of them presented a picture of pastoral ministry that muted the raw potential that I knew pulsed through the Scriptures.

So, I started reading the Bible, noting everything it said about pastoral leadership. What I found is that most of what the Bible has to say about pastoral leadership relates to the ministries of three main people: (1) Moses—the shepherd leader of Israel; (2) Jesus—the Good Shepherd and the mentor of the men who launched the first and prototypical church at Jerusalem; and (3) Paul—the radical church planter who coached the young pastors Timothy and Titus.

I was reminded again that the Bible clearly lays out three main responsibilities of a pastor: (1) pray, (2) teach the Word, and (3) lead and mentor leaders.

I also saw that effectively doing the work of pastor flowed from living the right type of life and being the right type of person—one with (1) clear calling, (2) Christlike character, and (3) consuming love for Jesus.

So the purpose of this book is to demonstrate from the godly examples of these men that the pastor's calling is shaped by three main responsibilities and that the effectiveness of the pastor's ministry depends (at least in part) on his character.

As you begin, let me give you a bit of advice.

You won't get it all at once.

Learning to lead a church with passion and confidence can seem a little like eating an elephant. You don't "get it" all down in one bite. You have to "eat it one bite at a time," learning a little more each week.

Chew it slowly.

This book was not designed to be rapidly read and quickly forgotten. It was prayerfully put together with the goal of changing your life. It will explain the what, why, and how of pastoral leadership. Read it with a pen in hand to mark it up and make notes in the margin. Personalize it. Let it mark your life by making it *your* book.

At the end of every chapter you will find "What Now?" challenges to challenge you to apply what you have just read. There will be some good quotes to encourage or motivate you.

Read it all.

I want to encourage you to read all thirty-one chapters. You may want to read one a day for the next month. You will want to make it a regular appointment in your schedule.

Get a cup of coffee, grab a pen for note-taking, and dive in.

I pray that this simple book will become a big book in your life. May it become your coach, equipping encourager, and idea catalyst for a lifetime of making an eternal difference for the glory of God.

—Dave Earley

1

Focusing on the Things Every Pastor Simply Must Do

Incredible!

Moses and the people of God had just experienced the incredible power of God as He delivered them from being the slaves of Egypt. Through the deliberate use of ten miraculous plagues, God had not only struck down the Egyptians' religion, but had shown His great power and His deep compassion for His people.

Annoying!

It would be easy to feel a little sorry for Moses. At this point, he was more than eighty years old and stuck in the desert with tens of thousands of irritable and immature people.

Instead of sitting back to enjoy retirement, he was leading one of the most frustrating mobs ever assembled. The Israelites had spent decades in slavery, and their new liberty quickly turned to license. Every time he turned around, Moses found them either rebelling or griping.

Moses felt the weight of the responsibility and the depth of the frustration of leading the Hebrew nation safely through the wiles of the wilderness into

5

the Promised Land when they would have preferred to return to the familiar bondage of Egypt. Shepherding them was like trying to herd cats.

Ridiculous!

Moses was trying to be everyone's pastor, chaplain, counselor, and judge. Jethro, his father-in-law, happened to be visiting. Jethro, a veteran shepherd who oversaw massive herds in Midian, noticed how Moses was shepherding Israel. He could see that Moses was not being very effective.

> When Moses' father-in-law saw everything he was doing for them he asked, "What is this thing you're doing for the people? Why are you alone sitting as judge, while all the people stand around you from morning until evening?" Moses replied to his father-in-law, "Because the people come to me to inquire of God. Whenever they have a dispute, it comes to me, and I make a decision between one man and another. I teach [them] God's statutes and laws." "What you're doing is not good," Moses' father-in-law said to him. "You will certainly wear out both yourself and these people who are with you, because the task is too heavy for you. You can't do it alone. (Exod 18:14–18)

Amnesia!

Moses knew better than to be the solo-shepherd for the flock of God. God had strategically placed Moses with Jethro for the previous decades in order for Moses to learn the nuances of leading a large flock in difficult terrain. But for some reason, when the people clamored for help, Moses forgot all he had learned and defaulted to trying to meet their needs himself. It was the pathway to burnout and the prescription for failure.

Avoiding the Trap

The majority of the churches in America are struggling. As many as 85 percent of the churches in the United States are plateaued or in decline.[1] Most of the struggling churches are led by a solo-pastor, who is falling into the same trap that swallowed Moses. Instead of leading a large, healthy, growing flock into the Promised Land, these "Lone Ranger" pastors are struggling to keep an aging flock of an average of seventy members alive. They are expending all of their energies trying to be everyone's pastor, chaplain, and counselor, all the while missing the three things every pastor simply must do.

Beyond the struggles of the churches, the majority of the pastors in the United States are struggling personally. The grind of the demands of the solo-pastor is burning American pastors out. Licensed professional counselor Michael Todd Wilson and veteran pastor Brad Hoffman report the following sobering statistics in their book *Preventing Ministry Failure.*

- 90 percent of American pastors surveyed feel inadequately trained to cope with ministry demands.
- 45 percent say they have experienced depression or burnout to the extent that they needed to take a leave of absence.[2]

Every month, 1,500 pastors leave the ministry permanently in America. Many more would leave if they could afford it. In a recent survey, more than 50 percent of pastors said they would leave their ministry if they could replace their income.[3]

In their book *Pastors at Greater Risk*, H. B. London and Neil Wiseman quote startling statistics from research conducted by Fuller Theological Seminary. These statistics are the reflection of the trap of the "Lone Ranger" pastor.

- 80 percent of pastors say they have insufficient time with spouse and that ministry has a negative effect on their family.
- 40 percent report a serious conflict with a parishioner once a month.
- 75 percent report they have had a significant stress-related crisis at least once in their ministry.
- 45 percent of pastors' wives say the greatest danger to them and family is physical, emotional, mental, and spiritual burnout.
- 21 percent of pastors' wives want more privacy.
- Pastors who work fewer than fifty hours a week are 35 percent more likely to be terminated.
- 40 percent of pastors considered leaving the pastorate in the past three months.
- 25 percent of pastors' wives see their husband's work schedule as a source of conflict.
- 48 percent of pastors think being in ministry is hazardous to family well-being.[4]

Of course, this is not the way God planned it. What is the problem? Part of the problem is too many pastors expend all of their energies trying to be the solo-pastor, chaplain, and counselor and are failing to focus on the three things every pastor simply must do.

A Plea for Sanity and the Three Things
Every Spiritual Shepherd Simply Must Do

Wise Counsel

God used Jethro to speak into Moses' life. As a wise advisor, he not only told Moses that what he was doing was wrong, but he also took the next step and told Moses what it was that he needed to do to correct it.

> Now listen to me; I will give you some advice, and God be with you. You be the one to represent the people before God and bring their cases to Him. Instruct them about the statutes and laws, and teach them the way to live and what they must do. But you should select from all the people able men, God-fearing, trustworthy, and hating bribes. Place [them] over the people as officials of thousands, hundreds, fifties, and tens. They should judge the people at all times. Then they can bring you every important case but judge every minor case themselves. In this way you will lighten your load, and they will bear [it] with you. If you do this, and God [so] directs you, you will be able to endure, and also all these people will be able to go home satisfied." (Exod 18:19–23)

Jethro's advice is crammed with insight and wisdom. Before we see the requirements, let's look at the results. Notice that in verses 22–23 Jethro promises Moses that if he focuses on doing the three things every pastor must do, leadership will be less stressful for him, and he will be able to endure the strain of shepherding a massive flock. On top of that, the people will prosper. That is better than a struggling flock with a burnt-out shepherd.

So what are the three things every spiritual shepherd simply must do?

1. Pray—"Be the one to represent the people before God and bring their cases to Him" (v. 19).
2. Teach the people how to live the Word of God—"Instruct them about the statutes and laws, and teach them the way to live and what they must do" (v. 20).
3. Equip and mentor the next layers of leaders—"Select from all the people able men, God-fearing, trustworthy, and hating bribes. Place [them] over the people as officials of thousands, hundreds, fifties, and tens" (v. 21).

Jesus and the Three Things Every Pastor Simply Must Do

Jesus is the Good Shepherd (John 10:11). If anyone can offer insight into that on which an effective spiritual shepherd should concentrate, it is Jesus. So what did Jesus focus on in His ministry? Did He attend board meetings, visit hospitals, or do counseling?

So what did He do?

You guessed it. Jesus primarily focused on the same three things Jethro told Moses to do: pray, teach the Word, and lead leaders.

1. Pray

Yes, Jesus is God, but do not miss the fact that Jesus Christ was also an amazing man of prayer. Samuel Dickey Gordon summarizes the prayer life of the leader Jesus when he writes, "The *man* Christ Jesus *prayed*; prayed *much*; *needed* to pray; *loved* to pray."[5] He added, "Jesus prayed. He loved to pray. . . . He prayed so much and so often that it became a part of His life. It became to Him like breathing—involuntary."[6] Edward M. Bounds concurs, "Prayer filled the life of our Lord while on earth. . . . Nothing is more conspicuous in the life of our Lord than prayer."[7]

Yes, I have heard the argument that we cannot pray like He did because He was the Son of God. But, that is the point. If Jesus Christ, the Son of God and the Son of Man, needed to pray, *how much more* do you and I?

In the Gospels there are fifteen accounts of Jesus praying. Eleven are found in Luke's Gospel. Why? The answer is that of the four Gospel writers, Luke focused most on the *human* aspect of Jesus. Luke wanted us to see that, as a *human* leader, Jesus lived a life of prayer. Jesus was fully God *and* fully man. If Jesus, the human, made time to pray, *how much more* should you and I?

2. Teach the Word

Jesus was a powerful biblical preacher. Jesus' first sermon was quoting the law to Satan (Deut 6:13,16; 8:3) and skillfully applying it to the situation (Matt 4:1–11). His second sermon was a dramatic reading of Isa 61:1–2 and the proclamation that this Scripture was being fulfilled as He spoke. As a rabbi, He had to know the Word of God thoroughly and teach it.

3. Equip and Mentor Leaders

Jesus was the master disciple-maker. Being Jewish, Jesus followed a rabbinical model of disciple development. He selected and called twelve to be with Him for training in ministry (Mark 1:16–20; 3:12–19). The climax of His ministry to them was His commissioning of them to be disciple-makers also (Matt 28:18–20). He developed His leaders, and they were able to carry on the ministry and take it to the world after He ascended into Heaven.

The Apostles and the Three Things Every Pastor Simply Must Do

The apostles started the church in Jerusalem with huge success—three thousand people baptized the first day and others saved daily (Acts 2:41–47). This amazing growth led to inevitable growing pains. Soon the apostles found themselves getting sucked into the trap of doing the ministry themselves and neglecting the three things pastors simply must do. This was not good for them, and it was causing some of the flock to be neglected.

Wisely, they called for an adjustment in priorities. They returned to prayer, teaching the Word, and leading by developing and deploying other leaders.

> Then the Twelve summoned the whole company of the disciples and said, "It would not be right for us to give up preaching about God to wait on tables. Therefore, brothers, select from among you seven men of good reputation, full of the Spirit and wisdom, whom we can appoint to this duty. But we will devote ourselves to prayer and to the preaching ministry." (Acts 6:2–4)

They chose to follow the same advice that Jethro had given Moses. They asked the church to help them to concentrate their energies on the things every spiritual shepherd simply must do.

1. Pray—"We will devote ourselves to prayer" (v. 4).
2. Teach the Word of God—"It is not right that we should give up preaching the word of God . . . we will devote ourselves to . . . the ministry of the word" (vv. 2–4 ESV).
3. Lead by developing and deploying other leaders—"Pick out from among you seven men of good repute, full of the Spirit and of wisdom, whom we will appoint to this duty" (v. 3 ESV).

How did it work? The good news is that the church agreed and supported them. As a result, God was able to richly bless them and grow the church.

> The proposal pleased the whole company. So they chose Stephen, a man full of faith and the Holy Spirit, and Philip, Prochorus, Nicanor, Timon, Parmenas, and Nicolaus, a proselyte from Antioch. They had them stand before the apostles, who prayed and laid their hands on them. So the preaching about God flourished, the number of the disciples in Jerusalem multiplied greatly, and a large group of priests became obedient to the faith. (Acts 6:5–7)

Paul and the Three Things Every Pastor Simply Must Do

Paul was the mentor of several young pastors, including Timothy. We are fortunate to have several of the letters Paul gave Timothy detailing how he was to fulfill his spiritual shepherding responsibilities. Like Jesus and the apostles, there is no mention of many of the responsibilities that we assume as essential for pastors in our Western context. Paul says nothing about committee meetings, hospital visitation, or performing funeral services.

Instead, just as we saw from Jethro and Moses, Jesus, and the apostles, Paul encouraged Timothy to focus on three essential tasks: pray, teach the Word, and lead leaders.

1. Pray

Paul intentionally reminded Timothy of the importance of prayer. He advised Timothy that as the spiritual shepherd for the church at Ephesus, one task was priority one—prayer.

> First of all, then, I urge that petitions, prayers, intercessions, and thanksgivings be made for everyone. . . . (1 Tim 2:1)

2. Teach the Word

Throughout his letters to Timothy, Paul reminds him of the importance of sound teaching. Paul commanded Timothy to "Do your best to present yourself to God as one approved, a workman who does not need to be ashamed and who correctly handles the word of truth (2 Tim 2:15 NIV). He further charged him to "preach the word" (2 Tim 4:2 NIV).

3. Lead

Paul had modeled the importance of mentoring rising leaders to Timothy when he took Timothy under his wing during his church-planting trips. In his letters, Paul told Timothy that one of his primary responsibilities was to also train faithful men who would be able to disciple others.

> And what you have heard from me in the presence of many witnesses, commit to faithful men who will be able to teach others also. (2 Tim 2:2)

Beyond that, Paul told Timothy's congregation, the Ephesians, that Timothy and the other pastor-teachers that might have been in their church were Christ's gift to the church (Eph 4:11). He also said that the responsibility of those pastors was to equip each member to do the work of ministry (Eph 4:12). Doing so results in the growth of the members *and* the increase of the body.

> And He personally gave . . . some pastors and teachers, for the training of the saints in the work of ministry, to build up the body of Christ, . . . From Him the whole body, fitted and knit together by every supporting ligament, promotes the growth of the body for building up itself in love by the proper working of each individual part. (Eph 4:11–12,16)

Warning!

While this book will discuss some of the pastoral responsibilities that fit within the cultural idea of an American pastor, that is not the emphasis. In an attempt to be as biblical as possible, the lion's share of this book will focus on inspiring and instructing pastors in the three tasks every effective spiritual shepherd simply must do: *Pray, Teach the Word,* and *Lead.*

Of course, we will also discuss the type of person a pastor must be. We will conclude with an overview of some of the other activities in which a shepherd-leader must be involved.

⁓ What Now? ⁓

I suggest that a pastor spends at least 25 percent of his time investing in prayer, 25 percent in studying and teaching the Word, and 25 percent equipping saints and developing leaders. This means in a sixty-hour work week, he's spending fifteen hours praying with and for people, fifteen hours studying and teaching, and fifteen hours developing potential multipliers. How can you begin to implement this ratio in your current ministry?

～ Quote ～

The timeworn work of the pastor, such as solid exegetical
preaching, prayer and disciple-making, [has] gone out of style.

—BILL HULL[8]

Notes

1. Win Arn, *The Pastor's Manual for Effective Ministry* (Monrovia, CA: Church Growth, 1988), 41, 43.

2. Michael Todd Wilson and Brad Hoffman, *Preventing Ministry Failure* (Downers Grove, IL: InterVarsity, 2007), 31.

3. *Focus on the Family*, 1998 as quoted by Ken Sande of Peacemaker Ministries in an article titled, "Strike the Shepherd," http://www.peacemaker.net/site/apps/nlnet/content3.aspx?c=aqKFLTOBIpH&b=1084263&ct=1245867 (accessed April 1, 2011).

4. H. B. London Jr. and Neil Wiseman, *Pastors at Greater Risk* (Ventura, CA: Regal, 2003), 33–60.

5. Samuel Dickey Gordon, *Quiet Talks on Prayer* (Grand Rapids, MI: Baker, 1980), 211.

6. Ibid., 209.

7. Edward M. Bounds, *The Reality of Prayer* (Grand Rapids, MI: Baker, 1978), 69, 73.

8. Bill Hull, *The Disciple-Making Pastor* (Grand Rapids, MI: Fleming Revell, 1988), 41.

Part 1
Being a Man of God

2

Abandoning All to Follow the Call

*The first and foremost of all the inward strengths of a pastor is
the conviction, deep as life itself, that God has called him
to ministry.*

—W. A. CRISWELL[1]

Moses

Poof!

Without warning, a muffled explosion shook the quietness of the morning.

The shepherd stopped and stared, stunned and silent.

A large acacia thorn bush had burst into flames. The golden tongues of fire danced in the sun above the floor of the desert. Amazingly, they did not consume a leaf, scorch a twig, or whither even one of the delicate flowers of the small tree.

This amazing phenomenon compelled the shepherd to draw closer to the bush. Mysteriously, there was no smoke—just flame . . . and a voice.

The voice called his name, "Moses, Moses!" (Exod 3:4).

For Moses this was his defining moment. He encountered the living God in the miraculous burning bush and his life would never be the same. In the next few moments, <u>the Lord called Moses to go back to Egypt to deliver the enslaved Hebrews from the Egyptians and to lead them to the Promised Land.</u>

After his initial reluctance, Moses abandoned his comfortable life in Midian, faced down the most powerful man on earth, and delivered God's people from slavery. Moses obeyed his calling, and the rest is history.

Before he was ready to shepherd God's flock passionately and effectively, Moses had to abandon his life to obey the call of God.

Nine Distinguishing Marks of the Call in the Bible

Reading through all the Bible passages describing the various calls extended to the characters of the Bible reveals nine challenging characteristics. As you read this summary of how God worked in the past, ask the Lord to speak to you about His call for your future.

1. The calling originates from God.

God approached Moses and got his attention through a burning bush. Over and over in the Bible, the Lord approached those He wanted *before* they approached Him. For example, Jeremiah described his calling with these words, "The word of the LORD came to me. . . . I set you apart before you were born. I appointed you a prophet to the nations" (Jer 1:4–5).

True pastoral leadership is a supernatural experience. It is a God-thing. It is born in the heart of God and is initiated by the promptings of God.

2. The calling comes to those who are listening with a heart to obey.

The Lord was looking for a prophet to speak to the wayward nation of Israel. He bypassed Eli, the priest, and his wicked sons. Instead, the Lord went to someone He knew who had the heart to obey, a young boy named Samuel. Notice Samuel's response.

> The LORD came, stood there, and called as before, "Samuel, Samuel!"
> Samuel responded, "Speak, for Your servant is listening." (1 Sam 3:10)

The Hebrew word "listen" (*shamah*) implies more than physical ability to process sounds. It speaks of a hearing *with the purpose of obedience*. God calls those willing to trust Him enough to say yes.

Years later when the Lord again needed a prophet to speak to His people, He again looked for someone who was fully available and had a heart to obey. When the Lord asked, "Who should I send? Who will go?" Isaiah's response was immediate availability, "Here I am. *Send me*" (Isa 6:8, italics added).

3. *The calling is often overwhelming.*

If the call is not so big that it overwhelms you, and if it does not scare you to death, you probably have not heard from God. When Moses received his calling from the Lord, he was crushed by the immensity of the challenge. His immediate response was, "Who am I that I should go to Pharaoh and that I should bring the Israelites out of Egypt?" (Exod 3:11).

Noah was called to the incredible task of building a huge boat in preparation for a global flood *in a world that had never even seen rain!* When the Lord called Gideon to defeat the terrifying Midianites, he was so overwhelmed he asked God for three specific signs of confirmation.

When the Lord asked Joshua to fill the shoes of the legendary leader Moses in order to lead the Hebrews to conquer a land full of strong enemies, Joshua was hesitant. So the Lord gave him a strong pep talk (Josh 1:1–9).

The call will humble you and scare you. It will demand everything out of you and drive you to greater dependency upon God.

4. *Obeying the call involves leaving your comfort zone.*

Obeying your calling is about abandoning yourself, not catering to yourself. Fulfilling your calling will involve taking risks. It will be inconvenient.

Too many miss their calling because they are addicted to their comfort zone. They fear pain or hardness or difficulty. They want to sit on the sidelines and soak in God.

But God is on the frontlines, not the sidelines. To follow Him you must *go* where it is not easy. Henry Blackaby and Claude King write, "You cannot continue life as usual or stay where you are, and go with God at the same time."[2]

One repeated theme seen in the various callings we see in the Bible is the command, "Go!" Look at these examples.

> The LORD said to Abram: *Go* out from your land, your relatives, and your father's house to the land that I will show you. (Gen 12:1, italics added)

> Then the LORD said . . . "Therefore, *go.* I am sending you to Pharaoh so that you may lead My people, the Israelites, out of Egypt. (Exod 3:7,10, italics added)

> The LORD turned to him and said, "*Go* in the strength you have and deliver Israel from the power of Midian. Am I not sending you?" (Judg 6:14, italics added)

Then I heard the voice of the Lord saying: Who should I send? Who will
go for Us? I said: Here I am. Send me. And He replied: *Go!* (Isa 6:8–9,
italics added)

The word of the Lord came to Jonah . . . "Get up! *Go* to the great city of
Nineveh and preach against it, because their wickedness has confronted
Me." (Jonah 1:1–2, italics added)

5. The calling is accompanied with the promise of God's protection and provision.

The calling is not to leave God in order to serve Him. Instead it is to go
with God as you serve Him. Obeying your calling draws you into a closer relationship with the Lord than you would experience otherwise.

To Moses, the Lord promised—"I will certainly be with you, and this will
be the sign to you that I have sent you" (Exod 3:12). In the face of Gideon's
protests, He said, "But I will be with you" (Judg 6:16). To Joshua God said,
"Do not be afraid or discouraged, for the Lord your God is with you wherever
you go" (Josh 1:9).

6. Obeying the calling unleashes your personality and makes you bigger and better than you could otherwise be.

When we first see Gideon, he is hiding in a hole, thrashing wheat in fear
that the enemy might see him. Yet, the call of God so transforms him that
he later earns the name "Mighty Warrior." Soon we see him taking down the
mighty Midian army with a tiny army of only three hundred men!

Noah saved humanity and animal life from destruction. Abraham became
the father of nations. Moses became the leader of an entire nation. David became
the king of Israel. Paul took the gospel to the world.

You have immense, untapped potential, but it will never be realized until
you take the bold step of faith to fulfill your calling. As you do, God will do
more in you, for you, and through you than you ever imagined possible.

7. A calling may take a long time to be fulfilled.

The ultimate fulfillment of a calling requires patience and perseverance.
God called Paul to take the gospel to the Gentiles. Before launching into his
mission, Paul spent the next three years alone in Arabia preparing for the ministry to which he was called (Gal 1:15–20). Joseph was called to be a leader as
a teen, but he was in slavery and prison until he became Egypt's prime minster
at the age of thirty.

David was called to be king when he also was a teen, but he lived as a fugitive until he was made Judah's king at age thirty and Israel's king at age thirty-seven. Abraham was called to father nations at the age of seventy-five (Genesis 12, 15). However, Abraham's son Isaac was not born until twenty-four years later when Abe was ninety-nine years old (Rom 4:19). The complete fulfillment of Moses' calling did not occur until forty years later when Joshua led the people into the Promised Land.

When God calls, be patient. Your responsibility is to take your next step.

8. The calling must be obeyed.

The primary issue for the servant of the Lord is *obedience*. The call must not only be heard, but it also must be obeyed. Noah, Abraham, Moses, Isaiah, and the rest are not distinguished because they heard the call of God. No, what sets them apart is that they took action and obeyed the call of God.

After God dropped the huge responsibility of building a gigantic boat and saving the world from the coming global flood, the Bible simply states, "And Noah did this. He did everything that God had commanded him" (Gen 6:13,22). After God called Abraham to leave his homeland and go to Canaan, the Bible simply says, "So Abram went" (Gen 12:1,4–5).

Gordon MacDonald writes, "Once you are called, financial security, location, notoriety, applause, and power become increasingly less important. Obedience becomes the primary issue. Let others feel free to build fortunes and empires; the call binds you to surrender to the will of God."[3]

When God calls, the only right response is yes. Your job is to obey and let God work out the details.

9. Running from your calling hurts you and others.

God called Jonah to go and preach repentance to the pagan people of Nineveh (Jonah 1:1–2). As you know, Jonah refused to obey and instead, tried to run from God by getting on a boat headed in the opposite direction (Jonah 1:3). As a result of Jonah's disobedience, a bunch of innocent sailors were nearly killed (Jonah 1:4–14). Jonah himself was thrown into a violent sea and only lived because God sent a big fish to swallow him (Jonah 1:15–17). On top of that, the people of the city of Nineveh would have missed hearing the Word of God.

Saying no to God's call is unwise and costly. Resisting God will leave you miserable or worse. Running from your calling will hurt others and cause many to miss out on what the Lord had for them through you.

The Call to Ministry Defined

A calling is different from a career choice. A career is what you're *paid* for, but a calling is what you're *made* for. Understanding the difference between the two can make all the difference between fulfillment and frustration.

Think of a calling as "a compelling invitation." The call to salvation is the compelling invitation to trust Jesus Christ as your Savior. The call to ministry is a compelling invitation to cooperate with God in advancing His kingdom and building His church as a vocational pursuit. A specific ministry call is a compelling invitation to cooperate with God in ministering: in a specific way (global missions, church planting, pastoring, preaching, worship leading); in a specific place (a city, a region, a country, or a people group); or to a specific group of people (such as children, teens, college students, or the least reached).

On rare occasions, a person may receive all three calls at once. But usually the calls are separate and spaced out somewhat in time.

Professor James Bryant and Pastor Mac Brunson state, "As much as anything, answering God's call is a step of faith. It is like enlisting in the army; you put your life and future in someone else's hands."[4]

I define and describe the call to church ministry as an inner conviction from God confirmed by the church, verified by giftedness, and supported by results. It is an unmistakable sense that I have been summoned by the Lord to lifelong vocational service in building His church.

The term *vocation* comes from the Latin word for *voice*. A *vocation* is an occupation that one does as a result of hearing God's voice. The initial use of the concept of the word *calling* was always tied to vocational Christian work, and the word *vocation* was only used to describe church ministry. Keith Drury writes, "While it is true God calls everyone to minister to others . . . God does not call everyone into professional ministry as a lifetime vocation."[5]

The Manner of Calling

Most of the examples of calling we see occurring in the Bible and especially in the Old Testament occurred in moments, often spectacular, extraordinary moments. However, this is not always the case. Longtime pastor and author Gordon MacDonald writes:

> For some of us, the call-story is dramatic. In one forceful moment, you gain a sense of conviction that God has spoken and directed. You are never the same again. For others, like myself, the call is like a continual dripping; it just beats on you until you capitulate.[6]

Glenn Wagner's call was on the lines of a continual dripping. He writes,

> There was for me a constant awareness that God was after me. No matter
> what I did, I couldn't escape the thought that God said, "You're mine."
> Right before I turned 21, I surrendered to the Lord, I could not get away
> from the impression that I was to be a pastor. It was an "F.I.F.," Funny
> Interior Feeling. It was constantly there. I could not see myself being
> anything else.[7]

Among my young pastoral students, the calling is mostly a continual dripping. However, among older pastors most state that their call was specific and
dramatic. According to research compiled by *Christianity Today*, 62 percent of
pastors surveyed indicated that calling was defined by specific events, but for
37 percent the call was a gradual process of slow realization.[8]

Paul instructed Timothy and Titus to select elders to lead the churches
(1 Timothy 3; Titus 1). The selection of these men was not a mystic, magical
moment as much as it was recognition of long-proven character.

Evidence of Calling

No one should pursue a life of vocational pastoral ministry unless they are
certain that it is what God wants them to do. There are several indicators that
help authenticate such a calling.

1. Results

Often the confirmation God grants comes to us through the results He
gives. For example, Jerry Falwell was wrestling with the call of God to be a pastor. He had been successfully working in the youth ministry when his senior
pastor asked him to preach. Falwell prayed that God would confirm or deny
the call through the results of that Sunday's message.

After Jerry's sermon, several people responded to his invitation to trust
Christ as Savior. But one of those coming to be saved was an elderly woman. She
told Falwell that, while she had been a member of the church for many years, she
had never been saved. That day it became clear to her that she was not saved and
needed to be. What the Lord did in her life that day was the confirmation Jerry
needed to know that he was indeed called into the pastoral ministry.

The person with the calling leaves a mark for God. Lives are impacted.
Lost people are drawn to Christ. Christians are encouraged, instructed, or
motivated.

2. Giftedness

With a call comes giftedness. The called person is divinely enabled to do what it is God has called him to do. It is obvious that the called person has received the God-given ability to serve Him with God-honoring impact and results.

3. Increased Intensity

The great preacher, pastor, and mentor Charles Spurgeon spoke to his pastoral ministry students of the intense nature of a calling. He said, "The first sign of a heavenly calling is an intense, all-absorbing desire for the work. . . . I have such a profound respect for this 'fire in the bones,' that if I did not feel it myself, I would leave the ministry at once."[9]

If someone is called and is walking with the Lord, the desire to serve the Lord deepens and continually intensifies. Drury writes,

> An authentic call gets stronger, not weaker over time. But a call does not grow in clarity all by itself. A call grows clearer as we respond to what we've already sensed. . . . Once we begin to respond to God's initial call, He often turns up the volume of His inner voice. . . . [M]ost of us move through several years of this "dance" with God.[10]

4. Sense of Completeness, Rightness, and Joy

You can know when you are fulfilling your calling because service in that area is accompanied by great energy and inner peace. You feel like "this is what God made me for." It feels right, and you feel complete. You can serve all day in that area and not be exhausted. Jeremiah said that obeying his calling and sharing the Word of God brought him great joy (Jer 15:16).

5. Consuming Conviction

Pastoral ministry is not glamorous. It is not easy. Stepping up to give leadership in a church puts a larger target on our backs for the enemy to attack us. The financial compensation rarely matches the work given. Therefore, it is no wonder that Spurgeon advised, "Do not enter the ministry if you can help it."[11]

But when you have a calling you can do nothing else. You will be inwardly miserable doing anything other than obeying the call. You have a consuming conviction and compulsion; you have a driving passion. There is a sense that this thing inside must be acted upon.

∼ What Now? ∼

Have you ever experienced the clear, unmistakable call of God? It can change everything. Maybe you have recognized the call to ministry in general as your life vocation and now you are wrestling with the call to a specific ministry. Maybe you still need some confirmation of your calling. Maybe you have said your yes to the Lord and are now awaiting more specifics.

If you are unclear, let me offer some advice. Take some extra time alone with God. Consider fasting as you pray.

Tell God, "Whatever You ask of me, I am willing to obey. Anywhere You want me, I am willing to go. Whatever the price, I will pay it."

"I need to know if this calling really is from You."

"If this calling is from You, please confirm it."

∼ Quote ∼

We are not workers for God by our own choice. . . . Never choose to be a worker, but when once God has put His call on you, woe be to you if you turn to the right hand or to the left. God will do with you what He never did with you before the call came. . . . Let Him have His way.

—J. OSWALD CHAMBERS[12]

Notes

1. Wally Amos Criswell, *Criswell's Guidebook for Pastors* (Nashville, TN: B&H, 1980), 345.

2. Henry Blackaby and Claude King, *Experiencing God* (Nashville, TN: B&H, 1988), 147–48.

3. Gordon MacDonald, "God's Calling Plan: So What Exactly Is 'A Call to Ministry?'" *Leadership Journal* (Fall 2003): 37.

4. Mac Brunson and James Bryant, *The New Guidebook for Pastors* (Nashville, TN: B&H, 2007), 16.

5. Keith Drury, *The Call of a Lifetime* (Indianapolis, IN: Wesleyan, 2003), 34.

6. MacDonald, "God's Calling Plan," 37.

7. Glenn Wagner, "Called to What?" *Leadership Journal* (Fall 2003): 26.

8. "Research Report on Pastoral Leadership, *Christianity Today,*" *Leadership Journal* (Fall 2003): 26.

9. Charles Haddon Spurgeon, *Lectures to My Students* (Grand Rapids, MI: Zondervan, 1954), 28.

10. Drury, *The Call of a Lifetime*, 38.

11. Spurgeon, *Lectures to My Students*, 38.

12. Oswald Chambers, *Approved Unto God* (Grand Rapids, MI: Discovery House, 1946), 9.

3

Cultivating
Godly Integrity

*Great achievement plus weak character equals disaster. Keep
your character strong and your influence will be irresistible.*
— STAN TOLER[1]

Several years ago, when I was a young pastor, one of my heroes fell. He was
the most gifted Bible teacher I had ever heard. Brilliant and full of charisma,
he was able to make even the oft overlooked sections of the Old Testament
burst into life. As a speaker, he was in demand all over the country.

Yet, the last time I had heard him speak I sensed something was wrong. It
was odd. Uncharacteristically, he labored through his message. I did not sense
the usual anointing that had always marked his delivery. What was wrong?

A few weeks later it all made sense.

The truth came out that he had been cheating on his wife.

The discovery of his lack of integrity was devastating for his children, his
wife, his health, and the many people who looked to him for leadership. Those
closest to him wrestled with intense feelings of shock, anger, betrayal, and deep
hurt. He had sinned, cheated, lied, denied, and deceived.

It did not have to happen. Of all people, he knew better. There were people
around him who loved and respected him and who would have gladly helped.
But it happened—leaving his family and his church struggling to get through
the aftermath of this awful, ugly episode.

Years later, he shared with me that he had become so busy in ministry that he had neglected his personal time with God. He started believing that he did not need this time anymore. He had experienced great success and possessed great gifting, and he began to think he could live above personal accountability.

The truth is, no one can survive ministry without being nurtured by God's word and living in loving accountability with other believers. Success and gifts cannot sustain moral character and protect us from temptation.

Personal integrity and godly character are the foundations for authentic, God-blessed pastoral leadership.

God's Measure of a Pastor

The expanding church of Ephesus and her daughter churches in Pergamum, Smyrna, Thyatira, Sardis, Philadelphia, and Laodicea needed leadership. The church at Crete also had similar issues. Paul told Timothy and Titus to look at their young disciples and select "overseers" or "elders" for each town.[2]

Then Paul gave Timothy and Titus a template to use in order to recognize godly, spiritually mature men.[3] He gave them a list of necessary character qualifications (1 Tim 3:1–7; Titus 1:5–9). The list Paul gave Timothy and the one given to Titus have many overlapping traits. Together, they give us a complete and comprehensive profile containing the requirements for recognizing a man of godly character.

1. The Focus Is on Godly Character and Christian Integrity

Reading through both lists (1 Tim 3:1–7; Titus 1:5–9) reveals that the focus is on godly character, not the level of education attained, knowledge of doctrine, spiritual gifts, or abilities. The qualifications focus on a man's reputation, ethics, morality, temperament, habits, and maturity.

In the early church, having a seminary degree was not a requirement for being a pastor, but being above reproach in your character was. I am a graduate of a great seminary. I have two sons currently enrolled as students in that seminary, and I earn my living teaching at that seminary. But, despite the obvious value of theological training for ministry, could it be that we have placed too much emphasis on education and not enough on character development?

I find it interesting and somewhat frustrating that too many modern-day ordination councils are focused almost exclusively on the candidate's knowledge of doctrine and his call to ministry. A clear call to ministry and sound doctrine are no doubt vital, but should we not also examine a candidate's fruitfulness and character?

2. The Nonnegotiable Is Blamelessness

It is worth noting that Paul's lists in 1 Tim 3:1–7 and Titus 1:5–9 start with the same characteristic—"blamelessness" or being "above reproach."

An overseer, therefore, must be *above reproach.* (1 Tim 3:2, italics added)

[A]ppoint elders in every town: someone who is *blameless.* (Titus 1:5–6, italics added)

[F]or an overseer, as God's manager, must be *blameless.* (Titus 1:7, italics added)

We can assume that Paul mentioned it twice to Titus because the people of Crete had such horrible reputations. They were infamous for their immorality. Attesting to this, Paul says, "One of their very own prophets said, Cretans are always liars, evil beasts, lazy gluttons" (Titus 1:12).

"Blamelessness" is the nonnegotiable criterion for qualifying as a pastor. It should be considered the overaching, summarizing foundation to all of the others. The other characteristics are simply descriptions of aspects of "blamelessness."

Blamelessness does not mean perfection, but it does mean being an outstanding example. It means having unquestionable integrity, such that accusations of wrongdoing do not stick. A blameless person is not vulnerable to attacks on his character. When you are blameless, your character is beyond criticism. There are no skeletons in your closet. The Greeks defined the term as "affording nothing of which an adversary can take hold."[4]

The blameless Christian leader offers the world a life of such purity that he leaves no place for accusation against him.

3. Snapshots of Blamelessness

What does blamelessness look like? How do you know it when you see it? Paul, following the custom of his day, gave Timothy and Titus a detailed list of criteria that paint a picture of exactly what it means for a godly leader to be above reproach.

The characteristics that Paul lists in 1 Tim 3:2–7 (AMP) are:

1. the husband of one wife
2. circumspect and temperate and self-controlled

3. sensible
4. well behaved and dignified and lead an orderly (disciplined) life
5. hospitable [showing love for and being a friend to the believers, especially strangers or foreigners]
6. a capable and qualified teacher
7. not given to wine
8. not combative but gentle and considerate
9. not quarrelsome but forbearing and peaceable
10. not a lover of money [insatiable for wealth and ready to obtain it by questionable means]
11. rule his own household well, keeping his children under control, with true dignity, commanding their respect in every way and keeping them respectful
12. not be a new convert
13. have a good reputation and be well thought of by those outside [the church]

He gives a very similar list in Titus 1:5–9:

1. the husband of [but] one wife
2. whose children are [well trained and are] believers, not open to the accusation of being loose in morals and conduct or unruly and disorderly
3. not self-willed or arrogant or presumptuous
4. not be quick-tempered
5. not given to drink or pugnacious (brawling, violent)
6. he must not be grasping and greedy for filthy lucre (financial gain)
7. be hospitable [loving and a friend to believers, especially to strangers and foreigners]
8. a lover of goodness [of good people and good things]
9. sober-minded [sensible, discreet]
10. upright and fair-minded
11. a devout man and religiously correct
12. temperate and keeping himself in hand
13. he must hold fast to the sure and trustworthy Word of God
14. able both to give stimulating instruction and encouragement in sound (wholesome) doctrine and to refute and convict those who contradict and oppose it [showing the wayward their error]

What Is Christian Character?

Through the years I have been collecting definitions and descriptions of Christian character. Some of my favorites include:

"Character is what a man is in the dark."

"Character is who you are when no one is looking."

"Character is measured by what you would do if you were never found out."

"Reputation is what men think you are. Character is what God knows you to be."

"Character is like a tree and reputation like its shadow.

The shadow is what we think of it; the tree is the real thing."

"The best index to a person's character is how he treats people

who can't do him any good, and how he treats people who can't fight back."

"There is never a reason to compromise God's standards

in order to maintain God's blessings."

—ANDY STANLEY[5]

The definition for character used at the United States Air Force Academy defines character as "the sum of those qualities of moral excellence that stimulates a person to do the right thing, which is manifested through right and proper actions despite internal or external pressures to the contrary."

Closely linked to Christian character is godly integrity, which I define as living life based on biblical principles and godly values. It is linked with responsibility, honesty, morality, loyalty, being trustworthy, and responding to temptation with incorruptibility. Integrity could be described as having the courage to always do the right thing because it is right, no matter what. Godly integrity is achieved by accountability.

You Must Have Integrity!

If a pastor lacks integrity, two things will happen. One, he will not be able to lead a church effectively because people will not trust him. Two, as he leads people, the people will ultimately be crushed by the leader's lack of integrity. When it comes to your Christian integrity, cutting corners is not an option.

Building a Life of Biblical Integrity and Godly Character

You do not just wake up one morning and look in the mirror to see a man or woman of biblical integrity. Integrity and godly character are built up little by little, day after day, choice by choice, incident by incident. Integrity is not automatic. It is consciously cultivated. It happens on purpose. Integrity is not a gift. It is a reward of discipline, sacrifice, honesty, consistency, and doing what is right no matter the cost.

After reading a friend's painful account of having to resign from his church because of moral failure, I wrote down the nonnegotiable commitments for my life to build and maintain biblical integrity and godly character.

1. Your Personal Time with God Is Vital—Prioritize It

When we consistently spend time with God, it enables us to notice and correct small cracks in our character before they become big ones. A lack of intimacy with God causes us to seek intimacy in all the wrong places, with the wrong people, at the wrong time, and in the wrong way.

2. You Have Emotional, Spiritual, and Physical Tanks—Keep Them Replenished

Human beings are made up of body, soul, and spirit. Yet we are more than isolated compartments. The state of one area of life does affect the other areas.

We are more susceptible to temptation when we are physically tired, emotionally drained, or spiritually spent. As leaders, we are expected to fill other people's tanks. We cannot expect others to take it upon themselves to fill ours. We must watch our gauges and learn what diminishes us.

For example, I have taken to monitoring how many hours of sleep I get each night. If I get less than seven hours of sleep too many days in a row, my physical tanks get low. If I exercise consistently, I feel better physically and emotionally, and I sleep better.

I also find that my emotional tanks get drained by unresolved conflict or broken relationships. For me, spending too much time with draining people can be hazardous to my emotional health. Trying to minister beyond my areas of giftedness also empties my tanks. On the other hand, quality time with my family fills my emotional tanks.

3. You Have a Few Priority Relationships—Build Them

Often leaders spend so much time ministering to everyone else that they have nothing left for their families. One way Cathy and I have tried to overcome this has been to minister together as a family. When my boys were in high school, together as a family we led a multi-celled Bible study group for high school kids in our house. We may have been going in many directions all week, but on Wednesday nights we knew we were at home doing ministry together.

Other family pegs we tried to keep nailed down were family dinner five nights a week around the kitchen table, family devotions a couple of nights every week, and prayer with each boy before bed several times a week. We also try to have some sort of family vacation each year, and we always make a big deal out of birthdays.

One of our favorite marriage-building priorities is a weekly date. It may be lunch and frozen yogurt, or a hike, or a bike ride, but three Fridays out of four we know we have at least had one good chunk of undisturbed time together each week.

4. You Ultimately Only Have to Please One Person—Choose the Right Person

Obviously we cannot live a life of godly integrity when we live to please ourselves. We can also get in trouble when we try to please others. Focusing on image and appearances will cause us to fudge truths and cover mistakes, which will eventually steal our integrity. The one person we ultimately must please is God.

5. Your Time on Earth Is a Blip on the Radar Screen of Eternity—Stay Focused

Eternity has been compared to the efforts of a parakeet picking up a single grain of sand in its beak and flying to the moon to drop it off before returning home to do it again. If each trip took a million years and the parakeet did it over and over until every single grain of sand was on the moon, all the billions and billions of years it would require would be just a moment in eternity.

Our lives down here on earth are merely a blip on the radar screen of eternity. We must refuse to be distracted by temporal temptations and worldly priorities. We must use each day to prepare for an eternal tomorrow.

6. You Are the Product of Your Daily Habits and Personal Disciplines— Develop Good Ones

The habits and decisions I made yesterday determine who I am today. The choices and disciplines I make today will determine my tomorrow. Basic habits such as Bible reading, prayer, journaling, reading, church attendance, tithing, and serving never go out of season.

7. You Need Accountability—Seek It

The Bible is clear about our need for one another. When God declared that it was "not good that the man should be alone" (Gen 17:18 ESV), He pointed to the essential relational side of our DNA. Just as we all have a genuine God-shaped void in our hearts, we also have a human-shaped one.

We were never intended to go it alone, and isolation often leads to our downfall. Hoffman and Wilson warn, "One of the fastest roads to moral failure in ministry is a lack of accountability."[6]

We can never reach our potential without the help of others. We need accountability. My friend Daniel Henderson writes, "Genuine accountability is a mirror to the soul, providing vital feedback. . . . Accountability fuels proper perspective and encourages authentic purity."[7]

I have discovered that the years when I have been intentional about finding an accountability partner, meeting regularly, and being utterly honest have been the years when I have enjoyed the greatest levels of personal growth and spiritual victory. I try to touch base with my current accountability partner on Mondays. Since we both travel to speak in churches most weekends, Monday is an especially good day for us. Either we eat lunch or, since his office is next door, he pops in and asks how I am doing. I have requested that he hold me accountable by asking me the following questions every week.

Sample Accountability Questions

- Have you consistently been spending time with the Lord?
- Have you been morally pure in thought, word, and actions?
- Have you watched anything, read anything, looked at anything, or visited any website you would be embarrassed to watch with Jesus?
- Have you said anything, written anything, talked to or touched anyone inappropriately?
- Have you honored and invested in your spouse?
- Have you lied about any of the above?

8. You Need Self-Examination—Do It

Frequently the toughest integrity test a leader faces is the challenge of "me." Often I discover that my biggest problem is . . . me. Too many times God cannot bless or use me as He would like because I am in the way. No wonder Jesus repeatedly encouraged His followers to deny themselves.

The last several years God has been repeatedly allowing circumstances in my life that test my character. Through these tests I have been led to practice the discipline of self-examination. Let me offer you a set of questions that comprise "the test of me."

1. How do I react when another is promoted over me, selected instead of me, or outshines me?
2. How do I feel when others evaluate me as harshly as I evaluate or criticize myself?
3. Do I think or speak too much about myself?
4. Do I see everything in reference to me?
5. Am I able to listen to the praises of a rival without detraction, rebuttal, or belittling?
6. Do I attach the affection of my followers more to Christ than to myself?
7. Do I give or accept exaggerated deference to or from other church leaders?
8. Do I cling to authority too long?
9. Am I actively training others to assume responsibility?
10. Do I take myself, and my success or failure, too seriously?
11. Can I admit when I am wrong?
12. Can I admit when I need to change?
13. Can I laugh at myself and go on?

— What Now? —

The best place to cultivate Christian character and learn to pass "the test of me" is at the foot of the cross. Take some time and pray through the above-mentioned questions. As you do, nail your pride and selfish ambition to the cross of the One who humbled Himself in order to give us the opportunity to make a difference.

⁓ Quote ⁓

*An unmistakable sense of authority accompanies leaders
with integrity.*

—HENRY AND RICHARD BLACKABY[8]

Notes

1. Stan Toler, *Stan Toler's Practical Guide for Pastoral Ministry* (Indianapolis, IN: Wesleyan, 2007), 28.

2. According to James Stitzinger, the terms elder, bishop or overseer, shepherd or pastor, preacher, and teacher are synonymous terms relating to the pastoral office. James Stizinger, "Pastoral Ministry in History," in *Pastoral Ministry: How to Shepherd Biblically*, ed. John MacArthur (Nashville, TN: Thomas Nelson, 2005), 30–31.

3. In this book, the pastor shall be referred to in the masculine gender.

4. William Barclay, *The Letters to Timothy, Titus, and Philemon* (Louisville, KY: Westminster John Knox, 2003), 75.

5. Andy Stanley, *Next Generation Leader* (Sisters, OR: Multnomah, 2006), 145.

6. Michael Todd Wilson and Brad Hoffman, *Preventing Ministry Failure* (Downers Grove, IL: InterVarsity, 2007), 45.

7. Daniel Henderson, *Defying Gravity: How to Survive the Storms of Pastoral Ministry* (Chicago, IL: Moody, 2010), 91–92.

8. Henry Blackaby and Richard Blackaby, *Spiritual Leadership* (Nashville, TN: B&H, 2002), 107.

4

Fleeing Greed and Pursuing Purity

The Jim and Tammy Faye Bakker story became one of the ugliest scandals ever to hit American Christianity. In 1967, the televangelist and his wife, Tammy Faye, started *The PTL Club*. (PTL is an acronym for "Praise the Lord" and "People That Love.") *The PTL Club* became one of the most popular televised ministries of its time. In 1984, their ministry added Heritage USA, a Christian theme park.

The way they told it, prosperity was a gift from God, and He had blessed them with an army of followers and immense personal fortunes. Everything seemed to be blessed until a series of scandals broke in 1987.

Bakker was caught funneling $265,000 in hush money to church secretary Jessica Hahn in order to cover up their adulterous tryst. Newspaper reporters began to investigate and discovered severe financial wrongdoings revealing that the Bakkers and their empire had blown through $158 million of their ministry's donations. Bakker was put on trial, and resigned from his position at PTL. He was convicted of fraud and conspiring to commit fraud. The court sentenced him to forty-five years in prison along with a $500,000 fine. He served almost five years in prison and was paroled for good behavior.

Bakker admitted squandering church money on luxury cars and six mansions. When he got caught, there were forty-seven separate bank accounts in Bakker's name.

Also convicted to prison was Richard Dortch, senior vice-president of PTL and associate pastor of Heritage Village Church. Dortch admitted, "Pride, arrogance and secrets led to the PTL scandal. While most people never face temptations on the same scale, the ingredients for seemingly smaller failures are the same."[1]

No one should ever fall because of mishandled money or messed up morality, especially a pastor. The exact opposite should be true. As a pastor, your godly character and integrity should set you apart.

Paul challenged Timothy that in order to be most useful and pleasing to the Lord, Timothy needed to flee lust and greed, and pursue purity.

> Now in a large house there are not only gold and silver bowls, but also those of wood and earthenware, some for special use, some for ordinary. So if anyone purifies himself from these things, he will be a special instrument, set apart, useful to the Master, prepared for every good work. Flee from youthful passions, and pursue righteousness, faith, love, and peace, along with those who call on the Lord from a pure heart. (2 Tim 2:20–22)

> But those who want to be rich fall into temptation, a trap, and many foolish and harmful desires, which plunge people into ruin and destruction. For the love of money is a root of all kinds of evil, and by craving it, some have wandered away from the faith and pierced themselves with many pains. Now you, man of God, run from these things; but pursue righteousness, godliness, faith, love, endurance, and gentleness. (1 Tim 6:9–11)

Pursue Purity

We live in a culture that glamorizes and celebrates what you can get away with. Dishonesty, lying, cheating, and stealing are expected as long as you don't get caught. Sex before marriage is expected. Extramarital affairs are common. Pornography is a multibillion dollar business. Statistics for Christian men trapped in pornography could make you cry.

For example, in a survey by Patrick Means of 350 men (10 percent pastors, 90 percent key laymen from twelve denominations), 64 percent admitted to struggles with sexual addiction or sexual compulsion, such as use of pornography, compulsive masturbation, or other secret sexual activity; 25 percent of married men admitted to having committed adultery; and another 14 percent confessed to sexual contact short of intercourse.[2]

In a survey of 800 active church members and leaders, 15 percent of the men and 11 percent of the women admitted to having been unfaithful to their spouses, and 49 percent had viewed pornography in the past year.[3] A more recent survey of 564 respondents found that 33 percent of pastors had visited a pornographic website in the past month.[4]

I feel their pain. I was exposed to pornography at the age of seven. Sadly, it left a deep scar on my heart and mind. Lust became an especially difficult challenge for me to overcome as a teenager. Yet it had to be overcome if I hoped to fulfill my calling as a Christian man, husband, father, and pastoral leader . . . and it has! Praise the Lord! My honesty, plus personal accountability, added to absolute dependency on God's all-sufficiency, has led to my on-going victory.[5]

Immorality is always very, very costly and spiritually deadly. No one can afford to pay its crushing price. One hour of pleasure can lead to years of agony.

Consider Joseph, who had the integrity not only to refuse the temptations of his master's wife, but to literally run out of the room when she would not take no for an answer. We must realize that, like Joseph, we are not strong enough to resist an all-out attack, so we must vigilantly avoid ever getting close to lust and immorality.

I find I can avoid lust as long as I refuse to get near it. Below is a list I have developed that keeps me pure.

I Will Never . . .

- gaze at a pornographic website.
- visit an "adult" bookstore.
- go to a "gentleman's" club.
- look at a "men's" magazine.
- watch an "adult" video or movie.
- read a questionable novel.
- engage in a personal phone call or email exchange with a female other than my wife without my wife's knowledge.
- look closely at a female below her chin.
- be alone with a woman in any setting for any reason at any time unless she is old enough to be my mother or grandmother.
- share my personal, emotional feelings with any female other than my wife.
- view another woman as anyone other than a person for whom Jesus bled and died.

The apostle Paul was clear that it is not enough to try to stop a negative. A positive must be put in its place. We put off the old by putting on the new. When it comes to morality, I have also developed a mental list that helps me. Instead of wasting thought, time, money, and energy on thoughts that are immoral . . .

I Will . . .

- wash my brain in the living waters of the Word of God each day.
- memorize the Word regularly.
- pray for my mate daily. (If you are single, pray for your *future* mate daily.)
- have a connecting conversation with God each day.
- have a connecting conversation with my mate each day.
- have a connecting conversation with a godly male friend often.
- remember that an earthly life of purity will enable me to better experience an eternity of ecstasy.

Flee Greed and Escape Financial Bondage

Many pastors who maintain moral purity stumble into financial problems. As Cathy and I teach and counsel dozens of pastors and their mates, we are shocked at the number of them who are in serious financial bondage.

Are You in Financial Bondage?

1. Do you and your mate often find yourselves arguing about money matters?
2. In your home, are discussions about money more common than discussions about God?
3. Are you not giving to God what you feel God wants you to give?
4. Are you content and at peace to live on what God has provided?
5. Are you considering or have you gotten a consolidation loan to reduce debt?
6. Do you receive notices of past-due accounts? Have you been turned over to a collections agency?
7. Do you charge items because you can't pay cash?
8. Do you or your mate use spending as emotional therapy?
9. Do you or your mate spend impulsively?
10. Do you or your mate invade savings to meet current expenses?
11. Is your net worth failing to increase annually?
12. Are you feeling like you "just cannot save"?
13. Do you wish you had a plan for spending and saving and are frustrated because you do not?

If you honestly agreed with several of the above statements you are heading toward financial bondage, if you are not already there. The truth is, you are not alone. Many find themselves in a similar situation. The good news is, many people have recovered from financial bondage. The reality is, if you do not act aggressively to address these issues, they can undermine and even destroy your ministry. The best news is with God's help you can break out of financial bondage.

Principles of Financial Freedom

The book of Proverbs is a great guide for avoiding financial bondage. In fact, the book of Proverbs offers nine clear principles to finding financial freedom.[6]

1. EARN MONEY DILIGENTLY

The first principle of financial freedom is to work hard to earn money. God has written into the code of this universe that *hard work* is honored and laziness is not.

> The soul of the sluggard craves and gets nothing. But the soul of the diligent is made fat. (Prov 13:4 NASB; see also 12:11; 12:24)

Of course the issue is more than merely effort expended. The type of work God blesses must be *honest work* (Prov 13:11). Being the best you can be at your work is also something God will bless. *Skilled labor* is increasingly rare. Developing your skills will lead to enhanced income, increased options, and more open doors for advancement (Prov 22:29).

Beyond hard, honest, and skilled work, God especially blesses the worker who has initiative and does not always need to be told what to do. On top of that, planning ahead is obviously a wise financial step to take (see Prov 6:6–11).

2. STAY OUT OF DEBT

> The rich rule over the poor, and the borrower is servant to the lender. (Prov 22:7 NIV)

Debt can be distressing, demoralizing, divisive, and devastating. Needless marital conflict, personal stress, guilt, shame, and the inability to obey God's call are the results of living with unnecessary debt. When you are facing overdue bills, debt for non-necessities, and credit on nonappreciating items—you are on the road to financial bondage.

This does not mean that you should never borrow, but borrowing to buy nonappreciating consumables such as gifts, vacations, and clothes should be avoided. This type of credit debt will push you into insurmountable debt faster than you can pay yourself out of it.

Cathy and I have been blessed by living extremely simply, refusing to go into debt for anything other than our first home. We do own a credit card (for convenient recordkeeping aid and the reward flier miles), but it is paid off every month. We have practiced the principle that *if we can't pay cash for something, we probably don't need it. If we do truly need it, God will provide it.* And He has.

3. KEEP GOOD RECORDS

> By wisdom a house is built, and by understanding it is established; by knowledge the rooms are filled with all precious and pleasant riches. (Prov 24:3–4 ESV)

> Be diligent to know the state of your flocks, And attend to your herds;
> For riches are not forever, Nor does a crown endure to all generations. (Prov 27:23–24 NKJV)

Recently it was discovered that less than two out of ten couples know how to actually balance their checkbooks. This means that many married couples seldom know how much money they have to spend or how much they are spending. Someone once stated a formula for financial disaster: Ignorance + easy credit = catastrophe.

The money we have in this life is not ours. It belongs to our Master. We are simply managers of *His* resources. One day we will give an account of what we did with His money. It is our obligation to keep careful track of what He has given us.

Let me encourage you to buy a budget book or use a software program in order to keep good financial records.[7] Revisit the budget each month at a regularly scheduled appointment.

4. PLAN YOUR EXPENSES

> The plans of the diligent lead surely to plenty, But those of everyone who is hasty, surely to poverty. (Prov 21:5 NKJV)

Which sounds better to you: plenty or poverty? The verse above clearly states that financial planning leads to plenty, while haste (unplanned, impulsive buying) leads to poverty.

Let me encourage you to plan your expenses in three areas:

1. How much you will give?
2. How much you will spend?
3. How much you will save?

Such a three-fold family financial plan is called a budget. If keeping a budget sounds restrictive, let me assure you that it is not. A budget, if properly used, does not enslave you; it will set you free. It does not take money away from you; it gives you more money to use for what you want.

Too often we put off planning until we are so deeply in debt that it seems impossible to get out. By then it is too late to plan, except for crisis planning. You should begin planning by writing down your financial goals and objectives into a monthly balanced budget. These goals and objectives need to be reviewed monthly.

5. SPEND WISELY

There is desirable treasure, And oil in the dwelling of the wise, But a foolish man squanders it. (Prov 21:20 NKJV)

Impulsive spending is often the fastest road to financial bondage. When we got married, Cathy and I practiced three rules to curb impulsiveness: (1) *Delayed action*—the bigger the purchase, the longer the delay before buying it. (2) *Limited spending without marital discussion.* For example, when Cathy and I were first married, neither of us was supposed to spend more than $20.00 without consulting the other first. Now the amount is $100. (3) *Question the purchase.* We found that by asking ourselves a simple set of questions we would ultimately be much happier with the things we did buy:

- Do I need it?
- Is the price reasonable?
- Can I substitute something cheaper for it?
- Have I shopped around?
- Will it put me into debt?
- Will it positively or negatively affect my/our spiritual life/lives?

6. BE CONTENT WITH WHAT YOU HAVE

Better is a little with the fear of the Lord, Than great treasure with trouble. Better is a dinner of herbs where love is, Than a fatted calf with hatred. Better is a dry morsel with quietness, Than a house full of feasting with strife. (Prov 15:16–17; 17:1 NKJV)

One of the secrets to financial freedom is learning to be content with what you have. We must have a healthy and realistic view of money. It is not a worthy end in itself, but rather is merely a necessary tool to be viewed and used skillfully.

7. HONOR GOD

Honor the Lord with your possessions, And with the firstfruits of all your increase; So your barns will be filled with plenty, And your vats will overflow with new wine. (Prov 3:9–10 NKJV)

Honoring God with our possessions means putting Him first. Elsewhere in the Old Testament this is expressed by giving God the first tenth (or tithe) of our income. I am not a legalist, but I am a fan of tithing. I found that by giving God the first tenth of my income I make three necessary and powerful statements:

- To God, I say thanks for past provisions.
- To others, I testify of my present priorities.
- To myself, I am demonstrating faith for future provisions.

When Cathy and I first were married, we were both full-time students. She was a part-time secretary and I was a part-time pastor. Our combined income was $117 a week or $6,084 for the year. We created a budget that included paying God first by giving our church one-tenth of our income. On paper, it seemed doubtful that we could make it on such meager income and tithe at the same time. But we were determined to put God first.

I cannot fully explain how it happened, but by the end of our first year of marriage, we had faithfully paid all of our bills and tithes without going into debt! On top of that, we had money left over which we put into our savings account. The amount left over was exactly ten percent of our income, or $608! Yes, both of us had been given raises from our jobs, but the best explanation is that God was faithful to provide for us.

8. GET EDUCATED AND FOLLOW WISE PRIORITIES

The naive believes everything, But the sensible man considers his steps. (Prov 14:15 NASB)

Most financially struggling persons are not stupid people. They just do not understand how money works. They often do not fully comprehend how borrowing and interest rates work. As a result, their primary concern becomes, "How much are the monthly payments?" rather than "How much is this going to ultimately cost?" They naively borrow more money than they can repay because they have no idea where their money goes each month or how much credit their income can support.

Often pastors fail to understand interest, investments, and priorities. Dave Ramsey offers a multi-tiered priority list of how we use our money. Following it closely leads to financial freedom.[8]

✳ Priorities for Financial Fulfillment ✳

Level one: Pay God first. If you expect God to honor your finances and efforts, you need to invite Him into the process by honoring him with your finances.

Level two: Start an emergency fund. Set aside the equivalent of two weeks' to one month's income into an emergency fund for those unexpected events in life that you can't plan for.

Level three: Pay off debt from smallest to largest. List your debts in order from smallest to greatest. Make paying off the smallest balance your number one priority. By knocking off the easiest debts first, you gain the momentum you need to make it all the way to being debt free.

Level four: Expand your savings. Once all nonappreciating debt is paid off, focus on slowly building up your savings to be large enough to cover three to six months of expenses in case you should lose your job. Basically this is money that you do not touch except in extreme circumstances.

Level five: Start investing in your retirement. If your only plan for funding your retirement is through Social Security, you need another plan. Even if Social Security is available when you retire, it probably won't nearly cover the lifestyle that you are currently enjoying. Therefore, most advisors suggest that you put 15 percent of your income each month into retirement.

Level six: Set aside funds to help pay for your children's college education. Some people use the husband's income for the first five priorities and the wife's income for the children's education. Many people use Education Savings Accounts (ESAs) and 529 plans to save for their children's education.

Remember, it does not hurt to have your children to provide for at least part of their own education. If your children help contribute to their education, they will probably appreciate it more and take their studies more seriously.

Level seven: Pay off your house. Being totally debt free provides a wonderful sense of freedom. You are free to obey anything the Lord asks of you.

Level eight: Give extragenerously. There is great joy in generous giving and financially investing in eternity.

9. ACT NOW

He who gathers in summer is a son who acts wisely, But he who sleeps in harvest is a son who acts shamefully. (Prov 10:5 NASB)

Notice the contrast in the verse above. The fool makes excuses and procrastinates, while the wise person takes action before it is too late. Don't wait. Act now.

— What Now? —

Which of the Proverbs principles to finding financial freedom do you need to adopt? Pick the one most necessary for your financial freedom and start following it today.

Notes

1. "The Re-education of Jim Bakker," in *Christianity Today Library* (December 7, 1998), http://christianitytoday.com/ct/8te/8te062.html (accessed September 21, 2011).

2. Pat Means, *Men's Secret Wars* (Ventura: Revell, 1996), 132–33, 255.

3. "Pastors and Internet Porn," *Leadership Magazine* (Winter 2001): 89.

4. Dr. Archibald D. Hart, *The Sexual Man* (Waco: Word, 1994), 95.

5. For help in this area visit www.xxxchurch.com.

6. Adapted from Dave Earley, *Small Group Leader's Toolkit* (Houston, TX: TouchUSA, 2008), 36–40.

7. Many practical aids for godly financial freedom are available at the Crown Financial Ministries website, www.crown.org. You can download helpful articles, charts, and recordkeeping systems.

8. These priorities were adapted from Dave Ramsey's "Seven Baby-Steps: Begin Your Journey to Financial Peace," http://www.daveramsey.com/new/baby-steps/ (accessed August 2, 2010).

5

Pastoral Leadership Is . . .

Being a
Faithful Servant

What makes a successful pastor?

In our day and time, pastors are often measured by the size of their churches, the books they have written, the number of people who follow them on twitter or read their weekly blog, and the conferences they are invited to address. Pastors are frequently evaluated based on the cost and size of their church's facilities, the number of people they have on their staff, the style of their preaching, the academic degrees they've received, the schools they attended, the particular scriptural emphasis that is associated with them, and their popularity with people. Some are measured by the attractiveness of their mate and the achievements of their children.

But how does God measure a pastor?

The Corinthian church was struggling mightily with this issue. They were ranking one man over another, and they were doing it based on human wisdom. The apostle Paul rebuked them for this, pointing out that the only one who has the right to evaluate is the Lord (1 Cor 4:3–5), and the primary measurement He uses is faithful service.

> A person should consider us in this way: as servants of Christ and managers of God's mysteries. In this regard, it is expected of managers that each one be found faithful. (1 Cor 4:1–2)

The Pastor Must Be a *Servant*

In his writings Paul never refers to the ministry as a career. The pastoral ministry is a high calling and a costly calling. It is not a profession to pursue, but a privileged call that must be obeyed no matter the price. It is not about gaining, but losing. It is not about getting, but giving.

In order to help his readers understand the notion that the greatest pastor is the greatest servant, Paul uses four different words to show the various sides of what it means for the faithful pastor to serve Christ. Understanding and applying these four concepts delivers us from the dangerous, damning, deadly desire to turn pastoral ministry into a profession. It frees us to become the holy, radical, reckless, righteous, rebels who snatch spiritual sheep from the teeth of wicked wolves.

1. Galley Slaves *Who Man the Oars for Jesus*

A person should consider us in this way: as servants of Christ. (1 Cor 4:1)

Servants of Christ. In the first century, Rome ruled the world. The primary ship in Rome's mighty navy was a galley, which is a large ship propelled by fifty human oarsman per floor. The word "servants" (ὑπηρέτης) that Paul selects in 1 Cor 4:1 can be translated "galley slaves, under rowers, subservient rowers." It speaks of the lowest level rower serving at the very bottom of a galley ship. These oarsmen's lives were extremely strenuous, difficult, dangerous, and lowly. There was no glamour in serving in the Roman galley—just backbreaking, thankless, hard work.

The word became synonymous with servant or subordinate. It spoke of the most menial person doing the most strenuous manual task. It was also used for the king's official soldiers. They did not serve each other. They served the wishes of their commander.

So the role of pastor is that of a hardworking, low-ranking slave carrying out the orders of King Jesus. He is a serving subordinate, charged with a responsibility. The emphasis is on his subservient role and his hard work.

2. Stewards *Who Serve Up God's Mysteries*

If you have ever travelled on a ship or a plane, you have been served by a steward or a stewardess. The steward does not own the boat. He also does not own anything on that plane. The company owns the plane and all that is on it. He just passes out the food and drinks. It is his responsibility to take the goods that belong to the company and dispense them to the people.

In 1 Corinthians 4, Paul said that the role of the pastor is not only to work as a galley slave for God, but also to *manage* the mysteries of God. The term "manager" or "steward" (οἰκονόμος) is a combination of two terms: οἰκο, which means "house"; and νόμος, meaning "to manage." Therefore, a steward is a slave entrusted to "manage a house."

A wealthy houseowner would have a steward to administer his household affairs, his property, his farm, his vineyards, his accounts, and his slaves. The steward's "responsibility was to devote his time, ability, and energy to his master's interests, not his own."[1]

The emphasis of this term is on his subservient role and his accountability to his master. "He must give an account for the manner in which he carries out his master's orders."[2]

Most of us try to live the Christian life backwards or upside down. Too often we ask God to care for *our* things instead of living as faithful managers of *His* things. We think we can choose to use our gifts, abilities, time, or money to serve God. But the truth is that because He owns us, our gifts, abilities, time, and money already belong to Him.

Paul notes that the steward is to manage *the mysteries of God*. What are the mysteries of God? The term "mysteries" (μυστήριον) speaks of "something hidden or secret which is now revealed." Here it refers to the word of God. So the responsibility is to take God's word and dispense it to God's people. As a steward, it is not his word that is significant, but rather it is the word of his master. Regarding this role of the pastor, John MacArthur has said,

> When I try to examine my ministry and say what I am to do, it's a simple thing. I simply say God has called me to take His word and pass it out to His people. That's all. I'm a waiter. He gives me the food. I get it out of His kitchen and I deliver it to the table.[3]

3. Servants Who Get Dirty for God . . . No Matter the Cost[4]

Prior to his statement regarding the true criterion of a pastor in 1 Corinthians 4, Paul used another term for the pastoral role in chapter three. He is responding to the silly arguing over who was greater, Apollos or Paul.

> So, what is Apollos? And what is Paul? They are *servants* through whom you believed. (1 Cor 3:5, italics added)

"Servants" (διάκονος) is the most common Greek term used in the New Testament for the pastoral leader (twenty times translated as "minister," plus eight times as "servant," and three times as "deacon"). In Phil 1:1 and 1 Tim 3:8–13 it denotes an office in the church. Almost everywhere else, however, the word is used in a more general sense.

Paul used the word to describe himself as a servant of the Lord (1 Cor 3:5), a servant of God (2 Cor 6:4), a servant of the new covenant (2 Cor 3:6), a servant of the gospel (Eph 3:7; Col 1:23) and "a servant of the church" (Col 1:25 GNB).

While we are not certain of its origin, it could be the product of compounding the words διά ("spreading") and κόνις ("dust"), so as to mean, properly, "raising dust by activity." Hence, being a minister is not merely having the title "minister" but serving so actively that a trail of dust follows in his wake. It is not about the title he is called, but rather the work that he does—serving. It is about getting dirty in order to make others clean.

Such service can be costly. Paul described himself as a minister (διάκονος) who was commendable to God (2 Cor 6:4). Why? Did he have a large church? Did he pack out concert arenas? Did everyone download his podcasts? No way! Notice what it was that made his ministry acceptable to God:

> But in everything, as God's ministers, we commend ourselves: by great endurance, by afflictions, by hardship, by pressures, by beatings, by imprisonments, by riots, by labors, by sleepless nights, by times of hunger, by purity, by knowledge, by patience, by kindness, by the Holy Spirit, by sincere love . . . through glory and dishonor, through slander and good report . . . as unknown yet recognized; as dying and look—we live; as being chastened yet not killed; as grieving yet always rejoicing; as poor yet enriching many; as having nothing yet possessing everything. (2 Cor 6:4-10)

Afflictions, hardship, pressures, beatings, imprisonments, sleepless nights, hunger—real ministry is not for cowards or wimps. It can be excruciatingly hard and extremely costly. But according to Paul, it is ultimately worth it as the real minister is known by God, is fully alive, is full of joy, is eternally rich, and ultimately possesses all things (see vv. 9–10).

4. Volunteer Slaves Who Get Their Ears Pierced for Jesus[5]

What would the apostle Paul have placed after his name on a business card? His academic degrees earned? He could have put "author of half of the New Testament" or "the evangelist to the Gentiles" or "the founder of the first churches in Europe" or "the most influential Christian in history."

But he did not. Notice the title he chose to give himself.

Paul, a *slave* of Christ Jesus . . . (Rom 1:1, italics added)
Paul and Timothy, *slaves* of Christ Jesus . . . (Phil 1:1, italics added)
Paul, a *slave* of God . . . (Titus 1:1, italics added)

Paul chose to identify himself as a "slave" of Jesus Christ. He was not the only one.

> James, a *slave* of God and of the Lord Jesus Christ . . . (Jas 1:1, italics added)
> Simeon Peter, a *slave* and an apostle of Jesus Christ . . . (2 Pet 1:1, italics added)
> Jude, a *slave* of Jesus Christ, and a brother of James . . . (Jude 1, italics added)
> The revelation of Jesus Christ . . . to His *slave* John . . . (Rev 1:1, italics added)

Wow! The most powerful men in early Christianity—Paul, James, Peter, Jude, and John—all had the same perspective. They each gave themselves the same title—"slave."

The word used in these verses for "slave" is *doulos*. This word has been described by Greek scholar Kenneth Wuest in the following manner:

> The word is doulos, the most abject, servile term used by Greeks to denote a slave, one who was bound to his master in cords so strong that only death could break them, one who served his master to the disregard of his own interests, one whose will was swallowed up in the will of his master.[6]

For those of us called into a life of pastoral ministry, we need to recognize that ministry means being the bond slave of Jesus. In the first century, slavery was common; there were 60 million slaves in the Roman Empire. A slave was viewed as a piece of property. Slaves belonged to the master.

In order to live as a slave of Jesus Christ, you must recognize the truth that God owns you. He created you. Every atom that makes you unique was made by the creative breath of God.

When you illegally sold yourself into spiritual slavery through sin, Jesus came along and saw you in your wretched state. He wept for your pain and hurt for your shame. There you were naked, filthy, broken, blind, and all but dead with the shackles of sin around your ankles, wrists, and neck. The Devil himself was jerking your chain however and whenever he wanted.

But one day, Jesus Christ rode into the slave market of sin and redeemed you with His own blood. He took upon Himself your filth and your sin. He bought you with His blood. He then declared that you are free.

Being a doulos of Christ is not the slavery of compulsion and law, but the willing and glad slavery of love. Slaves of Jesus are people who recognize that they owe Jesus an amazing debt and voluntarily sign up to serve Him. He is their rightful owner.

In the Old Testament, an Israelite was never born into being a slave but became a slave by choice. Samuel Brengle wrote,

There was a law among the Hebrews that for sore [great] poverty or debt or crime one man might become the servant of another, but he could not be held in servitude beyond a certain period. At the end of six years he must be allowed to go free (Exod. xxi. 1–6; Deut. xv. 12–17). But if he loved his master and preferred to remain with him as his slave, then the master, in the presence of judges, was to place the man against a door or door-post and bore a hole through his ear, and this was to be the mark that he was his master's servant forever.[7]

In other words, for the Israelite slave, the tool-pierced ear was a symbol of a love-pierced heart. Of course I am not talking about the literal piercing of your ear. I am speaking of the spiritual piercing of your heart and will. I am talking of viewing yourself as the slave of Jesus by choice out of love for Jesus.

The Pastor Must Be *Faithful*

In this regard, it is expected of managers that each one be found *faithful*. (1 Cor 4:1–2, italics added)

Note what Paul *did not* say. He did not say that it is expected that a pastor be found *brilliant* or *educated* or *clever* or *glib*. He did not say that pastors are expected to be *eloquent* or *gifted*. He did not say that pastors had to have a *great personality* or be *popular*. He did not even say the pastor had to be a *great leader*.

Paul *did* say that God expects pastors to, above all else, be *faithful*. He wants galley slaves who keep rowing without being whipped. He wants stewards that can be trusted. He wants servants who get things done. He wants bondslaves who serve because they love Him. He wants us to be faithful.

It is helpful to remember:

1. God grants us the privilege of being in ministry because of our faithfulness.

   I give thanks to Christ Jesus our Lord, who has strengthened me, because He considered me *faithful*, appointing me to the ministry. (1 Tim 1:12, italics added)

2. God will evaluate our faithfulness with what we have been given.

   Everyone to whom much was given, of him *much will be required*. (Luke 12:48 ESV, italics added)

3. God will one day commend and reward us based on our faithfulness.

> His master said to him, "Well done, good and faithful slave! You were faithful over a few things; I will put you in charge of many things. Share your master's joy!" (Matt 25:21, italics added)

4. Our faithfulness is ultimately rooted in the faithfulness of God to us.

> As *God is faithful* . . . (2 Cor 1:18, italics added)

> But *the Lord is faithful*; He will strengthen and guard you from the evil one. (2 Thess 3:3, italics added)

> [If] we are faithless, *He remains faithful*, for He cannot deny Himself. (2 Tim 2:13, italics added)

5. Our ability to be faithful in ministry flows out of our dependency on the faithfulness of God.

> *He who calls you is faithful*, who also will do it. (1 Thess 5:24, italics added)

6. Faithfulness starts and grows with the small things.

> Whoever is *faithful* in very little is also faithful in much, and whoever is unrighteous in very little is also unrighteous in much. (Luke 16:10, italics added)

— What Now? —

Are you being faithful with the responsibilities and ministries you already have? God's willingness to give you more depends on what you are doing with what you have now.

— Quotes —

> *I am a slave of Jesus, and a slave doesn't have problems. The only thing the slave has to do is what the master asks of him. He doesn't have to be successful, and when you really understand that, all of a sudden you don't have problems anymore. All that's left is opportunities to see God's work.*
> —Bill Bright[8]

*You don't exalt one galley slave over another. They're sort
of just lost in the mass of all of the slaves. . . . [As a galley
slave] Nobody gets glory for doing what they're told to
do. You just get in trouble for not doing it. So a man who
preaches because God has called him isn't worthy of any
special honor, he's just worthy of dishonor if he doesn't. . . .
We are nothing. The only reason we're even useful is because
the Lord chooses to use us.*

—JOHN MACARTHUR[9]

*Faithfulness is better than life. . . . Faithfulness to my call is
far more important than whether I live—live at all, not to
mention whether I live comfortably!*

—JOHN PIPER[10]

Notes

1. Frederick Fyvie Bruce, *1 and 2 Corinthians*, The New Century Commentary (Grand Rapids, MI: Eerdmans, 1971), 46.

2. Daniel Mitchell, *The Book of First Corinthians* (Chattanooga, TN: AMG Publishers, 2004), 62.

3. John MacArthur, "Examining the Servants of Christ," sermon preached Sunday, September 14, 1975, at Grace Community Church, http://www.gty.org/Resources/Sermons/1820_Examining-the-Servants-of-Christ (accessed May 16, 2011).

4. For more on the pastor as a *diakonos* see, Dave Earley and Ben Gutierrez, *Ministry Is . . .* (Nashville, TN: B&H Academic, 2010), 7–15.

5. For more on the pastor as a *doulos* see, Earley and Gutierrez, *Ministry Is . . .* , 16–23.

6. Kenneth Wuest, *Word Studies: Romans in the Greek New Testament for the English Reader* (Grand Rapids, MI: Eerdmans, 1956), 11.

7. Samuel Logan Brengle, *Love-Slaves* (Salem, OH: Schmul, 1996), 7.

8. "Bill Bright's Legacy: A Rev! Interview with Brad Bright," *REV!* (July/August 2007): 34.

9. John MacArthur, "Examining the Servants of Christ," sermon preached Sunday, September 14, 1975, at Grace Community Church, http://www.gty.org/Resources/Sermons/1820_Examining-the-Servants-of-Christ (accessed May 11, 2011).

10. John Piper, "Faithfulness Is Better Than Life," sermon preached April 9, 1989 at Bethlehem Baptist Church, http://www.desiringgod.org/resource-library/sermons/faithfulness-is-better-than-life (accessed May 24, 2011).

6

Engaging in
Spiritual Warfare

*There is no neutral ground in the universe; every square inch,
every split second is claimed by God and counterclaimed
by Satan.*

—C. S. Lewis[1]

This Is War!

Fifty years ago, pastor, author, and twentieth-century prophet A. W. Tozer observed that most believers live their lives as though there is not a spiritual battle. He said, "The idea that this world is a playground instead of a battleground has now been accepted in practice by the vast majority of Christians."[2]

Pastor and philosopher Francis Schaeffer noted, "We are locked in a battle. This is not a friendly, gentleman's discussion. It is a life and death conflict between the spiritual hosts of wickedness and those who claim the name of Christ."[3]

Pastor Ronnie Floyd writes, "We are in a war. Satan goes after your family with great intensity. His will is to destroy your family and your church."[4]

In speaking of spiritual warfare, pastor Charles Mylander noted, "Ignorance is not bliss, it is defeat. If you are a Christian, you are the target. If you are a pastor, you and your family are the bulls-eye."[5]

If we are to be biblical Christians and effective pastors, we must look at our lives through the lens of spiritual warfare. The most often used analogy for Christians in the Bible is that of soldiers. The words often used to describe the Christian life are war terms—*fight, conquer, strive, battle, overcome, victory.* We are living in enemy territory when we live in the world. The New Testament is a book littered with military imagery.

Paul referred to the Christians as "soldiers" (Phil 2:25; Phlm 2; 2 Tim 2:3–4). Christians are said to "wage war" (2 Cor 10:3–5). Christians are told to wear spiritual "armor" (Eph 6:11,13–17; Rom 13:12). "Weapons of our warfare" are to be wielded by Christians (2 Cor 10:3–5, see also Rom 6:13; 13:12; 2 Cor 6:7; 1 Tim 1:18). Paul referred to his own ministry as a military skirmish (2 Tim 4:7). The Christian life is called a military conflict or struggle (Eph 6:12; Col 1:29; 2:1; Heb 12:4; Jude 3).

Jesus declared that His mission was to liberate "captives" and proclaim liberty to "oppressed" prisoners of war (Luke 4:18). In Luke 11:21–22 Jesus referred to Satan as a "fully armed" strong man whom He (Jesus), as someone stronger, "overcomes" and takes his "armor" and divides his "spoil" (ESV).

Paul rejoiced that through the power of the cross and resurrection, Jesus "disarmed principalities and powers, He made a public spectacle of them, triumphing over them in it" (Col 2:15 NKJV) and that He "captured the enemy and seized the booty" (Eph 4:8 MSG).

Paul reminded Timothy that in order to be an effective pastor he would need to "wage the good warfare" (1 Tim 1:18 ESV), "fight the good fight for the faith" (1 Tim 6:12), and "share in suffering as a good soldier of Christ Jesus" (2 Tim 2:3). Make no mistake, pastoral leadership involves engaging in spiritual warfare.

The Wiles of the Devil

In order to win a battle, it is important to know our enemy. By looking at the five primary names and titles given to Satan, we can learn how he attempts to defeat us and destroy our churches.

1. Opposition

> So we wanted to come to you—even I, Paul, time and again—but Satan hindered us. (1 Thess 2:18)

Paul said that he wanted to come and visit the Thessalonians, "but Satan hindered us." The word "Satan" means "adversary" or "opposer." The word used for "hindered" means to "to stop, impede, prevent." It carries the idea of "chopping up the road so someone cannot pass." It was used to describe a runner being "cut off so they could not continue" the race.

God has called us to run the race for Him. Satan loves to oppose us by knocking us off stride, tripping us up, shoving us off the track, and even digging pits in the track so we have to stop. If he could slow Paul down, he can slow us down. We must be prepared. The Devil will oppose you and attempt to derail you, your marriage, your kids, your ministry, and your church.

The key is not always necessarily knowing *how* Satan is working, but knowing *when* he is working. We are not told how he hindered Paul, but that he did. Satan has influence over people, over nature, and over events (see Job 1–2). He will use them to try to derail us.

What do we learn?

First, expect opposition. Every time you take a step toward—a step to God, there will probably be opposition. I have seen too many derailed too easily. We must not be surprised that when things are going great, the enemy starts to work. We must not be shocked that when we start taking steps for God, the enemy tries to trip us. We must not be astonished that when we really start running the race well, the Devil gives us a big shove. We are in a war and he does not like to lose.

Second, do not let him stop you. I enjoy watching some of the races in the Olympics. A few years ago, an American runner was winning his heat when he got bumped hard by another runner. It shook him up so badly he went from first to seventh and failed to qualify. In the finals, however, another runner got bumped and used it to fuel his resolve and went on to win the race.

Opposition is what makes us strong. It is part of life. Do not let it stop you. Get back up and get going.

Third, remember that God is bigger than the enemy and can always turn it for greater good. Paul did not let Satan's attack stop him from doing what needed to be done. He stayed on track and God turned Satan's attempted derailment into our great victory. You see, Paul sent Timothy in his place with the letter we call 1 Thessalonians. It is a letter that would not have been written without Satan's hindrance. And it is a letter that has blessed thousands of Christians for nearly two thousand years!

2. Accusation

The name Devil, *diablos*, is used thirty-five times in the New Testament. It means "slanderer" or "accuser" (see Rev 12:9–10). The Devil uses several types of accusations against us.

First, he will accuse God to you. He denounces God before you. He whispers lies like, "God does not really care." Or, "God really cannot handle that." Or, "God really does not have your best interests in mind." Or, "God really doesn't know what He's doing." The Devil denounces God to you. He is trying to separate you from God.

Second, he will accuse you to others. The Devil will tell other people bad things about you. I recall a woman who had not attended a Sunday worship service in several weeks. I called her to inquire regarding her absence. She told me that she was not ever coming back because I did not like her. She told me that during a particular message one day she felt I was upset with her and never wanted her to come back. When I asked her where she got that idea, she said I had stared at her the whole time I spoke. This was interesting because I was not upset with her, and I can't really see that far back in the auditorium. What had happened? The enemy had accused me to her.

Third, he will accuse others to you. Ever get upset with someone and have every bad thing they have ever done to you come to mind? Or have you ever had wild notions about their motives or schemes come to mind? Where did that flood of negative thoughts come from? The accuser sent them.

When we were newly married, Cathy and I had a loud, heated "discussion." I went into the garage and all of a sudden my mind was flooded with thoughts like: *She does not love you. She has never loved you. She does not ever want to see you again. She wishes you were dead.*

Then the door between the garage and the kitchen opened. It was Cathy. She had a tear on her cheek.

"I am sorry," she said. "I don't even know why we're fighting. I love you."

"You do not want a divorce?" I asked.

"Of course not," she replied.

"You do not wish I was dead?" I asked.

"No!" she said. "Stop being silly and come back in the house."

Fourth, he will accuse you to yourself. The Devil will tell you bad things about yourself. He whispers that you can't or you aren't or that you never will. This is one of his favorite ways of devouring us.

Several years ago, I asked a group of forty teenagers if they had ever had a constant gnawing thought that they were worth less than others and would be better off dead. These were captains of sports teams, student council members, kids from very good homes, honor roll students. All were very attractive, intelligent, socially well-adapted kids. I was shocked as over half of them said they lived under the constant bombardment of thoughts that they were worthless, not acceptable, flawed, incapable, and unattractive.

Beware the accuser. <u>He wants to discourage you from being all you can for God</u>.

3. Temptation

> Then Jesus was led up by the Spirit into the wilderness to be tempted by the devil. . . . Now when the tempter came to Him . . . (Matt 4:1–3 NKJV)

The Bible teaches that Satan is the tempter. He takes our God-given drives and desires and twists them in such a way as to get us to seek to have them fulfilled in an unrighteous fashion. He whispers to our old nature an onslaught of tempting thoughts,

"What's so wrong with it?"
"Everyone else does it."
"No one will ever know."
"You need to do this."
"You will enjoy it."
"It will make you feel better."
"You deserve it."

He makes sin sound so good, but he never tells us the consequences of sin. He never tells us the full price. He always skips the fine print . . . that is until it's too late and you are caught. Then he laughs in your face.

4. Deception

> You are of your father the devil, and your will is to do your father's desires. He was a murderer from the beginning, and has nothing to do with the truth, because there is no truth in him. When he lies, he speaks out of his own character, for he is a liar and the father of lies. (John 8:44 ESV)

Jesus referred to the Devil as "the Father of Lies" (John 8:44 ESV). John called him "the deceiver" (Rev 12:9 ESV). One thing Satan consistently does is lie. He issues lies that attack our minds and lies that infiltrate our culture. He uses lies to trap us. Jesus told us that believing truth produces freedom and therefore implied that believing a lie produces bondage (John 8:32).

I remember the time the circus came to Chillicothe when I was a boy. My dad did a smart thing. He took me down to the city park the morning they were setting up. I will never forget walking around and being amazed at all the activity. I was especially captivated by the elephants. They were so big. I couldn't believe it. I was amazed. Then I noticed that the only thing holding them in the ground was a small chain fastened to a small metal stake. I was scared.

The man explained to us that the elephant would never get away from that little stake because elephants never forget. He told us how they stake an elephant to a little stake when they are still very young. The baby elephant pulls and pulls with all his might but cannot get away. He puts this in his mind and never forgets it. Even when he is grown up and is ten times the size he was when he was first staked, he does not pull away, even though he easily could. Why? It is because the elephant believes the lie that the same small stake that could hold him as a baby can hold him now. In reality that elephant is not in bondage to a stake. He is in bondage to a lie.

Satan wants to put you in bondage, and he will use lies to do it. The Devil uses lies to keep the lost from coming to God and to try to keep you from being effective for God. One reason we need to read the Bible every day is to rid our minds of lies that could put us in bondage.

5. Destruction

John referred to Satan as "Appolyon" or "the Destroyer" (see Rev 12:9; 20:3; John 10:10). Satan's goal is the ultimate destruction of you, your family, and your church. In order to bring destruction to your ministry, he often uses weapons of mass distraction to get you slightly off course, which will ultimately put you way off track. He also destroys through discouragement, distress, depression, and division.

Yet, do not fear. In Christ we have been given everything we need to live in spiritual victory.

In Him, We Win!

> No, in all these things we are more than victorious through Him who loved us. (Rom 8:37)

One of Satan's most powerful strategies is simply keeping us ignorant of the victory that is already ours through our position "in Christ." Because of our exalted position "in Christ" we do not fight *for* victory; we fight *from* victory. We do not fight in order to win because in Christ we have *already* "won."

In Rom 8:37 Paul reminds the Roman Christians that no matter what they faced, they were victorious "in Christ." When Paul referred to "all these things," he was referencing the challenges that are described earlier in this passage (8:35). These include "affliction," referring to the general outward pressures of life and to hard times; "anguish," describing the inner feeling of being trapped or hemmed in; "persecution," speaking of suffering because of your faith; "famine," which refers to hunger and distress resulting from natural disasters; "nakedness," which refers to not having enough or being in material need; "danger," speaking of peril from the criminal activity of others such as thugs, thieves, and bandits; and "sword," talking about political betrayal and attack.

Yet, these things cannot separate Christ's people from His love; for Paul boldly declares that "we are more than victorious." We have a *complete and overwhelming* victory, a victory that carries over into every possible aspect of life and every possible foe: life or death, angels or demons, the present or the future, power from on high or power from below, or anything else in the entire universe (8:38–39). Absolutely nothing can defeat us.

Obviously, we are easily defeated apart from Christ. We are helpless, hopeless victims of our circumstances and of the Enemy apart from Christ. But "through him who loves us," it is another story. Our victory comes through our unassailable, invincible position in Christ and through the undeniable, unrelenting, undeserved, invincible, inseparable love of Christ for us.

⚊ What Now? ⚊

Which of the wiles of the Devil are you struggling with the most right now? How can applying Rom 8:37 help you face and overcome the enemy's assault?

⚊ Quotes ⚊

The faithful Christian life is a battle; it is warfare
on a grand scale.

—John MacArthur[6]

Know it or not, like it or not, you and I are in a war! And we
need to begin living as if it were the battle of our lives. . . .
The life devoted to God is a soldier's life.

—Stu Weber[7]

Notes

1. C. S. Lewis quoted by Leland Ryken and Marjorie Lamp Mead in *A Reader's Guide Through the Wardrobe: Exploring C. S. Lewis's Classic Story* (Downers Grove: InterVarsity, 2005), 165.

2. Aiden Wilson Tozer, *This World: Playground or Battleground?* ed. Harry Verploegh (Camp Hill, PA: Christian Publications, 1989), 5.

3. Francis A. Schaeffer, *The Great Evangelical Disaster* (Wheaton: Crossway, 1984), 31.

4. Ronnie Floyd, *10 Things Every Minister Needs to Know* (Green Forest, AR: New Leaf Press, 2006), 61.

5. Neil T. Anderson and Charles Mylander, *Setting Your Church Free: A Biblical Plan to Help Your Church* (Ventura, CA: Regal, 1999), 24.

6. John MacArthur, *Ephesians*, MacArthur New Testament Commentary (Chicago: Moody, 1986), 331.

7. Stu Weber, *Spirit Warriors* (Sisters, OR: Multnomah, 2001), 10.

7

Training Yourself for Godliness

Complacency is a deadly foe of all spiritual growth.
— A. W. TOZER[1]

Timothy was a young pastor of the strategic church at Ephesus. His mentor, the apostle Paul, wrote him two letters of encouragement and instruction. Paul wanted Timothy to remember that one key to being a good pastoral servant of Christ was living a life of disciplined spiritual growth.

> If you point these things out to the brothers, you will be a good servant of Christ Jesus. . . . *Train yourself in godliness*, for, the training of the body has a limited benefit, but godliness is beneficial in every way, since it holds promise for the present life and also for the life to come. This saying is trustworthy and deserves full acceptance. . . . Practice these things; be committed to them, so that your progress may be evident to all. (1 Tim 4:6–9,15, italics added)

Athletes for God

Paul told Timothy that if he was to be "a good minister of Jesus Christ" (1 Tim 4:6 NIV) he would need to continue to make "progress" (1 Tim 4:15). The word "progress" means "pioneer advance into new territory." This would require maximum effort as he would have to "be committed" to give himself entirely to the process toward godliness (1 Tim 4:15).

Paul told Timothy that godliness was ultimately the result of disciplined exercise and intentional pursuits. Godliness would not just happen. It is not a sudden, magical, mystical experience for the spiritually elite. Rather, godliness is the fruit of a spiritually disciplined life.

The word for "train" is *gymnazo*. From it we get our word, "gymnasium." It has been translated "to exercise vigorously, to train diligently, to discipline." It was used for Olympic athletes who spent their lives training for the competition of the games. So, Paul told Timothy that in order to be a good pastor, he needed to live the dedicated, disciplined life of a spiritual athlete. Training is not a one-time event. It is not a once-a-month activity. It is not a once-a-week event. It is a daily discipline.

The DNA of a Champion

Peter tells his readers that God has already given us everything we need to please God and live godly. Beyond that, because we are born again by the Spirit of God, we are partakers of the very nature of God (1 Pet 1:3). In other words, in Christ we have divine DNA. God has given us the DNA of a champion. But we must make every effort to bring it out.

> His divine power has given to us all things that pertain to life and godliness, through the knowledge of Him who called us by glory and virtue, by which have been given to us exceedingly great and precious promises, that through these you may be partakers of the divine nature. . . . But also for this very reason, *giving all diligence, add to your faith.* . . . (2 Pet 1:3–5 NKJV, italics added)

It is great to have the DNA of a champion. But such an astounding DNA will do us no good unless we add diligence, determination, and discipline to bring it out. Great talent only yields great achievement when it is linked with great discipline and persistent practice.

Imagine having the USA Olympic committee show up at your door. Excitedly they say to you, "Congratulations! We have been looking for someone to run the twenty-six-mile marathon in the next Olympics. We have statistics on every person in the entire nation on computer. We have checked everyone's body type, bone structure, and DNA. We have determined that out of 300 million people, you are the one person in America with a chance to bring home the gold medal in the marathon. So you are on the squad. You will run the race. This is the chance of a lifetime."

While you initially are surprised by this information, you start to get excited. You see yourself in the Olympic stadium bursting across the finish line in world record time. You imagine your mom in the stands with tears running down her proud face. You picture your face being shown on the television sets of every home in America.

Then it dawns on you. You have never even run twenty-six miles before, let alone at world record pace. How can you expect to run a marathon when you get out of breath walking from the couch to the refrigerator? John Ortberg writes:

> If you are serious about seizing this chance of a lifetime, you will have to enter into a life of training. You must arrange your life around certain practices that will enable you to do what you cannot do now by willpower alone. . . . Training is necessary for anyone who wants to change deeply and do things exceptionally well. Whether it is running a marathon, or hitting a golf ball, or playing a musical instrument, or learning a new language, or running a successful business, training is required. Trying harder won't get it done. Training is necessary.[2]

Training is necessary. The only way to experience fully the potential of your amazing DNA is living a life of diligence and discipline. Maybe you are thinking, *I'm not so sure about this. Discipline is so hard.* Yes, discipline is hard, but ultimately living without discipline is harder. Ortberg writes:

> People sometimes think that learning how to play Bach at the keyboard by spending years practicing scales and chord progressions is the "hard" way. The truth is the other way around. Spending years practicing scales is the easy way to learn to play Bach. But imagine sitting down at a grand piano in front of a packed concert hall and having never practiced a moment in your life. That's the hard way.[3]

Run on the Treadmill

Cathy and I have (and use) a collection of exercise equipment we bought gently used and in great condition. Why is it so easy to get great exercise equipment so cheap? It is because people want a quick fix and fail to invest the time and perseverance needed to discipline themselves to burn off calories.

Typically someone decides that they need to lose some weight so they get a treadmill for Christmas. Determined to lose weight, they use it the first few weeks of January. Then they miss a few days and stop all together, having lost no weight. Of course some blame the treadmill for their failure to lose weight.

The problem was not with the treadmill, it worked fine. The problem was that they did not use it. As Francis Chan states, "It takes participation on our part. We have to get on the treadmill and run—merely looking at a machine doesn't do a whole lot."[4]

Often we ask the Lord to make us more loving, or to free us from lust, or deliver us from gluttony without apparent success. Why? The reason is that growth and freedom don't just happen. The path to freedom and godliness takes time and perseverance.

Personal Growth Is One Thing You Can Control

Most things are out of our control. About the only thing you can directly improve is yourself. However, when you do improve yourself, everything else within your sphere of influence begins to get better. When you grow yourself as the leader, you allow God to grow your ministry and your people through you. You could say that the key to changing the ministry is changing the minister, the key to improving the ministry is improving the minister, and the key to growing the ministry is growing the minister.

Paul told Timothy, "train *yourself* in godliness" (2 Tim 4:7, italics added). No one else could do it for him. As Christians, we understand that we are not the victims of our environment. What we are is more the product of our decisions than our conditions.

God says that we will have to give an account *of ourselves* when we stand before Him (Rom 14:12). No one else is responsible for our personal growth. No one else can grow for us, learn for us, and improve for us. We have to grow, learn, and develop for ourselves.

Highly effective pastoral leaders know the value of investing in their personal growth. They intentionally plan to maintain and grow their spiritual lives. They build time into their schedules to help them grow as a leader and as a person.

Intentional Growth Prevents Unintentional Decline

If you stop going forward, you quickly go back. This is true of our character, knowledge, and especially our skills. When we stop learning, growing, and developing, we will not remain the same. We will quickly begin to lose ground. Note the attitude of the apostle Paul.

Not that I have already attained, or am already perfected; but I press on, that I may lay hold of that for which Christ Jesus has also laid hold of me. Brethren, I do not count myself to have apprehended; but one thing I do, forgetting those things which are behind and reaching forward to those things which are ahead, I press toward the goal for the prize of the upward call of God in Christ Jesus. (Phil 3:12–14)

Think about it. If the apostle Paul, who was probably in his sixties when he wrote these words, felt the need to continue to grow, how much more do you and I?

John Maxwell noted, "Developing as a leader is a lot like investing successfully in the stock market. If you hope to make a fortune in a day, you are not going to be very successful."[5] He also said, "[T]he learning process is ongoing, a result of self-discipline and perseverance. The goal each day must be to get a little better, to build on the previous day's progress."[6]

The Secret Is in Your Daily Habits and Weekly Plan

Several years ago, I began to feel the need to increase all of my levels of personal effectiveness. This included leadership effectiveness, physical health, spiritual capacity, and the quality of my relationship with my wife and sons. I made the choice to invest time aggressively in a more disciplined and challenging personal growth plan that addressed the areas in which I needed to grow.

I made it a goal to build several daily disciplines into my schedule. Daily, I would set aside time either to serve or really listen to my wife. I set a goal of having at least one thirty-minute personal prayer time daily and to fast one day a week. I read my Bible each day. I attempted to exercise at least five days a week. I severely limited the time I spent watching TV. We tried to have family devotions four nights a week. I listened to two teaching podcasts a week and read one book a week. Later, I added the goal of writing an hour a day.

Sometimes I did not quite reach all my goals, but by the end of a few months, I could tell the difference. I was making progress in all the key areas of my life. When one area seemed like it needed to be addressed, I would hit it harder the next month.

Over the next few years of being aggressive with my growth plan, I slowly made big strides in all the key areas of my life. I had read hundreds of books. I had listened to hundreds of hours of Bible teaching and leadership training. I had written several books. I had read through the Bible several times. I saw answers to prayer almost every day.

When I got intentional about my personal growth, every part of my life became better, including my ministry. My church doubled in attendance. God multiplied my small group numerous times. I enjoyed life more than ever.

The secret of growth and long-term effectiveness is found in your daily habits and weekly plans. Effective ministry leaders build necessary disciplines into their lives and live those disciplines daily. Personal, spiritual, and professional fitness are like physical fitness. They come from learning the right exercises and doing them regularly until they become habits.

"By Failing to Prepare, You Are Preparing to Fail"

Benjamin Franklin, one of the founding fathers of the United States, was a leading printer, satirist, political theorist, politician, scientist, inventor, civic activist, statesmen, and diplomat. He also published *Poor Richard's Almanac*. In between each dated calendar page, he sprinkled his various bits of wisdom including: "There are no gains, without pains," "One today is worth two tomorrows," "Have you somewhat to do tomorrow, do it today," and "Early to bed, and early to rise, makes a man healthy, wealthy, and wise."

Most importantly for this discussion, he also noted, "By failing to prepare, you are preparing to fail." If you are serious about reaching your ministry potential, you need to have an aggressive growth plan.

1. Make a few growth goals. Start with a few goals that you can work on every day or every week. Make them as simple, yet measurable as possible. For example, "read the Bible for fifteen minutes a day" or "read two chapters of the Bible each day." Pick goals that address the areas in which *you* need to grow.

2. Gather necessary tools. There may be some tools you need in order to get the maximum benefit from your growth plan. For me, the key tool is my notebook/journal with my growth plan chart written into the back pages. I check things off every morning as I read my Bible, pray, and journal. Then I check off the reading, exercise, and family relationship investments from the previous day. Other tools may be a good Bible, a prayer notebook, exercise clothes or equipment, and other good books. I have the Bible on CD and now listen to two chapters a day when I drive to work every morning.

3. Develop a plan that fits you. Those who are effective in personal growth do not adopt someone else's plan. They prayerfully develop a plan that fits them. They adjust their plan each month with new goals and disciplines. As you grow, your goals may grow. As your schedule changes, so must your plan.

4. Schedule time to grow. Henry Ford said, "It is my observation that most successful people get ahead in the time other people waste." Growth takes time. Make appointments with yourself to work on your growth plan. Earl Nightingale stated, "If anyone will spend one hour a day on the same subject, that person will be an expert on that subject." Try to find approximately an hour a day to work on personal growth. This time can include Bible reading, prayer, book reading, and exercise. It can be broken into increments of 10–30 minutes. You may do some in the morning and some in the evening.

5. Get started. The best time to get started is *now*. You have to sow *in order to* reap. If no seed is sown, no harvest will be reaped. You have to sow *before* you reap. You cannot cram for harvest. You need to plant in the spring or you will never reap in the fall. Cutting corners and waiting till that last minute just won't work. Start working hard now in order to enjoy the positive results later. Look at the time you spend on personal growth as seeds sown that will in time yield a great multiplying harvest.

Sample Growth Goals

Grow mentally by:
    Reading a _____ a _____.
    Listening to _____ podcast (s) _____.

Developing spiritual fitness by:
    Reading the Bible _____ minutes daily or _____ chapters daily.
    Praying _____ minutes daily.
    Journaling _____ minutes daily.
    Leading family devotions _____ minutes a day, _____ days a week.
    Fasting _____ days a month.

Increasing physical fitness by:
    Exercising _____ minutes _____ days a week.
    Sleeping _____ hours a night.
    Eating healthy by eating less _____ and more _____.

Investing in relationships with:

Disciples _____ minutes a day / hours a week.

Mentor _____ minutes a day / hours a week.

Spouse _____ minutes a day / hours a week.

Children _____ minutes a day / hours a week.

Others _____ minutes a day / hours a week.

Sample Personal Growth Plan

GOAL	Mon	Tues	Wed	Thurs	Fri	Sat
Bible	2 chapters	2 chapters	1 chapter	0	2 chapters	0
Prayer	30 minutes	30 minutes	20 minutes	30 minutes	10 minutes	0
Journal	X	X	0	X	X	0
Exercise	30 minutes	30 minutes	0	30 minutes	0	120 minutes
Meet w/ Disciple	Josh	Jason		Chad		
Fasting	yes					
Reading	2 chapters	2 chapters	1 chapter	0	2 chapters	0

⁓ What Now? ⁓

List some growth goals you should shoot for in the next month. Now plan them into your daily schedule. Update your plan every month, adding and subtracting goals based on your schedule and needs.

⁓ Quotes ⁓

Effective leadership results from hard work and a continuing effort to learn . . . leaders grow. They learn. They continue to change until they have the character and walk with God that is required to lead their organization effectively. Leaders who are willing to make the effort will experience the joy and satisfaction of being used by the Lord to make significant difference in their world.

—HENRY AND RICHARD BLACKABY[7]

Leadership develops daily, not in a day.

—JOHN C. MAXWELL[8]

The secret of our success is found in our daily agenda.

—TAG SHORT[9]

Notes

1. A. W. Tozer quoted by Stan Toler in *Stan Toler's Practical Guide to Pastoral Ministry* (Indianapolis, IN: Wesleyan, 2007), 13.

2. John Ortberg, *The Life You Have Always Wanted* (Grand Rapids, MI: Zondervan, 2002), 55.

3. Ibid, 56.

4. Francis Chan, *Crazy Love* (Colorado Springs, CO: David C. Cook, 2008), 200.

5. John C. Maxwell, *The 21 Irrefutable Laws of Leadership* (Nashville, TN: Thomas Nelson, 1998), 23.

6. Ibid., 24.

7. Henry and Richard Blackaby, *Spiritual Leadership* (Nashville, TN: B&H Publishing, 2002), 285–86.

8. Maxwell, *21 Irrefutable Laws*, 21.

9. Tag Short, quoted by Maxwell, *21 Irrefutable Laws*, 23.

Part 2
Praying with Power

8

Prioritizing Prayer

If a pastor does nothing else, what is the one thing he must do? If a pastor does not do anything else well, what is the one thing he has to do well?

The answer to both questions is the same: *pray*.

What was the very first thing the Lord told Moses to do through his father-in-law Jethro? The answer is to pray (Exod 18:19).

What was it that Jesus modeled before His disciples so faithfully that it was the one thing they asked Him to teach them? The answer is to pray (Luke 11:1).

When the apostles felt that church growth was pulling them away from their priorities, what was the first thing they devoted themselves to? The answer is prayer (Acts 6:4).

When Paul advised Timothy regarding leading the strategic church of Ephesus, what was the first task he gave Timothy to do? The answer again is to pray (1 Tim 2:1).

> First of all, then, I urge that petitions, prayers, intercessions, and thanksgivings be made for everyone. (1 Tim 2:1)

The first priority for every effective spiritual shepherd is to pray.

Do You Truly Believe It?

Do you *really* believe that God can accomplish *more* than you can? Are you convinced that He can produce positive changes *faster* than you can? Would you say that God can do things much *bigger* than you ever could? Do you believe that what God wills and accomplishes *last much longer* than the things that we desire and do?

If so, then your belief will demand that you make prayer a primary priority in your ministry. If you truly believe that God can do things bigger, faster, and better than you can, you will pray. God can do more in seconds than we can accomplish in years. He can do it better, bigger, and more lastingly than we can even imagine.

So the question becomes, how can we somehow cooperate with God to be more influential in the lives of the people we pastor? The answer, of course, is prayer. If you really believe it, you will pray.

But Most Don't

I have trained pastors, missionaries, church staffs, and small group leaders all over the nation and in many parts of the world. When we discuss prayer, all will nod their heads and agree that prayer is important. Yet too often North American Christian leaders are guilty of doing nearly everything else but prayer. One survey said the average pastor prays only seven minutes a day![1] Another said that 80 percent of pastors surveyed spend less than fifteen minutes a day in prayer.[2]

The most generous survey said that pastors pray all of thirty-seven minutes a day. But it also showed that only 16 percent of Protestant ministers across the country are very satisfied with their personal prayer life. This survey stated that a disheartening 21 percent typically spend fifteen minutes or less per day in prayer.[3]

I am not sure which survey is most accurate, but at any rate they all tell us the same thing. Most pastors pray too little. No wonder so many pastors are discouraged. No wonder so many will burn out. No wonder so many quit.

Prayer Is the Common Denominator

Over the past thirty years, I have studied nearly one hundred high impact Christian leaders and pastors. I started with the patriarch Abraham in the Old Testament and went through to the twentieth-century pastor/evangelist Billy Graham. They all had differing backgrounds, abilities, gifts, experiences, and levels of education. But they all had one common denominator—strong prayer lives. Prayer is certainly not the only act of pastoral leadership, but it is the indisputable common denominator of spiritual difference-makers in every generation and in any setting.

Henry Blackaby states, "More than any other single thing leaders do, it is their prayer life that will determine their effectiveness."[4] Nineteenth-century author Andrew Murray said that prayer in the life of the pastor should be regarded "as the highest part of the work entrusted to us, the root and strength of all other work . . . there is nothing we need to study and practice as the art of praying aright."[5]

John Charles Ryle, another well-known nineteenth-century Christian leader, writes:

> I have read the lives of many eminent Christians who have been on earth
> since Bible days. Some of them, I see, were rich, and some poor. Some
> were learned, some unlearned . . . some were Calvinists, and some were
> Arminians. . . . But one thing, I see, they all had in common. They all had
> been men of prayer.[6]

Prayer Is the Determining Factor

Prayer is the determining factor. The more we pray the more God works. We often fail to realize the astounding way our omnipotent God has limited His activity to our prayers.

For example, the prophet Ezekiel showed how the prayers of a single intercessor would have been the determining factor in delivering Israel from the Babylonian Captivity.

> *I searched for a man among them who would repair the wall and stand
> in the gap before Me on behalf of the land so that I might not destroy it,
> but I found no one.* So I have poured out My indignation on them and
> consumed them with the fire of My fury. I have brought their actions
> down on their own heads. [This is] the declaration of the Lord God.
> (Ezek 22:30–31, italics added)

Read verse 30 again, slowly. Think about the fact that one single gap-stander could have stopped the Babylonian captivity. But the last five words of verse 30 tell the sad story, *but I found no one.*

Through the years, I have found that I was not alone in my belief that prayer was the determining factor. "Words fail to explain how necessary prayer is," writes John Calvin. "Although [God] never either sleeps or idles, still very often [he] gives the impression of one sleeping or idling in order that he may thus train us, otherwise idle and lazy, to seek, ask, and entreat him to our great good."[7]

John Piper observed, "Prayer . . . is the splicing of our limp wire into the lightning bolt of heaven. . . . God loves to bless His people. But even more He loves to do it in answer to prayer."[8]

Great praying pastor and author E. M. Bounds wrote,

> God has of His own motion placed Himself under the law of prayer, and has obligated Himself to answer the prayers of men. He has ordained prayer as a means whereby He will do things through men as they pray, which He would not otherwise do . . . man has it in his power to by prayer, move God to work in His own way among men, in which way He would not work if prayer was not made.[9]

Prioritize Prayer in Order to Maximize Impact

R. A. Torrey made an astounding observation when he wrote:

> Prayer is the key that unlocks all the storehouses of God's infinite grace and power. All that God is and all that God does is at the disposal of prayer. But we must use the key. Prayer can do anything God can do, and as God can do anything, prayer is omnipotent.[10]

Hudson Taylor was an English missionary to China. He founded the China Inland Mission which became miraculously influential for God in China. At his death, the mission included 205 mission stations with more than 800 missionaries and 125,000 Chinese Christians. How did he do it? He said that he discovered, "It is possible to move men through God by prayer alone."[11]

Wise spiritual shepherds learn to prioritize prayer in order to maximize their impact.

God Does Nothing in Ministry Apart from Prayer

Pastoral ministry, at its core, is spiritual work. Spiritual work requires spiritual tools. David Jeremiah leads a large church in Southern California and a Christian college. Regarding the essential role of prayer in ministry, he writes,

> I scoured the New Testament some time ago, looking for things God does in ministry that are not prompted by prayer. Do you know what I found?
> Nothing.
> I don't mean I had trouble finding an item or two: I mean I found nothing. Everything God does in the work of ministry, He does through prayer. Consider:

- Prayer is the way you defeat the Devil (Luke 23:31–32; Jas 4:7).
- Prayer is the way you get the lost saved (Luke 18:13).
- Prayer is the way you acquire wisdom (Jas 1:5).
- Prayer is the way a backslider gets restored (Jas 5:16–20).
- Prayer is how saints get strengthened (Jude 20; Matt 26:41).
- Prayer is the way to get laborers out to the mission field (Matt 9:38).
- Prayer is how we cure the sick (Jas 5:13–15).
- Prayer is how we accomplish the impossible (Mark 11:23–24).

. . . everything God wants to do in your life; He has subjugated to one thing: Prayer.[12]

Billy Graham was one of the best-loved spiritual leaders of the twentieth century. He has been called "the nation's pastor" and "America's pastor." He believes in the untapped power of prayer. He wrote, "More can be done by prayer than anything else. Prayer is our greatest weapon. . . . Very few of us have learned how to fully develop the power of prayer."[13]

Too Busy *Not* to Pray

Jesus bit off life in big chunks, and often ministered at an intense pace. The demands on His time and energy were immense. How did He survive it, let alone thrive through it and rise triumphantly above it all?

Jesus viewed prayer as the secret source of spiritual strength and the reservoir of real refreshment. Even when He was very busy, He was never too busy to pray. If nothing else would get done that day, prayer would get done.

When the apostles were experiencing church growing pains and began running into their own limitations, they decided that they were "too busy not to pray," declaring, "But we will devote ourselves to prayer and to the preaching ministry" (Acts 6:4).

The pastor of a huge church in South Korea in writing on the importance of leaders taking the time to pray has written,

One of the greatest lies of Satan is that we don't have enough time to pray. However, all of us have enough time to sleep, eat, and breathe. As soon as we realize that prayer is as important as sleeping, eating, and breathing, we will be amazed at how much time we have to pray.[14]

Prayer Saves Time

Charles Spurgeon, the incredibly successful and busy English pastor, agreed. When preaching on the subject of prayer he observed,

> Sometimes we think we are too busy to pray. That also is a great mistake, for *praying is a saving of time.* . . . God can multiply our ability to make use of time. If we give the Lord his due, we shall have enough for all necessary purposes. In this matter seek first the kingdom of God and his righteousness, and all these things shall be added to you. Your other engagements will run smoothly if you do not forget your engagement with God.[15] (italics added)

George Muller was one of the most amazing spiritual leaders the world has ever seen. He was a gifted pastor, educator, philanthropist, and evangelist. As a young pastor, he went through a very busy season. In fact, he often found himself too busy to pray as he ought. His biographer writes,

> After learning the lesson of being busy in the work of the Lord, too busy in fact to pray, he told his brethren that four hours of work after an hour of prayer would accomplish more than five hours without prayer. This rule henceforth he faithfully kept.[16]

Prayer allows God to do more in days, hours, minutes, or even seconds than we could accomplish without Him in months, or even years, of work. How often we have taught, encouraged, and counseled people with little or no result? How often have we shared our faith with seemingly little or no breakthrough in the other person's defenses? But, when God moves, He helps people make changes in seconds that we could not get them to do in years. Prayer is a powerful time saver. Once we understand this principle, we will learn to say, "I am too busy *not* to pray."

Martin Luther towers as a giant in church history. The highly active and influential pastor, professor, author, and father of the Protestant Reformation understood the power of prayer to save time and effort. When asked of his plans for the coming week, Martin Luther mentioned that he generally spent two hours a day in prayer, but his coming week was extra busy. Therefore, he said, "Work, work from early till late. In fact I have so much to do that I shall spend the first three hours in prayer."[17]

Three hours in prayer on a busy day!

Martin Luther understood something we need to grasp. Time spent praying can be the best time-saving device we have.

Prioritize Prayer in Your Daily Schedule

The biographers of Hudson Taylor, the intensely busy founder of the China Inland Mission, described the priority Taylor gave to prayer and Bible study. Taylor found it necessary to meet God very early in the day. His biographers write, "From two to four A.M. was the time he usually gave to prayer, the time when he could be most sure of being undisturbed to wait upon God."[18]

Stan Toler is a gifted leader, author, and pastor. In his *Practical Guide for Pastoral Ministry* he offers more than three hundred pages of common sense for pastors stating, "Prayer is the most important thing a pastor has to do every day."[19]

Set a Time to Pray

Jerry Falwell was the highly influential founder and pastor of Thomas Road Baptist Church, which has a membership of tens of thousands. He also founded Liberty University, which has more than 50,000 students. When Falwell was a college student, he learned the immense value of having a daily prayer time. He went to the dean of students and asked for a key to the third floor of the administration building. There he prayed from 1:30 to 5:00 every weekday afternoon, crying out to God to bless his ministry as a fifth-grade Sunday school teacher. It paid off. The class grew from two boys to fifty-seven by May.[20]

Most of us need to set a daily prayer time or times if we hope to build a dynamic prayer life. We may choose morning, afternoon, or evening, but we need to at least choose a time, or several times, for prayer.

Set an Amount of Time to Pray

Effective spiritual leaders not only establish a time for prayer but also usually set *an amount of time*. Most set aside an hour; many set aside even longer. The pattern of spending an hour in prayer goes back to the garden of Gethsemane when Jesus confronted the sleeping apostle Peter, "Then He came to the disciples and found them sleeping. He asked Peter, 'So, couldn't you stay awake with Me *one hour*?'" (Matt 26:40, italics added). Just think what God can do through you, for you, and in you, and those you pray for if you prayed at least an hour every day!

Determine a Place to Pray

Almost as important as the time of prayer is the *place* of prayer. The best example of a leader having a special place for prayer is Moses. The people Moses led were mostly spiritual infants. He had to teach them everything, including how to relate to God.

Moses used a tent and pitched it outside the camp and called it "the tent of meeting" (Exod 33:7–11). That tent was a place made sacred as a spot where divine dialogue occurred. When Moses went inside, distractions were minimized and prayer was maximized.

⚊ What Now? ⚊

Determine a time or times when you will pray each day. Get a place or places for your daily appointment with God. Start praying more than you ever have before.

⚊ Quotes ⚊

Much time spent in prayer is the secret of all successful praying. Prayer that is felt as a mighty force is the mediate or immediate product of much time spent in prayer. Our short prayers owe their point and efficiency to the long ones that have preceded them.

—E. M. Bounds[21]

The greatest problem we face is not unanswered prayer but unoffered prayer.

—Adrian Rogers[22]

We not ought only to pray more, but we **must***! The fact is, the secret of all ministerial success lies in prevalence at the mercy seat.*

—C. H. Spurgeon[23] (emphasis his)

Notes

1. William Brehm, *Why Should We Pray?* Be Ready! http://www.be-ready.org/whypray.html (accessed February 12, 2007).

2. "Statistics about Pastors," Maranatha Life, http://www.maranathalife.com/lifeline/stats.htm (accessed February 14, 2007).

3. "Study shows only 16% of Protestant ministers are very satisfied with their personal prayer lives," Ellison Research, http://www.ellisonresearch.com/ERPS%20II/release_16_prayer.htm (accessed May 11, 2007).

4. Henry Blackaby and Richard Blackaby, *Spiritual Leadership* (Nashville, TN: B&H, 2001), 151.

5. Andrew Murray, *With Christ in the School of Prayer* (Grand Rapids: Zondervan, 1983), xii.

6. John Charles Ryle, *A Call to Prayer* (Grand Rapids: Baker, 1976), 14–15.

7. John Calvin, *Institutes of the Christian Religion*, 2 vols., ed. John T. McNeill, trans. Ford Lewis Battles (Philadelphia: Westminster, 1960), 2:851, 853.

8. John Piper, *Brothers, We Are Not Professionals* (Nashville, TN: B&H, 2002), 53.

9. Edward Mckendress Bounds, *The Weapon of Prayer* (Grand Rapids, MI: Baker, 1931), 21.

10. R. A. Torrey, *The Power of Prayer* (Grand Rapids, MI: Zondervan, 1924), 17.

11. Hudson Taylor as quoted in J. O. Sanders, *Spiritual Leadership* (Chicago, IL: Moody, 1974), 82.

12. David Jeremiah, *Prayer: The Great Adventure* (Sisters, OR: Multnomah, 1997), 40–41.

13. Billy Graham quoted by Cort Flint, *The Quotable Billy Graham* (Anderson, SC: Droke House, 1966), 153.

14. Paul Y. Cho, *Prayer: Key to Revival* (Waco, TX: Word, 1984), 18.

15. Charles Spurgeon, "Pray without Ceasing," Metropolitan Tabernacle Pulpit, A Sermon Delivered on Lord's Day Morning, March 10, 1872, http://www.spurgeon.org/sermons/1039.htm (accessed May 16, 2007).

16. Basil Miller, *George Muller: Man of Faith and Miracles* (Minneapolis, MN: Bethany Fellowship, 1941), 49.

17. Martin Luther quoted in Edward Mackendree Bounds, *Power Through Prayer* (Grand Rapids, MI: Zondervan, 1962), 37 (italics added).

18. Howard and Geraldine Taylor, *Hudson Taylor's Spiritual Secret* (Chicago, IL: Moody, 1932), 235.

19. Stan Toler, *Stan Toler's Practical Guide for Pastoral Ministry* (Indianapolis: Wesleyan, 2007, 2011).

20. Jerry Strober and Ruth Tomczak, *Jerry Falwell: Aflame for God* (Nashville, TN: Thomas Nelson, 1979), 25–26.

21. Edward Mackendree Bounds, *Preacher and Prayer* (Grand Rapids, MI: Zondervan, 1982), 36.

22. Adrian Rogers, *Adrianisms: The Wit and Wisdom of Adrian Rogers* (Memphis, TN: Love Worth Finding Ministries, 2006), 44.

23. Charles H. Spurgeon, *Lectures to My Students* (Grand Rapids, MI: Zondervan, 1954), 49.

9

Interceding
for Your People

The Hebrew people whom Moses was called to lead were a notoriously rebellious lot whose propensity to wander angered the Lord. In fact, on more than one occasion, He was so angry with them that He planned to destroy them. Yet He never did, despite having good reason to do so.

What affected His decision?

The determining factor was the intercessory prayers of the leader, Moses.

> The LORD also said to Moses: "I have seen this people, and they are indeed a stiff-necked people. Now leave Me alone, so that My anger can burn against them and I can destroy them. Then I will make you into a great nation." *But Moses interceded with the* LORD *his God. . . .*So the LORD changed his mind about the disaster He said He would bring on His people. (Exod 32:9–11,14, italics added)

Read that again slowly. God said He was going to destroy the Hebrews, but Moses interceded on their behalf. As a result, God changed His mind! Intercessory prayer is a *powerful* gift from God to His people that He uses to allow them to participate in His saving work.

What is amazing is that this display of the power of intercession was not a one-time event. Again and again, the people whom Moses led complained to God. Again and again, Moses prayed for his people. Again and again, God responded to his intercessory prayers (Num 14:11–20). The psalmist summarizes the power of Moses' gap-standing intercession in one dynamic statement:

So He [God] said He would have destroyed them—if *Moses* His chosen
one had not stood before Him in the breach to turn His wrath away from
destroying [them]. (Ps 106:23, italics added)

The term *intercede* means "to go between." Used for prayer it describes the
act of going to God and pleading on behalf of another.

The word "prayer" is a general term meaning "talking to God." "Intercession" is more specific. It describes coming to God *on behalf of another*. Therefore, while all intercession is prayer, not all prayer is intercession.

Missionary leader Wesley Duewel writes, "You have no greater ministry or
no leadership more influential than intercession."[1] It was E. M. Bounds who
said, "Talking to men for God is a great thing. But talking to God for men is
greater still."[2]

Jesus Intercedes for Us

Jesus lived intercession. His entire ministry is identifying with us, standing
in our stead, and going to God the Father on our behalf. As a leader, He often
went away by Himself in part, to pray for His followers.

In speaking of the twelve disciples, He said, "I pray for them" (John 17:9).
In speaking of His then future followers, like us, He said, "I pray not only for
these, but also for those who believe in Me through their message" (John 17:20).

Even now in His exalted home in heaven, Jesus is interceding for us.

Christ Jesus is the One who died, but even more, has been raised; He also
is at the right hand of God and *intercedes for us.* (Rom 8:34, italics added)

Therefore He is always able to save those who come to God through
Him, since He always *lives to intercede* for them. (Heb 7:25, italics
added)

Spurgeon Advised Pastors to Be Intercessors

Charles Spurgeon is recognized as one of the greatest pastors who ever
lived. He led one of the first megachurches since Pentecost, with as many as
ten thousand people gathering weekly to hear him preach. He started a seminary and personally trained hundreds of pastors and missionaries. Beyond that,
he led his church to send out teams of members to plant dozens of churches
around metropolitan London. His leadership also produced dozens of justice
ministries such as orphan homes, ministries to widows, food and clothing for
the poor, help for poverty-stricken pastors, and much more. He also was a
prolific and popular author.

Spurgeon was adamant that great pastoral leadership and preaching flowed from serious prayer. He told his young pastoral students, "None is so able to plead with men as those who have been wrestling with God on their behalf."[3] As a great believer in the importance of intercession in the life of the pastor, he said:

> My brethren, let me beseech you to be men of prayer. Great talents you may never have but you will do well without them if you abound in intercession.[4]

Keys to Powerful Intercession

Sacrificial Selflessness

Why were the prayers of Moses so powerful? The secret is uncovered at the end of Exodus 32. Moses was not only selflessly willing to give up being the father and king of a great nation of his own, but he was willing to give up his own pass to paradise. Look carefully at Moses' prayer.

> So Moses returned to the LORD and said, "Oh, this people has committed a great sin; they have made for themselves a god of gold. Now if You would only forgive their sin. But if not, please *erase me* from the book You have written." (Exod 32:31–32, italics added)

I am amazed at the sacrificial selflessness of Moses — *"Forgive their sin — but if not, please erase me!"* He was willing to lose his own reservation in heaven if it would keep them from being destroyed.

Dick Eastman is the president of the large mission agency Every Home for Christ. He also is a prayer warrior and catalyst. He has taught me much about intercession. He writes, "An intercessor must bid farewell to self and welcome the burdens of humanity."[5] Elsewhere he states, "As intercessors who bear our crosses of sacrifice, we too stand between hurting humanity and a loving Father, carrying their concerns to God."[6]

Relentless Boldness

Abraham was a flawed, but highly influential spiritual leader. He was the spiritual father of the faithful and the biological father of the Jews.

As you may recall, God and two angels had cloaked themselves in human form in order to visit Abraham and Sarah to tell Sarah that she would bear a child within a year. After dinner, the three guests got up to leave and the Lord confided in Abraham that they also were investigating the extreme wickedness

of Sodom. Realizing that judgment was about to come, Abraham valiantly posi-
tioned himself between the Lord and Sodom. There he interceded on behalf of
the people of Sodom.

> But Abraham still stood before the LORD. And Abraham came near and
> said, "Would You also destroy the righteous with the wicked? Suppose
> there were fifty righteous within the city; would You also destroy the
> place and not spare it for the fifty righteous that were in it? Far be it from
> You to do such a thing as this, to slay the righteous with the wicked, so
> that the righteous should be as the wicked; far be it from You! Shall not
> the Judge of all the earth do right?" (Gen 18:22–25 NKJV)

Notice his position—"standing before the Lord." That is a physical example of the spiritual positioning of an intercessor. Notice also that he gave God
a definite challenge to respond to: "would You also destroy the place and not
spare it for the fifty righteous that were in it?" (v. 24). Beyond that, note that he
appealed to the Lord's righteous and just character: "Far be it from You to do
such a thing as this, to slay the righteous with the wicked, so that the righteous
should be as the wicked; far be it from You! Shall not the Judge of all the earth
do right?" (v. 25).

God noticed and it profoundly affected Him.

> So the LORD said, "If I find in Sodom fifty righteous within the city, then
> I will spare all the place for their sakes." (Gen 18:26 NKJV)

Abraham's intercessory prayers potentially saved an entire city! His bold
directness made a difference. Yet Abraham was not through. He was not blind
or naïve. He also knew the wicked nature of Sodom. He cared enough for the
people of Sodom that he had to be sure of their deliverance. So he asked the
Lord to spare Sodom again, this time for the sake of forty-five righteous people. And God said yes!

> Then Abraham answered and said, "Indeed now, I who am but dust and
> ashes have taken it upon myself to speak to the Lord: Suppose there were
> five less than the fifty righteous; would You destroy all of the city for
> lack of five?" So He said, "If I find there forty-five, I will not destroy it."
> (Gen 18:27–28 NKJV)

I probably would have stopped there, content to leave well enough alone.
But not Abraham; he was relentlessly aggressive in his prayers. Four more
times he sought God on behalf of Sodom. Each time he appealed for greater
grace and mercy.

And he spoke to Him yet again and said, "Suppose there should be forty found there?"

So He said, "I will not do it for the sake of forty."

Then he said, "Let not the Lord be angry, and I will speak: Suppose thirty should be found there?"

So He said, "I will not do it if I find thirty there."

And he said, "Indeed now, I have taken it upon myself to speak to the Lord: Suppose twenty should be found there?"

So He said, "I will not destroy it for the sake of twenty."

Then he said, "Let not the Lord be angry, and I will speak but once more: Suppose ten should be found there?"

And He said, "I will not destroy it for the sake of ten." (Gen 18:29–32 NKJV)

One man's persistently insistent prayers secured the safety of an entire city . . . *if* the city had a representation of a mere ten righteous souls. It took faith to keep coming back to God and asking for more. It took serious concern for those people. It also took holy stubbornness.

And it worked! God agreed to Abraham's requests.

Unfortunately, Abraham was overly optimistic in his view of Sodom. He must have assumed that surely his nephew Lot would have been able to convert a few others to join him on behalf of God and righteousness. But sadly, Lot had failed to convert even his own wife. There were not even a handful of righteous people in Sodom. So it was destroyed.

But don't miss the bigger issue. Abraham's intercession had potentially spared Sodom from destruction. Persistent petition made a difference.

Brokenhearted Tears

Jesus had a huge heart for people. His heart is well summed up in two words: "Jesus wept" (John 11:35). Consider how He became a man of sorrows and acquainted with grief (Isa 53:3). Notice the tears tracing down His cheeks when He contemplated the pain of the people: "Now as He drew near, He saw the city and wept over it" (Luke 19:41).

Jesus, the brokenhearted intercessor, shed tears for those He came to serve.

When he looked out over the crowds, *his heart broke*. So confused and aimless they were, like sheep with no shepherd. (Matt 9:36 MSG)

During the days of Jesus' life on earth, he offered up prayers and petitions with *loud cries and tears* to the one who could save him from death, and he was heard because of his reverent submission. (Heb 5:7 NIV)

There is no great servant leadership without brokenhearted tears. God told the prophet Joel that He wanted His spiritual servants to intercede for their people *with tears* (Joel 2:17). He gave the same message through Isaiah (Isa 22:12). When they refused to do so, God saw their selfishness as sin that "will not be atoned for" (Isa 22:13–14 ESV). Likewise, the prophet Samuel took his role in praying for God's people very seriously when he wrote, "As for me, far be it from me that I should sin against the LORD by failing to pray for you" (1 Sam 12:23 NIV).

A study of the great servant leaders in the Bible is a study in tears:

- David wept over insults to God's name (Ps 69:9–10).
- Isaiah wept over the plight of his enemies (Isa 16:9–11).
- Josiah wept for his people (2 Kgs 22:19).
- A crowd gathered as a result of Ezra's tears (Ezra 10:1–2).

The Weeping Prophet. One of the great servant intercessors is the prophet Jeremiah. Jeremiah has been labeled "the weeping prophet." Hear the deep burden in his words as he writes, "Since my people are crushed, I am crushed; I mourn, and horror grips me" (Jer 8:21 NIV) and "Oh, that my head were a spring of water and my eyes a fountain of tears! I would weep day and night for the slain of my people" (Jer 9:1 NIV).

Out of anguished love he warned his people, "If you do not listen, I will weep in secret because of your pride; my eyes will weep bitterly, overflowing with tears, because the LORD's flock will be taken captive" (Jer 13:17 NIV).

Jeremiah wrote another book of the Bible that, because of its tear-stained content, became widely known as Lamentations. In it he records God's grief over the sinfulness of His people and the destruction of Jerusalem. One of its astounding features is that the weeping of God results in tears streaming down Jeremiah's cheeks.

This is why I weep and my eyes overflow with tears.... (Lam 1:16 NIV)

My eyes fail from weeping, I am in torment within; my heart is poured out on the ground because my people are destroyed, because children and infants faint in the streets of the city. (Lam 2:11 NIV)

Streams of tears flow from my eyes because my people are destroyed.
My eyes will flow unceasingly, without relief, until the LORD looks down
from heaven and sees. (Lam 3:48–50 NIV)

The Weeping Apostle. Paul's intercessory ministry is splattered with tears.
He summarized his ministry in Ephesus by reminding the elders that he "served
the Lord with great humility *and with tears*" and "that for three years I never
stopped warning each of you night and day *with tears*" (Acts 20:18–19,31 NIV,
italics added). He told the Corinthians, "I wrote you out of great distress and
anguish of heart and *with many tears*" (2 Cor 2:4 NIV).

The thought of his people, the Jews, not coming to Christ caused him to
write:

> I tell the truth in Christ, I am not lying, my conscience also bearing
> me witness in the Holy Spirit, that I have great sorrow and continual
> grief in my heart. For I could wish that I myself were accursed from
> Christ for my brethren, my countrymen according to the flesh, who are
> Israelites. . . . (Rom 9:1–4 NKJV)

"Try Tears." In more recent history, the founder of the Salvation Army was
a man of tear-stained intercession. William Booth was an unconventional, con-
troversial zealot for Jesus. He lived the life of a spiritual soldier as the founder
of the Salvation Army and preached to the least of the least.

Two of his protégés set out to found a new work, only to meet with failure
and opposition. Frustrated and tired, they appealed to Booth to close the rescue
mission.

General Booth sent back a telegram with two words on it:

TRY TEARS

They followed his advice and they witnessed a mighty revival.[7]

"Let my heart be broken." Bob Pierce, the founder of World Vision, a
huge Christian relief and development organization that works in more than
one hundred countries to tackle poverty, once wrote on the flyleaf of his Bible,
"Let my heart be broken with the things that break the heart of God."[8] God's
leaders pray out of hearts crushed by the people and situations that cause
God's heart to break.

Wesley Duewel adds,

We must so identify with those we lead, both by love and by commitment, that we carry them on our hearts every day of our leadership. . . . We must touch His throne constantly for our people. We sin against the Lord if we fail to do so.[9]

Refusal to Quit

Persistent faith-based intercession produces results. No one symbolizes this better than George Muller. He was preaching in 1884 and testified that forty years prior, in 1844, five individuals were laid upon his heart and he began to intercede for them to come to Christ.

Eighteen months passed before one of them was converted. He prayed on for five years more and another was converted. He continued to pray.

At the end of twelve and a half years, the third was converted.

During his message given in 1884, Muller stated that he had continued to pray for the other two, without missing a single day, but they were not yet converted. But he was encouraged that the answer would come. In fact Muller said, "They are not converted yet, but they will be."[10]

Twelve years later, at his death, after interceding for them daily for a total of fifty-two years, they still were not yet converted. But one came to Christ at Muller's funeral and the other shortly thereafter![11] Resilient, persistent intercession makes a difference.

A Guide to Praying for Your Church

1. Sanctify us and free us through the truth (John 8:32; 17:16).
2. We would truly love and serve one another (John 13:14).
3. We would be protected from the evil one (John 17:15).
4. We would be united (John 17:21–23).
5. We would be and make disciples (Matt 28:19–20).
6. We would be devoted to the Word, prayer, fellowship, worship, ministry, and evangelism (Acts 2:42–47).

~ What Now? ~

How can you make intercession a more central part of your ministry now?
What could happen if you would begin to pray for others like you wish others
would pray for you?

Notes

1. Wesley Duewel, *Mighty Prevailing Prayer* (Grand Rapids, MI: Zondervan,
1990), 22.

2. Edward Mackendree Bounds, *Power Through Prayer* (Grand Rapids, MI:
Zondervan, 1962), 27.

3. Charles Spurgeon, *Lectures to My Students* (Grand Rapids, MI: Zondervan,
1954), 45.

4. Ibid., 47.

5. Dick Eastman, *Love on Its Knees* (Tarrytown, NY: Fleming Revell, 1989), 56.

6. Ibid., 17.

7. Story told by H. Begbie in "The Life of General William Booth" as recorded at
http://www.jesus-is-savior.com/Great%20Men%20of%20God/general_william
_booth.htm (accessed Feb. 12, 2009).

8. Kenneth Boa, "The Heart of God," World Vision Resources, http://www
.worldvisionresources.com/product_info.php?products_id=289 (accessed Feb. 12,
2009).

9. Wesley Duewel, *Ablaze for God* (Grand Rapids, MI: Zondervan, 1989), 243.

10. Dwight L. Moody, *Prevailing Prayer* (Chicago, IL: Moody, 1987), 100–101.

11. Basil Miller, *George Muller: Man of Faith and Miracles* (Minneapolis, MN:
Bethany House, 1943), 146.

10

Following Paul's Example in Praying for Your Flock

If you are like I am, you have to admit that you need all the help you can get to be an effective biblical pastor. Maybe like me you really want to be a man of prayer but have not had many examples to model your prayer life after. Fortunately for us, one of the greatest mentors of all time has offered to help us. His name is Paul, and he has extended this invitation.

> Be imitators of me, as I also am of Christ. (1 Cor 11:1)

The apostle Paul was an outstanding spiritual leader to the young Christians in the churches he started. Fortunately for us, he recorded many of the prayers he regularly offered on behalf of his churches. From those prayers we learn from his example how we can pray for those we serve.

In one sitting, I read the content of each of Paul's prayers, in four translations. Reading them all at once shook me, convicted me, challenged me, and powerfully encouraged me as I pray for others. They are found in Rom 1:8–10; 15:5–6,13; Eph 1:15–19; 3:14–19; Phil 1:9–11; Col 1:9–12; 1 Thess 1:2–3; 3:11–13; 2 Thess 1:11–12; Phlm 4–6. In looking at them as a group, I saw several powerful insights into how a pastor can most effectively pray for his flock.

Paul's Keys to Effective Intercession

Consistency in Prayer

The first thing that jumps out as you study Paul's prayers is his repeated mention of how consistently and constantly he prayed for others. Obviously Paul viewed regular, relentless, persistent, persevering, frequent, fervent prayer as a primary responsibility for his spiritual children. Note the words that are italicized.

> *Without ceasing* I make mention of you always in my prayers. (Rom 1:9 NIV)

> *Do not cease* to give thanks for you, making mention of you in my prayers. (Eph 1:16 NKJV)

> *Praying always* for you . . . (Col 1:3 NKJV)

> We give thanks to God *always* for you all, making mention of you in our prayers, *remembering without ceasing.* (1 Thess 1:2–3 NKJV)

> *Night and day praying exceedingly* . . . (1 Thess 3:10 NKJV)

> We also pray *always* for you. (2 Thess 1:11 NKJV)

> *Without ceasing* I remember you in my prayers night and day. (2 Tim 1:3 NKJV)

> I thank my God, making mention of you *always* in my prayers. (Phlm 4 NKJV)

Look back through those verses and observe the drumbeat repetition describing the consistency of Paul's prayers for his spiritual children—"without ceasing," "always," "do not cease," "always," "without ceasing," "night and day," "exceedingly," "always," "without ceasing," and "day and night." You get the idea that he never missed a day, let alone an opportunity to pray for his spiritual children. Every time they came to mind, he offered a prayer on their behalf.

Maybe you are like me. I will pray often when there are emergencies or crises, but I tend to slack off when the pressure lets off. I need to learn to pray consistently even when there is no crisis. If I did, maybe there would be fewer crises.

We often think about the people we are called to lead, talk about them, and even spend time with them, but how much time do we actually spend praying for them? I would guess that most of us would have to say that the frequency of our prayers is too little, too rare, and often, too late. I want to strongly encourage you to have a set time, at least once a day, when you pray Scripture for the people you pastor.

If you have a large church, allow me to suggest to you a pattern for praying effectively for your flock each week. The idea is to divide the names of your prayer list into seven separate lists. Then pray for each of the seven lists once a week. For example, you would pray for list number 1 on Monday, list number 2 on Tuesday, and list number 3 on Wednesday. This way you can get to each one on your prayer list once a week with greater depth than if you tried to get to all of them every day.

Constancy in Gratitude

Paul was not only consistent in his prayers, but he was constant in his gratitude. Again and again he mentioned how thankful he was for his spiritual children and the work God had already done and was doing in them. Read these verses and note Paul's heartbeat of gratitude, italics added.

> First, I *thank* my God through Jesus Christ for all of you, because your faith is being reported all over the world. (Rom 1:8 NIV)

> I *thank* my God always concerning you for the grace of God which was given to you by Christ Jesus, that you were enriched in everything by Him in all utterance and all knowledge, even as the testimony of Christ was confirmed in you, so that you come short in no gift. (1 Cor 1:4–7 NKJV)

> [A]fter I heard of your faith in the Lord Jesus and your love for all the saints, do not cease to *give thanks* for you. (Eph 1:15–16 NKJV)

> I *thank* my God upon every remembrance of you, always in every prayer of mine making request for you all with joy, for your fellowship in the gospel from the first day until now, being confident of this very thing, that He who has begun a good work in you will complete it until the day of Jesus Christ. (Phil 1:3–6 NKJV)

> We give *thanks* to the God and Father of our Lord Jesus Christ, praying always for you, since we heard of your faith in Christ Jesus and of your love for all the saints. (Col 1:3–4 NKJV)

> We give *thanks* to God always for you all, making mention of you in our prayers, remembering without ceasing your work of faith, labor of love, and patience of hope in our Lord Jesus Christ in the sight of our God and Father. (1 Thess 1:2–3 NKJV)

For this reason we also *thank* God without ceasing, because when you
received the word of God which you heard from us, you welcomed it
not as the word of men, but as it is in truth, the word of God, which also
effectively works in you who believe. (1 Thess 2:13 NKJV)

For what *thanks* can we render to God for you, for all the joy with which
we rejoice for your sake before our God? (1 Thess 3:9 NKJV)

We are bound to *thank* God always for you, brethren, as it is fitting,
because your faith grows exceedingly, and the love of every one of you
all abounds toward each other. (2 Thess 1:3 NKJV)

I *thank* God, whom I serve with a pure conscience, as my forefathers did,
as without ceasing I remember you in my prayers night and day . . . when I
call to remembrance the genuine faith that is in you. (2 Tim 1:3–5 NKJV)

I *thank* my God, making mention of you always in my prayers, hearing
of your love and faith which you have toward the Lord Jesus and toward
all the saints. (Phlm 4–5 NKJV)

Do you thank God for your church every day? Or do you take for granted
that God has given them to you as a gift? Are you taking for granted the work
He is doing in their lives? We should learn from Paul to spend time each day
thanking God for our people.

Pastoral leadership can be the most discouraging responsibility we ever
face. Some of our people go through stretches when it is, at best, three steps
forward, two steps back. Paul served as the pastor for Christians who could
have easily worn him out and driven him crazy.

But amazingly they did not make him bitter or cynical or discouraged.
Why? He always thanked God for them.

What I find challenging is that he not only was thankful for the faithful
Romans and the spiritually influential Thessalonians, but he was also grateful
for the carnal Corinthians. His Corinthian church members struggled to follow his leadership. They continually fought with each other. They got off track
easily, quickly, and often.

We should not only note *that* Paul was grateful, but also observe *that for
which* he was grateful. He did *not* mention thanks for their good health or easy
lives. Instead he was grateful to God for what He had done in their lives, what
He was doing in their lives, and what He would do in their lives. Paul's gratitude was spiritual, not physical or material. I am not saying that we should not
thank God for the physical, material, educational, and vocational blessings He

gives our flock. But the primary content of our gratitude should be focused on the spiritual work God has done, is doing, and will do in their lives.

Confidence in Expectation

Paul was not only consistent in his prayers and constant in his gratitude, but he was also confident in his expectation. He prayed for each of his churches, believing that God was not finished yet. God still had more and better ahead. Let's look at several examples.

> Now may the God of hope fill you with all joy and peace in believing, that you may abound in hope by the power of the Holy Spirit. Now I myself am confident concerning you, my brethren, that you also are full of goodness, filled with all knowledge, able also to admonish one another. (Rom 15:13–14 NKJV)

Notice that Paul based his prayers on the assurance he had in God's work in their lives. Because God was at work in them, they had goodness, knowledge, and ability.

Paul prayed with confident expectation even when he prayed for the Corinthians, his most troublesome group of spiritual children. Yet he was positive that one day even they would end up blameless *because God is faithful.* We can pray for our church members with great anticipation because we are praying to our great and faithful God.

> I thank my God always concerning you for the grace of God which was given to you by Christ Jesus, that you were enriched in everything by Him in all utterance and all knowledge, even as the testimony of Christ was confirmed in you, so that you come short in no gift, eagerly waiting for the revelation of our Lord Jesus Christ, who will also confirm you to the end, that you may be blameless in the day of our Lord Jesus Christ. God is faithful, by whom you were called into the fellowship of His Son, Jesus Christ our Lord. (1 Cor 1:4–9 NKJV)

Paul prayed with firm anticipation that the God who began the work in the lives of his church members would complete it.

> I thank my God upon every remembrance of you, always in every prayer of mine making request for you all with joy, for your fellowship in the gospel from the first day until now, being confident of this very thing, that He who has begun a good work in you will complete it until the day of Jesus Christ. (Phil 1:3–6 NKJV)

Note carefully verse 6. Eugene Petersen renders this verse as "There has never been the slightest doubt in my mind that the God who started this great work in you would keep at it and bring it to a flourishing finish on the very day Christ Jesus appears."[1]

Certainly there will be times when our children disappoint us. We must be like Paul and remember that our faith is not in them but in the God who is at work in them. As long as they are breathing, He is not finished working.

Too often the aim of our prayers is much too low. Paul prayed expectantly that his spiritual children wouldn't barely make God's team and ride the bench, but that they would hit spiritual homeruns and end up in the Hall of Faith. God is able and willing to work. He can do more than we can ask or imagine.

Consumed with Their Spiritual Progress

Paul was not only consistent in his prayers, constant in his gratitude, and confident in his expectation, but he was also consumed with the spiritual progress of his people. He prayed that they would know God and all God had available for them (Eph 1:17–19); that they would have inner strength and live open to Christ, experiencing the full dimensions of His love (Eph 3:14–20); that they would learn to live well and wisely, bearing spiritual fruit (Phil 1:9–11). Paul prayed that they would be in step with God's will and live well as they worked for Him with glorious and joyful endurance (Col 1:9–12); that they would overflow with love, strength, and purity (1 Thess 3:11–13); and that God would make them holy and whole inside and out (1 Thess 5:23–24). Paul prayed that they would be fit for what God had called them to be, and God would energize their efforts (2 Thess 1:11–12); that they would experience spiritual encouragement and empowerment in their words and works (2 Thess 2:16–17); and that as they shared their faith they would understand just how amazing it is (Phlm 6).

Unlike most of our prayers that tend to be based on our members' physical needs, vocational challenges, and financial situations, Paul's prayers are consumed with the spiritual state of his spiritual children. I am sure that he did mention other areas of need on occasion, but what comprised the vast majority of his requests was their spiritual condition.

Beyond that, he prayed that they would not remain at their current levels of spiritual maturity. Repeatedly his prayers are entwined with requests for their ongoing spiritual development and progress. For example, he asked that they would be "increasing in the knowledge of God" (Col 1:10 NKJV); that they would "increase and abound in love to one another and to all" (1 Thess 3:12

NKJV); and told them that he prayed that their "faith grows exceedingly, and the love of every one of you all abounds toward each other" (2 Thess 1:3 NKJV).

Do not allow the content of your prayers to be overly focused on temporal, external, and superficial needs. Learn from Paul to fix your prayers on what is most important: the spiritual development of your church members.

A Summary of the Requests Paul Made for His Flock

We are fortunate that Paul recorded so many of his prayer requests. They show us that he prayed for every possible aspect of his flock's relationship with God and their spiritual development. I have summarized them below. Read slowly through the list of twenty-six requests and mark the ones that you feel would be especially appropriate to pray for your flock at this time.

Paul prayed that his spiritual children would . . .

Rom 15:5–6	Learn to live in unity and harmony with others
Rom 15:13	Be filled with joy, peace, and spiritual energy
Eph 1:17	Know God personally
Eph 1:18	Know what God is calling them to do and be, all that is available to them in God, and how great God's power can be in them as they believe in Him
Eph 3:16	Be inwardly strengthened with Spirit-imparted power
Eph 3:17	Have faith to be fully open to Christ and make Him welcome in their hearts
Eph 3:18	Experience an ever-growing realization of every possible dimension of Christ's extravagant love
Eph 3:19	Live full of God
Phil 1:9	Possess abounding, insightful, discerning, appropriate love
Phil 1:10	Wisely prioritize the best things
Phil 1:10	Be blamelessly pure
Phil 1:11	Be filled with righteous fruits
Col 1:9	Be filled with a clear knowledge of God's will

Col 1:10	Live worthy of the Lord consciously
Col 1:10	Fully please Him in everything
Col 1:10	Bear fruit in good works
Col 1:10	Be filled with a clear knowledge of God
Col 1:11	Be invigorated with glorious strength and endurance
Col 1:12	Joyfully thank God for all He has made available to them
1 Thess 3:12	Abound in and overflow with love
1 Thess 3:13	Be infused with strengthened and blameless holiness
1 Thess 5:23	Be made holy and whole inside and out
2 Thess 1:11	Be made fit for what God has called them to be
2 Thess 1:11	Be energized by God to and fulfill their spiritual ideas and efforts
2 Thess 2:17	Experience spiritual encouragement and empowerment in their words and works
Phlm 6	Share their faith and understand just how amazing it is

Don't Forget . . .

As you consider how the Lord would like you to pray scriptural prayers for your church, be reminded of two very encouraging truths. First, as we are faithful in praying, God will be faithful in working. As Paul reminded the Corinthians, "God, who has called you into fellowship with his Son Jesus Christ our Lord, is faithful" (1 Cor 1:9 NIV).

Second, God is able to do more than we have asked for or have even imagined. We pour our hearts out to God on behalf of our people, and it not only makes us feel better, it accomplishes something. God is able. He can do far more than we could ever request or even imagine in our wildest dreams. He is powerful. Remember the promise Paul gave the Ephesians,

> Now to him who is able to do immeasurably more than all we ask or
> imagine, according to his power that is at work within us, to him be glory
> in the church and in Christ Jesus throughout all generations, forever and
> ever! Amen. (Eph 3:20–21 NIV)

Read the words of verse 21 again slowly: "to him be glory in the church and in Christ Jesus throughout all generations, forever and ever!" Remember, the ultimate point of all of our prayers for our church members is that Jesus would receive such awesome glory through their lives that it would span the generations.

~ What Now? ~

Adopt Paul's prayer patterns into your ministry. Set aside a time to pray for your people each day. Paul was not only consistent in his prayers, constant in his gratitude, and confident in his expectation, but he was also consumed with the spiritual progress of those he was called to pastor.

~ Quote ~

Are you overwhelmed by ministry demands? Pray. Are you under spiritual attack? Pray. Is temptation about to get the best of you? Pray. Are you lacking? Are you anxious?
Pray, pray, pray.

—CHARLES SWINDOLL[2]

Notes

1. Eugene Petersen, *The Message//Remix: The Bible in Contemporary Language* (Colorado Springs, CO: NavPress, 2003), 2134.

2. Charles Swindoll and Gary Matlack, *Excellence in Ministry* (Fullerton, CA: Insights for Living, 1996), 25.

11

Fasting
and Praying

Fasting has long been an ally in the pastoral ministry. Great pastors know what it is to feel the burden of the Lord and hear Him call them away into extended seasons of fasting and prayer. The Bible and history are littered with examples of how the power of prayer and the discipline of fasting turn the tide and make a difference in someone's ministry.

It was after forty days of fasting that Moses came down from Mt. Sinai with the Ten Commandments and a face that radiated the glory of the Lord (Exod 34:27–29). Samuel fasted and cried out to the Lord, and the Lord gave Israel a thunderous (literally) victory over the Philistines (1 Sam 7:5–11).

God promised to reverse the plight of His people if they would repent (Joel 2:12–27). In response, King Josiah proclaimed a fast (Jer 36:9).

Ezra called a fast and as a result the pilgrims were able to travel safely from Babylon to Jerusalem (Ezra 8:21–24). Other leaders such as David, Elijah, Ezra, and Daniel discovered the power available to those who cry out to God through fasting. Yet they are not alone.

After having fasted forty days, Jesus resisted the Devil's temptations and launched his ministry in the power of the Spirit (Luke 4:1–14). Frequent fasting marked the prayer life of the apostle Paul (Acts 9:9; 2 Cor 6:5; 11:27).

For centuries early church leaders fasted twice every week. Epiphanus, who authored what could be considered the first Christian encyclopedia, asked rhetorically,

> Who does not know that the fast of the fourth and sixth days of the week
> (Wednesday and Friday) are observed by Christians throughout the world?[1]

John Calvin, long considered one of the most influential leaders and theologians in history, habitually fasted. He viewed fasting as a necessary aid to the earnestness and fervency of his prayers.[2]

History views John Wesley as an inspiring preacher, wise organizer, relentless social activist, challenging writer, historic church builder, and world-shaking reviver. The man rode 250,000 miles on horseback, preached 40,000 sermons, gave away £30,000, and left behind 132,000 followers. He also was a strong advocate for fasting.

When he led the Holy Club, or Methodists, of Oxford, Wesley followed the pattern of the early church and fasted two days a week, Wednesdays and Fridays. Later in life, he always fasted on "Fridays." His Friday fast was conducted according to the Jewish "day"—stretching from sundown to sundown. Therefore, Wesley gave himself to fasting and prayer each Thursday evening, after the evening meal, until late afternoon on each Friday. As a leader, he expected all of his "preachers" to participate. In fact, he wanted all of the Methodist leaders and people to follow this discipline.

Biblical Fasting

Fasting as used in the Bible means "not to eat" or "self-denial." In the Old Testament the word "fast" is derived from the Hebrew term *tsom*, which refers to the practice of self-denial. In the New Testament, the word is *nestia*, which also refers to self-denial. Fasting is choosing not to partake of food because spiritual hunger is so deep, determination in intercession is so intense, or spiritual warfare so demanding that you temporarily set aside even fleshly needs to give yourself more wholly to prayer.[3]

A normal fast involves fasting from all food, but not from water (Matt 4:2). An absolute fast is very rare and involves abstaining from food *and* water in the face of spiritual emergency (Exod 34:28; Deut 9:9,18; 1 Kings 19:8; Ezra 10:6; Esth 4:16; Acts 9:9). Because the body needs fluids to survive, one would need to be very sure of the leading of God to undertake such a fast for any period longer than three days. A partial fast is the restriction of one's diet as opposed to complete abstention (Dan 10:3). Fasting may also include skipping a meal consistently or abstaining from certain foods or other activities. Many of us have enjoyed the benefit of a media fast from television, movies, cell phones, and the Internet.

Typically, biblical fasting lasted for one complete 24-hour period, usually from sundown to sundown. As we previously mentioned, the early church fasted two days every week, Wednesday and Friday. Pharisees fasted Tuesday and Thursday. Other biblical fasts extended from three to forty days. Both individual and corporate fasts are seen in the Scriptures.

The early church practiced fasting for several days prior to Easter. Later, this fast took the form of fasting one day per week for the weeks leading up to Easter. It was also customary for Christians to fast in the post-apostolic period in preparation of their baptism.

In the Bible, there are individual and corporate fasts. Corporate fasts could involve the whole church (Acts 13:1–4) or even the entire nation (Jonah 3; Esther 4; 2 Chronicles 20).

Add Fasting

Wesley Duewel has given himself to the cause of missions for more than sixty-six years. Following ministry in India for nearly twenty-five years, he served as president of OMS (Oriental Missionary Society) for thirteen years. OMS was a pioneer missions agency in the area of training nationals as church leaders which has seen seven thousand churches planted with a combined membership in excess of one million people in more than forty countries. About 1.7 million of his books are now in circulation in sixty-one languages or national editions.

Duewel is an ardent believer in the unbreakable link between effective spiritual leadership and prayer, especially as prayer is wed with fasting. He writes,

> When you long to strengthen and discipline your prayer habits and to add a new dimension to your prevailing in prayer, *add fasting*. When you seek to humble yourself before God in total submission to His will and in total dependence on His almighty power, *add fasting*. When you face an overwhelming need, a human impossibility, and your soul hungers to see God intervene by supernatural power, *add fasting*.[4] (emphasis original)

My Four Big Requests

My first serious fast of more than one day was as a junior in college. I felt led to pursue a three-day fast with lots of intense prayer. I had four major requests that I needed/wanted to see happen within thirty days:

1. God would miraculously provide me with enough money to give to help some of my friends pay their school bills and stay in school.
2. I would lead fifty souls to Christ in the next month.

3. God would give me a mentor.
4. God would spare the lives of and heal three students who were
   severely injured in an automobile accident.

Within thirty days the answers started coming in: First, all three students turned the corner and we knew they would all live. Second, one of my professors agreed to mentor me (although he did not follow through, I do believe God did His part). Third, I unexpectedly received a check in the mail for $500, which was just enough to help several guys pay their school bills.

But it looked like the fifty souls saved request was too much to expect. What was I thinking? I lived in dorm with eighty Christian young men, on a mountain with only Christian students, teachers, and staff. Who was I going to lead to Christ?

I did witness to the telephone repairman, and he prayed to accept Christ. I was asked to fill in as a last minute replacement at a Christian haunted house. My job was to share the gospel at the end of the tour through the house. That weekend, twenty-one people prayed to accept Christ.

That brought my total to twenty-two. That was amazing, but a very long way from fifty.

The last weekend of the month, I drove seven hours to speak at a youth retreat in a very remote part of southeastern Ohio. Several small churches had joined together and there were nearly 150 teens there. There were two other speakers, so I had one chance to speak to the group.

I started my talk that night and it was going badly. To be honest, it was horrible.

So I stopped.

Out of nowhere, I got the idea to have everyone stand up, one by one and rate themselves spiritually as either hot, cold, or lukewarm. Conviction settled down on the group, and the presence of God filled the room. After the first few students stood and stated their cold or lukewarm spiritual condition, teens started crying. Then kids got down on their knees. Soon everyone was on their knees. It went on for nearly an hour.

The ringleader of the unsaved, wild, rebellious kids had fallen on the floor and started shaking. Other kids started praying for him. He was unable to speak for half an hour. Then he came to his senses, got on his knees, and cried out to God to save him.

The next morning the leader came up to me with a big smile on his face, "Twenty-eight!" He said.

"Twenty-eight what?" I asked.

"Twenty-eight kids gave their hearts to Christ last night," he said. "We have been fasting and praying for a breakthrough and God gave it to us last night. Twenty-eight kids got saved, and I mean saved. Most of them were the roughest kids at the high school. They have been bringing me cigarettes, alcohol, and pot all night, asking me to destroy it."

I smiled. "Thank God," I thought. "He did an unusual work last night."

Then it hit me. *Last night was the thirtieth day since my fast. Twenty-two people were saved before last night, twenty-eight more were saved last night. That equals fifty—not forty-nine, not fifty-one, but fifty. God answered all four of my impossible requests.* Fasting makes prayer more effective.

Fasting for a Miracle

In 1971, Jerry Falwell started Thomas Road Baptist Church, *The Old Time Gospel Hour*, and Liberty University. During the first twenty-five years of its existence, Liberty grew rapidly from a handful of students to more than ten thousand in its various programs. Classroom buildings and dorms were built on a cash-only basis, with most of the cash coming from supporters of Falwell's television program.

When scandals rocked the religious broadcasting world, contributions to every ministry decreased dramatically, including Falwell's. Yet the university continued to grow and build. Soon the university was staring at more than $100 million in debt. Liberty risked losing its accreditation because of its excessive debt. The loss of accreditation would spell the end of the school. Falwell said, "With this crisis, I had to fast, and fast seriously."[5]

Falwell felt impressed by the Lord to go on a forty-day fast to pray for miraculous financial provision. He began July 20, 1996, and abstained from all food until September 1, 1996. He drank water, took a vitamin daily, and drank some vegetable juice every few days. The fast, however, did not go as he had planned.

> I kept asking God for money, but He impressed upon my heart that I needed to get close to Him, to listen to Him, and trust Him. When I asked for money, God told me not to ask for money, but to learn to know Him better. I had several lessons to learn before I could ask for money. As I ended that first 40-day fast, I felt I had learned what God wanted to teach me. But I did not have an answer about money.[6]

God is not a slot machine where we put in prayer and/or fasting and automatically get back what we want. God is God. Jerry needed to learn that on a deeper level. Then he was ready to proceed.

After resuming my normal diet for 25 days, God told me I could ask Him for money. So I went back on another 40-day fast that began September 25, 1996, ending on November 4.[7]

God responded.

First, Falwell received a huge cash gift that erased the long-term mortgage debt of the university. Second, their monthly income increased dramatically, putting the university into a place of financial health. Third, all accreditation sanctions were removed and it was affirmed for the next decade.

The last several years the answers from Falwell's fasts continue to roll in. The university has continued to grow to more than twelve thousand residential students and more than seventy thousand online distance learners, the facilities on campus have more than doubled, and financial health has been maintained.

Never Underestimate the Power of Prayer and Fasting

Bill Bright was one of the most effective spiritual leaders in history. Started in 1951 at UCLA, his ministry, Campus Crusade for Christ, has grown incredibly. Campus Crusade was originally a ministry for college students but has since expanded its focus to sixty different ministries, including ministry to adult professionals, families, athletes, and high school students in 9,190 different countries. Campus Crusade employs more than 27,000 full-time staff and has trained 2,225 volunteers.

Bright could be called the greatest evangelist of the twentieth century. His booklet "The Four Spiritual Laws" and his ministry Campus Crusade for Christ have influenced astounding numbers of people to receive Jesus Christ around the world.

Bright was a man who deeply valued the power of prayer and fasting. He wrote,

Fasting is the most powerful spiritual discipline of all the Christian disciplines. Through fasting and prayer, the Holy Spirit can transform your life. . . . Fasting and prayer can also work on a much grander scale. According to Scripture, personal experience, and observation, I am convinced that when God's people fast with a proper Biblical motive— seeking God's face not His hand—with a broken, repentant, and contrite spirit, God will hear from heaven and heal our lives, our churches, our communities, our nation, and world. Fasting and prayer can bring about revival—a change in the direction of our nation, the nations of earth, and the fulfillment of the Great Commission.[8]

Fasting More Effectively

Before You Begin Fasting

1. Determine what and how long you plan to fast. Will you be fasting for one meal, or one full day, or three days, or a week? Will you be abstaining from just solid food, or food *and* juice, or just sweets? From the TV, or the Internet, or the newspaper?
2. Go through some of the reasons for fasting mentioned in this chapter and set some objectives for your fast.
3. Prepare yourself spiritually by repenting of any and every possible sin. Fasting cleanses your body while confession cleanses your heart.
4. Prepare yourself physically by cutting down to smaller meals a few days prior. Especially prior to taking long fasts of a week or more, start shrinking your stomach by eating smaller amounts. Don't gorge the meal before you start fasting.
5. Try to plan to be less busy during the period you will be fasting. One of the goals is to be able to concentrate on God as much as possible.
6. Set aside ample time to spend with God.
7. Consider the effect fasting may have on prescription medications. Some things must be taken with food. Can you skip a day or two? Can you take it with juice?

Other Practical Advice and Observations

1. Try to limit physical activities.
2. Drink a lot of liquid and expect to visit the facilities more frequently.
3. Be prepared for some headaches or joint pain as your body detoxes. The headaches may be worse if you use a lot of nicotine and/or caffeine.
4. Build up gradually. Start with one meal. The next time go for a whole day. Then fast for three days. Then a week.
5. Most people can fast one to three days regardless of the busyness of their schedule.
6. You may tell others about your fast but do not boast.
7. The longer the fast, the more gradually it needs to be broken. Do not break a longer fast with a heavy meal.
8. Consider fasting one day a week for 24 hours from sundown the first day to sundown the next day. That is the model practiced by the disciples.

9. Remember, the God who sees in secret will reward openly. Fasting is a secret service that can aid in bringing revealing answers to prayer.[9]

— What Now? —

When are you going to start developing the discipline of fasting? Can you name one good reason for not starting this practice as soon as possible?

What are some prayer requests that prompt you to consider fasting? Why shouldn't you fast at least one day a week for God's blessings upon your pastoral ministry?

Notes

1. Epiphanus, as quoted in Wesley Duewel, *Mighty Prevailing Prayer* (Grand Rapids: Zondervan, 1990), 180.

2. John Calvin, *Institutes of the Christian Religion*, book 4, chap. 12, http://www.island-of-freedom.com/CAQUOTES.HTM (accessed Feb. 14, 2009).

3. Arthur Wallis, *God's Chosen Fast* (Fort Washington, PA: Christian Literature Crusade, 1968), 29–30.

4. Duewel, *Mighty Prevailing Prayer*, 183.

5. Jerry Falwell, quoted in Elmer Towns, *Fasting Can Change Your Life* (Ventura, CA: Regal Books, 1998), 19.

6. Falwell, quoted in Towns, *Fasting Can Change Your Life*, 19–20.

7. Ibid., 20.

8. Bill Bright, "Your Personal Guide to Fasting and Prayer," http://www.billbright.com/howtofast (accessed Mar. 29, 2012).

9. For more on fasting, see Dave Earley, *Prayer: The Timeless Secret of High Impact Leaders* (Chattanooga, TN: AMG Publishers, 2008), chap. 6.

12

Pastoral Leadership Is . . .

Making Prayer Your Church's Top Priority

The man who mobilizes the Christian church to prayer will make the greatest contribution to world evangelization in history.

—ANDREW MURRAY[1]

Paul wrote a letter to Timothy, the young pastor leading the strategic church at Ephesus. From the site, Paul wanted to evangelize all of Turkey and much of Asia. In a letter of advice for Timothy, Paul told Timothy to make one activity his top priority.

> First of all, then, I urge that petitions, prayers, intercessions, and thanksgivings be made for everyone, for kings and all those who are in authority, so that we may lead a tranquil and quiet life in all godliness and dignity. This is good, and it pleases God our Savior, who wants everyone to be saved and to come to the knowledge of the truth. For there is one God and one mediator between God and man, a man, Christ Jesus, who gave Himself—a ransom for all, a testimony at the proper time. For this I was appointed a herald, an apostle (I am telling the truth; I am not lying), and a teacher of the Gentiles in faith and truth. Therefore I want the men in every place to pray, lifting up holy hands without anger or argument. (1 Tim 2:1–8)

One of the most important responsibilities of a pastor is cultivating his prayer life. But beyond that, he must also develop the prayer ministry of his church.

Pray First

First of all, then, I urge that petitions, prayers, intercessions, and thanksgivings be made for everyone. (1 Tim 2:1, italics added)

The phrase, "first of all" speaks of both chronology and priority. Paul wanted Timothy to make evangelistic prayer the first thing on the schedule and the number one priority of his life and his church.

"Supplications" speaks of asking God to meet a need and refers primarily to your own needs. "Prayers" is a general term and can include prayer gatherings. "Intercessions" refers to petitions for others. "Thanksgivings" refers to expressing gratitude to God for blessings received and anticipated. The point is not that Paul is listing four ways to pray as much as he is piling up various terms for prayer to make his point—the church must focus on prayer.

One of the primary reasons a church exists is to bathe its city in prayer. But prayer must not be an end in itself. Prayer must prepare people for evangelism and disciple-making. Prayer is offered to make it hard for people to go to hell from your city. Without strong prayer support, all of your evangelistic efforts will bear little lasting fruit.

Pray for All of the Lost to Be Saved

I urge that supplications, prayers, intercessions, and thanksgivings be *made for all people* . . . God our Savior, who *desires all people* to be saved and to come to the knowledge of the truth . . . Christ Jesus, who gave himself as a *ransom for all* . . . (1 Tim 2:1,3–6, italics added ESV)

Evangelistic prayer for all people is rooted in the fact the God wants all people to be saved and that Jesus died for all people. Barclay writes, "Few passages in the New Testament so stress the universality of the gospel. Prayer is to be made for *all* men; God is the Savior who wishes *all* men to be saved; Jesus gave his life a ransom for *all*. As Walter Lock writes: 'God's will to save is as broad as his will to create.'"[2] Paul wanted Timothy to know that for the gospel to spread out, prayer needed to be offered up. The church must have followed his command. The book of Revelation shows that the gospel not only spread through Ephesus, but also to the towns surrounding it—Smyrna, Pergamum, Thyatira, Sardis, Philadelphia, and Laodicea.

A pastor who was working on his doctorate asked me, "What is the ideal evangelistic strategy for my local church?" My answer, "Jesus said, the great command is to love God and to love your neighbor as yourself. Therefore, maybe the best strategy is that every member of your church invests in and intercedes for their friends and neighbors every day until they get saved."

Sadly, even in American churches that still have a midweek gathering, the prayer meeting is no longer a *prayer* meeting. Usually it is primarily a Bible study and not a prayer service. During that time, a minimal amount of prayer is offered for people who are sick. Yet, as James Bryant notes, "Seldom does the church pray for the lost to be saved. We spend more time praying to keep Christians out of heaven than we do praying to keep lost people out of hell!"[3]

What if your church began to view it as your responsibility to pray for everyone in your community to be saved and to keep on praying until they all were?

Pray for Favor from Civil Authorities so Your Church May Share the Gospel

> First of all, then, I urge that petitions, prayers, intercessions, and thanksgivings be made for everyone, *for kings and all those who are in authority*, so that we may lead a tranquil and quiet life in all godliness and dignity. (1 Tim 2:1–2, italics added)

Public authorities can either aid the spread of the gospel or hinder it. Permissions, permits, and policies often restrict the ministry or bless it at the whim of the authority. We must pray that the Lord would give the church favor and turn the hearts of leaders to knowingly or unknowingly make decisions that help us fulfill the Great Commission.

Pray for Yourselves as You Share the Gospel

> For there is one God, and there is one mediator between God and men, the man Christ Jesus, who gave himself as a ransom for all, which is the *testimony* given at the proper time. For this I was appointed a *preacher* and an *apostle* (I am telling the truth, I am not lying), a *teacher* of the Gentiles in faith and truth. (1 Tim 2:5–7 ESV, italics added)

The church is to make it a priority to pray for all of the lost people in its community that they might all be saved because Jesus died for all of them. We must not only pray for them to be saved, but also be willing to testify, proclaim, share the message, and teach them the truth (1 Tim 2:6–7).

Think about the first church. Two of its leaders, Peter and John, were dragged before the authorities and told to stop preaching the gospel of Jesus. What was the church's response? They prayed for more boldness to keep on preaching (Acts 4:24–31)! They not only practiced evangelistic prayers for lost souls, but also focused on praying for themselves that they would be fearless to share the gospel with the lost people they were praying for.

Pray Throughout Your Community for All of the Lost in the Community

I desire then that in every place the men should pray, lifting holy hands without anger or quarreling. (1 Tim 2:8 ESV)

Since the days of Joshua, Christian leaders have led their people to take literal steps of faith. It has not been uncommon for pastors to lead their people to walk around a piece of property while claiming it for the Lord and as the site of their new church facilities. Others have prayed in every seat of their sanctuary, asking God to fill those seats and touch everyone who would be seated in them on Sunday. Paul seemed to be encouraging Timothy to get the men in his church praying for lost people from every part of the city.

In recent days some have adapted the principles applied by Joshua as a means of evangelism and spiritual warfare. They call it "prayer walking." Prayer walking has been defined as "praying onsite with insight." Done corporately or as individuals, prayer walking is a form of discreet intercession that takes the intercessor to the battle. As people walk through a neighborhood, they pray for every home, every family, every business, every school, and every church—that God's name would be honored, that His kingdom would come and His will would be done for that person, family, or business.

You could give every member a map of your city and ask them to pray over part of it every day, neighborhood by neighborhood. You could rip pages from the phone book, hand them out to your members, and ask your people to pray for the people whose names are on the sheet given them. You could lead your people to pray over every "For Sale" sign they pass in your city. Pray that these transitional properties would be purchased in complete alignment with God's will.

The Early Church Made Prayer Their Top Priority

Acts 1 Must Happen Before Acts 2 Occurs

I love Acts 2:41–47. It is the portrait of a healthy, dynamic, missional, evangelistic church on fire. In it we see radical evangelism, radical discipleship, radical community, radical generosity, radical power ministry, and radical praise ushering in explosive evangelism.

Acts 2 tells the story of the birth of the first church in history. It is the exhilarating tale of the church that God had in mind. It is the account of a group of imperfect people turning the world upside down. It describes the church *as it should be*; the church as an unstoppable force, created to change the world; the church as a tiny acorn becoming a mighty oak; and the church as a spiritual oasis in the desert wasteland of moral bankruptcy and cultural relativism.

The very first church in the world experienced incredible growth and impact. "Scholars estimate that over the thirty year span of the book of Acts, the Christian movement grew from 120 to 100,000 among the Jews alone."[4]

All of us love Acts 2. In Acts 2 we see a church-planting movement that swept tens of thousands of souls into the kingdom of God. It was a movement that eventually led to the gospel spreading through the world.

How could anyone not love Acts 2?

But that leads me to a question—*If the church was born in Acts 2, what was happening in Acts 1?*

> They went to the room upstairs where they were staying. . . . All these were continually united in prayer, along with the women, including Mary the mother of Jesus, and His brothers. . . . The number of people who were together was about 120. (Acts 1:13–15)

Before the first church in history was ready to experience tremendous evangelism, growth, and impact, it first practiced tremendous prayer. We must learn to prioritize the prayer ministry of the church if we hope to maximize the evangelistic impact of the church. In other words, there is no Acts 2 without Acts 1.

If we want what they had, we must do what they did. There is no healthy ministry without prayer, and there will never be a healthy church without prayer.

Addressing his Monday night prayer meeting, Charles Spurgeon said,

> How could we expect a blessing if we were too idle to ask for it? How could we look for a Pentecost if we never met with one accord, in one place, to wait upon the Lord? Brethren, we shall never see much change for the better in our churches in general till the prayer-meeting occupies a higher place in the esteem of Christians.[5]

They Prayed Before Doing Anything Else

For seven days the disciples focused everything entirely on prayer *before* doing anything else. They spent a week in intense prayer *before* attempting to preach the gospel and plant a church. And it was worth it. Those seven days of intense prayer preceded the coming of the Holy Spirit as flames of fire over the heads of the apostles and the explosive birth of the church as three thousand were baptized!

Jesus spent forty days in prayer and fasting *before* launching His three-year ministry. Paul told Timothy to pray *first*. Too often we make prayer our last resort instead of our first response.

The largest and fastest growing churches in the world put prayer first by holding several prayer meetings each morning. For example, the largest church in Columbia with more than 45,000 active members holds prayer meetings at 5:00, 6:00, 7:00, and 8:00 AM each day.

They Prayed Together

All these were continually *united*. . . . (Acts 1:14, italics added)

When we read the book of Acts, we see that the primary pattern of prayer they established was corporate prayer. United prayer birthed the church (1:14; 2:1). Corporate prayer was their method of dealing with problems, pressure, and persecution (4:24–31). Praying together was modeled by the apostolic leadership team (6:4). Earnest united prayer by the church miraculously freed Peter from prison and execution (12:5–12). United prayer was the means by which leaders received divine instruction and ministry direction (13:1–2).

Wise pastors unite the prayers of their church to unleash the power of God through their church. We need to lead our churches creatively to pray *together*.

They Prayed in Concentrated Seasons

That first prayer meeting was literally 24/7. They prayed all day for seven days. I doubt that any one person prayed all of that time, but I am sure that most of them prayed most of the time. The church might have prayed 168 hours in the week before their launch (that is more than most American pastors pray in a year)!

The largest and fastest growing churches in the world are known for their all-night prayer meetings. At one point, Paul Cho's church in Seoul, South Korea, was seeing twelve thousand souls saved each month. The church has well over half a million active members. Alongside of their vibrant cell ministry is their powerful prayer ministry. Even though Saturday is often a work day in South Korea, thousands of people gather every Friday night for an all-night prayer meeting. Cho writes, "Although it is not easy to spend the night in prayer, it has been the means by which we have been able to maintain revival."[6]

The Prayer Ministry of the Church Was Led by the Leaders of the Church

> When they arrived, they went to the room upstairs where they were
> staying: Peter, John, James, Andrew, Philip, Thomas, Bartholomew,
> Matthew, James the son of Alphaeus, Simon the Zealot, and Judas the son
> of James. All these were continually united in prayer. . . . (Acts 1:13–14)

Note the role of those in active attendance at the first prayer meeting of the first church. It is a who's who of first-century Christian leaders—Peter, James, John, and Andrew. Any pastor who hopes to experience the blessings of God will not delegate the leadership of the prayer ministry to others.

They Devoted Themselves to Prayer

> And *they devoted themselves* to the apostles' teaching, to fellowship, to
> the breaking of bread, and *to prayers*. (Acts 2:42, italics added)

The first church was a church on fire because it was a church on its knees. Prayer was built into the DNA of the first church. It was a priority, a practice, a lifestyle, a habit, and a passion. It is impossible to read the book of Acts without repeatedly running into prayer, as prayer is mentioned thirteen times in the first fourteen chapters (see Acts 1:14–15; 2:42; 3:1; 4:25–31; 6:4,6; 9:40; 10:2,4,31; 11:5; 13:2–3; 14:23).

When we look at the church globally, we see that where the church devotes itself to prayer, the lost are being saved and the church is strong and growing. Where prayer is neglected, the church is in decline.

They Devoted Themselves to the Prayers

Notice the plural ending on the word "prayers." Possibly because they were motivated by the example of David and Daniel, the pattern of establishing three daily prayer times was adopted by the Jews and was regularly practiced by the early church (Ps 55:17; Dan 6:10). Regarding the Jewish pattern of prayer, church father Tertulian says,

> As regards the time, there should be no lax observation of certain
> hours—I mean of those common hours which have long marked the
> divisions of the day, the third, the sixth, and the ninth, and which we may
> observe in Scripture to be more solemn than the rest.[7]

At the time he wrote those words, the day started at 6:00 a.m. Therefore, the third, sixth, and ninth hours represent 9:00 a.m., noon, and 3:00 p.m. So everyone in the church devoted themselves to praying three times a day—9:00, 12:00, and 3:00. The Jewish world also offered prayer three times daily in the temple—during the morning sacrifice, during evening sacrifice, and at sunset

The early church enjoyed the manifold blessings of seeing God work mightily in their midst and the lost saved daily *because* they were devoted to prayer and prayers. They lived a prayer commitment every day at least several times a day. One church leader (Hippolytus, in the beginning of the third century) advocated praying at least six times a day. If we want what they had, we must do what they did.

> If you are home, pray at the third hour [9 nine o'clock in the morning] and bless God. But if you are somewhere else then, pray to God in your heart. . . . Pray likewise at the sixth hour [noon]. . . . Let a great prayer and a great blessing be offered also at the ninth hour [three o'clock in the afternoon]. . . . Pray as well before your body rests on its bed. But toward midnight rise up, wash your hands and pray. . . . And at the cockcrow rise up and pray once more.[8]

— What Now? —

Out of what was discussed in this chapter, what principles will you apply to your personal prayer life? What can you apply to your church's prayer ministry?

— Quotes —

Prayer is the key to the successful fulfillment of the Great Commission.

ED SILVOSO[9]

If pastors would mobilize their people to pray, the world would be transformed.

DANIEL HENDERSON[10]

If you want to see your church grow, teach your church to pray.

KEN HEMPHILL[11]

Notes

1. Andrew Murray quoted in the *IFCA Voice*, September 2, 2003.

2. William Barclay, *1 Timothy* (Louisville, KY: John Knox, 1975), 55.

3. James Bryant and Mac Brunson, *The New Guidebook for Pastors* (Nashville, TN: B&H, 2007), 47.

4. C. Peter Wagner, *Acts of the Holy Spirit* (Ventura, CA: Regal, 1994), 16.

5. Charles Spurgeon, *It Is Only a Prayer Meeting* (Clover, SC: Christian Heritage, 2006), 3.

6. Paul Y. Cho, *Prayer: Key to Revival* (Waco, TX: Word, 1984), 112.

7. Tertullian, *De Oratione*, xxiii, xxv, in P.L., I, 1191–(3).

8. Hippolytus, *Apostalic Tradition*, quoted in Boniface Ramsey, *Beginning to Read the Fathers* (Mahwah, NJ: Paulist, 1985), 165–66.

9. Ed Silvoso, *That None Should Perish: How to Reach Entire Cities for Christ Through Prayer* (Ventura, CA: Regal, 1994), 64.

10. Daniel Henderson, *Fresh Encounters* (Colorado Springs, CO: NavPress, 2004), 33.

11. Ken Hemphill, *The Antioch Effect: 8 Characteristics of Highly Effective Churches* (Nashville, TN: B&H, 1999), 27.

13

Pastoral Leadership Is . . .

Building a
House of Prayer

*The dynamic church of the twenty-first century will be first
a house of prayer.*

—THOM RAINER[1]

Rambo Jesus

Cathy and I love to walk together. One day we happened to be walking around the campus of a small, used-to-be religious, private college. We stopped in the chapel for a few minutes to get out of the sun. At the front of the chapel sanctuary was a mural of a man walking through a field of flowers. He was wearing a silky white robe and had beautiful, long, flowing light-brown hair, flawless olive skin, and a sweet smile.

"That has got to be the most effeminate looking picture of Jesus I have ever seen," I exclaimed.

"It is creepy," Cathy said.

Feeling awkward and uncomfortable, we left and went back to our walk.

The sad thing is, someone actually thought Jesus was like that. I guess they never read Mark 11.

They came to Jerusalem, and He went into the temple complex and began to throw out those buying and selling in the temple. He overturned the money changers' tables and the chairs of those selling doves, and would not permit anyone to carry goods through the temple complex. Then He began to teach them: "Is it not written, My house will be called a house of prayer for all nations? But you have made it a den of thieves!" (Mark 11:15–17)

I cannot wait to get to heaven and see the video of this event! Imagine Jesus bursting into the temple, and, like a bar bouncer, grabbing men by the scuff of the neck and tossing them out the door. Picture Him turning over their tables, and gold coins rolling everywhere. See Him pulling chairs out from under the money changers. Imagine Him standing with His arms outraised, refusing to permit anyone from even walking through the temple area if not there on spiritual matters. He refused to allow anyone to use it for a travel or transportation short-cut.

Now picture Jesus doing all of this with a whip in His hands (see John 2:15)!

Sounds more like "Rambo Jesus" than "wimpy Jesus."

Something must have really ticked Him off.

Let me give you a bit of context. The temple complex was divided into four primary sections. In the rear and elevated above the others was the Court of the Priests, containing the Holy of Holies. Next to it was the Israel's Court, where Jewish men were permitted. Then the Women's Court, which was as far as Jewish women were allowed. Below these, and larger than all of them combined, was the vast Court of the Gentiles. The Jews had lost respect for what this court was intended to be—a place where Gentiles from all nations could come and meet with God.

Jesus was incredibly passionate about the things of God (John 2:17). The Jews behind the money tables, on the other hand, were passionate about making money. They were extorting the spiritual pilgrims by exchanging their currency into "special temple coins." They were selling to the pilgrims overpriced, "approved" oxen, sheep, and birds for sacrifices. Jesus said that they had made God's house into a den of thieves. In doing this, they had lost the purpose for which the temple existed—to be a place where people from all nations could come and meet with God.

Understanding this makes it obvious why Jesus was so upset. When the temple was being used for something less than a house of prayer, it so infuriated Jesus that He drove the defilers out. He then predicted that the physical temple would soon be destroyed. Seeing such a display of His authority, plus losing their source of extra income, so angered the priests that they plotted to have Jesus killed (Mark 11:18).

This was an extremely important incident in the life of Jesus that is often overlooked. Jesus was willing to make a spectacle in the temple and face death in order to remind people that God's house must be a place of prayer, and not for personal gain at the expense of others.

If Jesus took the prayer ministry of His people that seriously, how much more should you and I!

Today the House of Prayer *Is the Church*

What did Jesus mean when He referred to God's "house"? The most obvious meaning is that God's house is the place where God lives. Prior to Pentecost, God's house was primarily the tabernacle, which was built by Moses so God could dwell among His people (Exod 25:8). After that, the temple was where God manifested His glory (1 Chr 7:1–3).

Yet God also promised to dwell in humble, broken people: "I live in a high and holy place, and with the oppressed and lowly of spirit, to revive the spirit of the lowly, and revive the heart of the oppressed" (Isa 57:15). According to Denis Fuqua, "People have always been God's most desired dwelling place . . . in the New Testament believers are referred to as being the temple of God, the place where His Spirit lives today. . . . A shift has taken place. God's primary dwelling place . . . was once a building, now it is a people."[2]

In a parallel passage to Mark 11, John 2 adds these words: "Jesus answered, 'Destroy this sanctuary, and I will raise it up in three days.' Therefore the Jews said, 'This sanctuary took 46 years to build, and will You raise it up in three days?' But He was speaking about the sanctuary of *His body*" (John 2:19–21, italics added).

During the time Jesus walked the earth, His physical body was the primary dwelling place of God (John 1:14). If you wanted to get to God, you went to Jesus. But since Pentecost, *the church is the body of Christ* (1 Cor 12:12–27). The church is the sanctuary of God both individually (1 Cor 6:19–20) *and* collectively (1 Cor 3:16–17). Clearly since the day of Pentecost, *the church is to be a house of prayer for all nations.*

Therefore, since the church must be a house of prayer, it only makes sense that when the disciples went to launch the first church in history, they first spent an intense week in corporate prayer (Acts 1:13–15). It explains why the first church devoted themselves to prayer (Acts 2:42). We should not be surprised that when faced with persecution, the church corporately cried out for greater boldness to witness (Acts 4:25–31). It is only to be expected that when faced with a choice between two good things, the apostles choose the best thing as they devoted themselves to prayer and the ministry of the Word (Acts 6:1–4). No wonder when its leaders were thrown in prison the church banded together and cried out to God (Acts 12:1–5). Of course, when Paul advised Timothy, he told him that as pastor, his first priority was to see that prayer was being offered by his church for all people to be saved (1 Tim 2:1–8). He wanted Timothy to build a house of prayer for all peoples.

If the first-century church was determined to be a place of prayer for all peoples, how much more should the twenty-first-century church!

A Brooklyn House of Prayer

In 1972, twenty-nine-year-old Jim Cymbala became pastor of the struggling, broken down, nearly bankrupt Brooklyn Tabernacle. Only two dozen people made up the church, and on his first Sunday as pastor, the offering was $85. Jim had only a secular university education and felt incapable of leading such an unhealthy church in such a tough neighborhood. Humbled, broken, and realizing that the church was doomed without a breakthrough of God, he began to cry out to God in prayer.

During a vacation trip to Florida, Jim sensed God speaking to him deep within his spirit.

> If you and your wife will lead my people to pray and call upon my name, you will never lack for something fresh to preach. I will supply all the money that's needed, both for the church and for your family, and you will never have a building large enough to contain the crowds I will send in response.[3]

Jim went back to his people with renewed hope. Standing in front of them, he told them of his new resolution.

> From this day on, the prayer meeting will be the barometer of our church. What happens on Tuesday night will be the gauge by which we judge success or failure because that will be the measure by which God blesses us.[4]

They began to pray seriously—whether by crying out to the Lord as a group, by holding hands in a large prayer circle, or by individuals asking for prayer for special burdens. The methods varied, but the focus was the same: prayer.

God responded. In the next few weeks answers became noticeable.

The lives of his congregation were powerfully changed. Excited about what God was doing, they began to bring friends, neighbors, and family members. Hopeless, hurting, broken people began to come and find radical deliverance and transformation.

God began to send in junkies, prostitutes, homosexuals, lawyers, business men, and bus drivers. There were Latinos, African Americans, Caribbean Americans, whites, and more. People began to stream in from Manhattan, the Bronx, Queens, and Long Island. Within a few years, they had outgrown the church building and were meeting in a local high school. A few years later, the high school had become too small.

So they prayed.

God responded, giving them a 1,400-seat theatre on the main street coming into Brooklyn. In spite of sending out teams to start new churches around the city, they had to hold four Sunday worship services to get everyone in who wanted to come.

The ragtag band with no trained musicians and choir that could not read music began each practice with a lively thirty-minute prayer meeting. The music ministry began to improve and expand. The power in their worship was so thick that often Jim would skip his sermon and go straight to the invitation.

Maybe you know the rest of the story. The choir eventually became world famous, turning out Grammy Award-winning albums. Jim's story of the church, *Fresh Wind, Fresh Fire*, became a bestselling book.

What was the secret?

As Cymbala writes, "God had formed a core group of people who wanted to pray, who believed that nothing was too big for him to handle."[5]

A South Korean House of Prayer

The Yoido Full Gospel Church of Seoul, South Korea, is the largest church in the world with more than five hundred thousand active members. At one point it was growing at a rate of twelve thousand new converts a month!

What is the secret?

They are a house of prayer. Their pastor writes, "We have learned not only to pray, but we have learned how to live our lives in prayer."[6] Early morning prayer meetings begin each day at 5:00 a.m. and continue at 6:00 a.m., 7:00

a.m., and 8:00 a.m. The church also holds an all-night prayer meeting each Friday. They have an average of three thousand people during the week and ten thousand on weekends who are fasting and praying on the church's Prayer Mountain.

Their pastor believes that the reason the church has become so mighty in prayer and evangelism is because the prayer ministry of his church is an overflow and reflection of his own prayer life. He writes, "I am not able to do all I have been called to do without spending the minimum of an hour a day in prayer. . . . I must spend my life in prayer. . . . If I did not pray, they would not pray."[7]

A Historic House of Prayer

Many Christian leaders consider Charles Haddon Spurgeon to be the greatest pastor in history. He grew one of the first modern-day megachurches in London in the nineteenth century. Though commonly known as the "Prince of Preachers," it was not preaching that made Spurgeon great. It was leading a praying church.

Spurgeon frequently commented that his success was the direct result of his congregation's faithful prayers. When visitors would come to Spurgeon's church he would take them to the basement prayer-room where people were always on their knees interceding. Then Spurgeon would declare, "Here is the powerhouse of this church."[8]

Even though he had 5,000 in attendance on Sunday mornings and another 5,000 Sunday evening for an evangelistic service, he regarded his church's Monday night prayer meeting as the most important meeting of the week. Every Monday night, a large portion of Spurgeon's huge sanctuary was filled with 1,000 to 1,200 earnest and fervent intercessors. His biographers noted, "In Spurgeon's eyes the prayer-meeting was the most important meeting of the week."[9]

Regarding church prayer meetings, Spurgeon stated,

> The condition of the church may be very accurately gauged by its prayer meetings. So is the prayer meeting a grace-ometer, and from it we may gauge the amount of divine working among a people. If God be near a church, it must pray. And if he be not there, one of the first tokens of his absence will be slothfulness in prayer.[10]

In his autobiography, Spurgeon described his gratefulness for being blessed with such a praying church, saying, "I always give all the glory to God, but I do not forget that He gave me the privilege of ministering from the first to a praying people. We had prayer meetings that moved our very souls, each one appeared determined to storm the Celestial City by the might of intercession."[11]

In his book *Only a Prayer Meeting*, Spurgeon offered several reasons for the success of his church's weekly prayer meeting and suggestions for making prayer meetings effective. These include:

1. The pastor must make the prayer meeting his priority. His obvious love for prayer will "foster a corresponding love for the prayer-meeting" among his people.
2. Work on having concise prayers. "Length is the deathblow to earnestness, and brevity is the assistant to zeal."
3. Persuade all to pray aloud. "It gives a reality and life to the whole matter, to hear those trembling lips utter thanks for new life just received, and to hear that choking voice confessing the sin from which it has just escaped."
4. Encourage the attendants to send in special requests for prayer as often as they feel constrained to do so. "These little scraps of paper, in themselves most truly prayers, may be used as kindling to the fire in the whole assembly."
5. "Do not allow singing, scripture reading, or preaching to take the place of prayer. Remember that we meet for prayer; and let it be prayer."[12]

A Small-Town House of Prayer

Jefferson, Oregon, has a population of 2,200 people. Several years ago it also had a very discouraged pastor. Dee Dukes had given up his first love—farming—to take over the role of pastor for the struggling Jefferson Baptist Church. After 12 years, he was burnt out and bitter, and planning on resigning.

But during a four-day conference, all of that changed. At the pastors' prayer summit, Pastor Dukes realized that he had tried everything but prayer. Convicted of spiritual arrogance, prayerlessness, an independent spirit, and the belief that he could accomplish anything by hard work, he resolved to change. He returned to his church, confessed his prayerlessness to his congregation, and dedicated himself to prayer and to leading his church to become a house of prayer. In doing so, he made seven specific goals:

1. Spend one uninterrupted hour per day praying by himself.
2. Spend one hour per day praying with a partner.

3. Pray for everyone in the church by name weekly.
4. Pray at least once a month with other pastors.
5. Preach on prayer for three months.
6. Plan at least four major church prayer events each year (always to precede a major evangelistic thrust).
7. Identify the church's "farm" (twenty miles in every direction from the church), claim it, and target prayer for it.[13]

Prayer changed everything. Dukes says, "The more we prayed, the more God put it on our hearts to reach the lost. We experienced a growing sense of urgency to reach our neighbors and the world. We grew in creative ways to reach out to the lost. Almost everyone in the church began praying for lost friends, work associates, family members, mission efforts, and countries around the world."[14]

Since Dukes got serious about prayer, the church has grown to an average Sunday morning attendance of 1,400 people in a town of 2,200. It has forty prayer times that take place each week. They also pray around the clock for lost people the ten days before Easter and with twenty-four hours of fasting and prayer the day before Easter. They pray for every single person within twenty miles of their church by name. Every morning, their high school students "prayer walk" around the school track, praying for their fellow students.

Dukes strongly believes that in order for a church to become a house of prayer the pastor must understand the difference between believing that prayer is important and that it is essential. "Those who believe that prayer is essential—not just important," Dukes says, "will have passion and fervency that will persuade others to join them."[15]

— What Now? —

Determine to lead your church to become a house of prayer for all nations. In order for this to happen, decide that prayer is not only important, but it is essential. Choose to give yourself to prayer. Like Pastor Dukes, make some tangible resolutions and specific, measurable goals.

∽ Quotes ∽

All of our past failure, all of our past inefficiency and insufficiency, all of our past unfruitfulness in service, can be banished now, once and for all, if we only give ourselves to prayer.

—THOM RAINER[16]

Never underestimate the power of the praying church!

—WARREN WEIRSBE[17]

Prayer-less ministry is powerless ministry.

—DAVID KORNFIELD[18]

The ministry of the church is prayer—not the ordinary kind consisting of small prayers but the kind which prepares the way of God. It is God who first desires to do a certain thing, but the church prepares the way for it with prayer so He may have a thoroughfare. The church should have big prayers, terrific and strong prayers.

—WATCHMAN NEE[19]

History would teach us that there is no revival or spiritual awakening unless churches begin to pray. In addition, most churches will not become houses of prayer unless pastors lead the way through their personal example and through skilled and strategic leadership in prayer.

—PAUL CEDAR[20]

Notes

1. Thom Rainer, *Giant Awakenings: Making the Most of Nine Surprising Trends That Can Benefit Your Church* (Nashville, TN: B&H, 1995), 23.

2. Denis Fuqua, "The Meaning of 'A House of Prayer,'" in *Giving Ourselves to Prayer: An Acts 6:4 Primer for Ministry* (Terre Haute, IN: PrayerShop, 2008), 293.

3. Jim Cymbala and Dean Merrill, *Fresh Wind, Fresh Fire* (Grand Rapids, MI: Zondervan, 1997), 25.

4. Ibid., 27.

5. Ibid., 38.

6. Paul Y. Cho, *Prayer: Key to Revival* (Waco, TX: Word, 1984), 14.

7. Ibid., 18–19.

8. Arnold Dallimore, *Spurgeon: A New Biography* (Carlisle, PA: Banner of Truth, 1985), 125.

9. Ibid., 126.

10. Tom Cater, *Spurgeon at His Best* (Grand Rapids: Baker, 1988), 155; selections from the 1873 edition of *The Metropolitan Tabernacle Pulpit: Sermons Preached by C. H. Spurgeon, Revised and Published during the Year 1873*, vol. XIX (repr., Pilgrim Publications, 1971), 218.

11. Charles Haddon Spurgeon, *C. H. Spurgeon's Autobiography,* comp. Susannah Spurgeon and Joseph Harrald (Toronto, Canada: University of Toronto Libraries, 2011), 77.

12. Charles H. Spurgeon, *Only a Prayer Meeting* (Hagerstown, MD: Christian Heritage, 2010), 8–11.

13. Dee Dukes, quoted in Daniel Henderson and Elmer Towns, *Churches That Pray Together* (Colorado Springs, CO: NavPress, 2009), 18.

14. Ibid., 19.

15. Ibid., 21.

16. Rainer, *Giant Awakenings*, 4.

17. Warren Wiersbe, *Be Dynamic (Acts 1–12): Experience the Power of God's People* (Colorado Springs, CO: David C. Cook, 2009), 174.

18. David Kornfield, *Church Renewal: A Handbook for Christian Leaders* (Grand Rapids, MI: Baker, 1989), 40.

19. Watchman Nee, *The Prayer Ministry of the Church* (Richmond, VA: Christian Fellowship, 1973), 31.

20. Paul Cedar, quoted in Daniel Henderson, *Fresh Encounters* (Colorado Springs, CO: NavPress, 2004), 11.

Part 3
Teaching the Word of God

14

Preaching
the Word

*There is enough power in the preaching of God's Word alone
to build a church from nothing.*

— MARK DRISCOLL[1]

Famous Last Words

A person's last words are significant. Often, in that defining moment, their heart, passion, and priorities come together with great clarity. Many agree that of all the advice Paul gave to his protégé, Timothy, in the letters of 1 and 2 Timothy, perhaps the most valuable is the last thing he said.

These final words of Paul are filled with emotion. He is coming to the end of his life. He is a prisoner. He is older now. He knows he will soon lose his life in martyrdom. What we have in 1 and 2 Timothy is his final appeal to the young man whom he has trained and mentored.

Paul sums up everything he had taught Timothy in one final sentence. In this his final address to a young pastor, Paul leaves him with a solemn, serious, severe, and significant commission.

> I charge you in the presence of God and of Christ Jesus, who is to judge
> the living and the dead, and by his appearing and his kingdom: *preach the*

word; be ready in season and out of season; reprove, rebuke, and exhort, with complete patience and teaching. (2 Tim 4:1–2 ESV, italics added)

Throughout their letters, Paul gave Timothy several solemn charges (1 Tim 1:3–4; 1:18; 5:21; 6:13–14). Yet none of them is treated as solemnly and forcefully as this one simple exhortation: "Preach the Word." This pastoral priority fits in line with Jethro's advice to Moses when he told him to "instruct them about the statutes and laws, and teach them the way to live and what they must do" (Exod 18:20).

The first commitment every pastor must make is to be a man of God. The second commitment every pastor must make is to live a life of prayer. And the third commitment every pastor must make is to preach the Word.

Preaching the Word Is a Serious Responsibility

As you just read, Paul set up the command to "preach the word," by first pointing out the supreme seriousness of the exhortation. He said, "I charge you in the presence of God and of Christ Jesus, who is to judge the living and the dead, and by his appearing and his kingdom: preach the word" (2 Tim 4:1–2 ESV).

"*I charge you:*" To "charge" means to command solemnly or urge strongly. The idea was that this charge to preach the Word was of utmost importance, and Paul could not impress this on Timothy too strongly.

"*. . . in the presence of God:*" Paul wanted Timothy to know that his ministry had a constant observer. God was looking over his shoulder.

"*. . . of Christ Jesus, who is to judge the living and the dead:*" Paul also wanted Timothy to know that not only would Jesus watch his ministry, but that Jesus would also carefully evaluate it.

The solemn charge given Timothy parallels a common format used in court cases. The statement, "I solemnly charge you in the presence of God and of Christ Jesus" (v. 1 NASB), takes a format that archeologists have discovered was used in the typical subpoenas and legal documents of ancient times. Paul therefore used the terminology of a subpoena to, in essence, state, "The case will be drawn up against you in the court of Christ Jesus who is the judge."[2] It is a solemn subpoena for the preacher to come to court to face the legal evaluation of God with reference to his ministry.

"*. . . Jesus, who is to judge:*" Paul wanted Timothy to take seriously the command to preach the Word because Jesus would closely evaluate him and would render the verdict on his ministry. He was under divine scrutiny. Let me remind you that when it comes to the evaluation of your life and ministry there is only one Judge and one person whose opinion really matters—Jesus. We must seek to please Him.

"*. . . and by his appearing and his kingdom:*" If you knew that one month from now a king was coming to your house for a visit, what would you do? You would clean the house, fix the hole in the wall, and get new carpet. Paul wanted Timothy to know that even more important than the appearance of a king was going to be the coming of the King *of kings*. When the King of kings comes, He will call Timothy into account for his ministry, especially as it related to if and how he preached the Word.

"*Preach* the Word"

The New Testament speaks of "preaching" with a variety of words:

1. announcing of good news *(euangelizein)*
2. conversing *(homilien)*
3. witnessing *(martyrein)*
4. teaching *(didaskein)*
5. prophesying *(propheteuein)*
6. exhorting *(parakalein)*

A good pastor does all of the above. Paul in 2 Timothy uses another term that is significant. Paul commanded Timothy to "preach" the word. The word translated "preach" is the verb *kerusso*, which means "to proclaim publicly or announce." In the first century, there obviously was no Internet, no newspapers, no television, no cell phones, and no radio. If the emperor wanted to make a public announcement, he sent a public herald into the community and there he would proclaim the message of the emperor to the people.

John Piper states that preaching is announcing and exulting. The herald brings good news and the people cheer as a result. Piper says,

> Preaching is more than teaching. It is exultation in the Word. "Preach the Word," means "exult in the Word." That is, announce it and revel in it. Speak it as amazing news. Speak it from a heart that is moved by it.[3]

Piper gives two reasons why God commands pastors to herald and exult when they preach the Word. First, the nature of the truth calls for something more than mere explanation, discussion, or conversation. The magnificence of the truth calls for a heartfelt heralding and passionate exultation. Second, "our hearts will not be drawn out to worship if someone just dissects and analyzes the worth and glory of God but does not exult in it before us. Our hearts long for true preaching."[4]

"Preaching" has been defined as "the oral communication of a biblical truth by the Holy Spirit through a human personality to a given audience with the intent of a positive response."[5] It is called the "responsible, passionate, and authentic declaration of the Christ-exalting Scriptures, by the power of the Spirit, for the glory of God."[6]

"Preach the Word"

When Paul referred to "the Word," what did he mean? What was he commanding Timothy to herald?

We can see two clues in the immediate context. The first is found immediately before the command to "preach the Word."

> . . . from childhood you have been acquainted with *the sacred writings*, which are able to make you wise for salvation through faith in Christ Jesus. All *Scripture* is breathed out by God and profitable for teaching, for reproof, for correction, and for training in righteousness, that the man of God may be competent, equipped for every good work. . . . *Preach the word* (2 Tim 3:15; 4:2 ESV, italics added)

Obviously, when Paul said "preach *the Word*," he was telling Timothy to preach the God-inspired Scriptures. The word "Scripture" means simply "writing" or "letter." This means that the Word of God has come to us in a written form captured in a book—God's book. This means that your preparation and your preaching should be Word-based, Word-driven, Word-saturated, Word-balanced, and Word-faithful. Because it was God's Spirit who inspired the Word, your sermon preparation and delivery should also be Spirit-given, Spirit-shaped, Spirit-carried, and Spirit-anointed.

Paul wanted it to be crystal clear to Timothy. As a pastor, *preach* is what you do, and *the Word* is what you preach.

Why Preach the Word?

Paul wanted Timothy to focus his preaching on the Word of God because God's Word is a spiritual shepherd's primary food for his flock and his chief tool for leading them. No other book in the world is like it. The Bible itself uses several metaphors to show us how important it is in the life of the believer.

The Word of God Is . . .

1. Spiritual bread (Matt 4:4)
2. Spiritual milk (1 Pet 2:2)
3. Spiritual meat (Heb 5:14)
4. Spiritual seed (Mark 4:14)
5. A spiritual lamp (Ps 119:105)
6. A spiritual sword (Eph 6:17)
7. A spiritual scalpel (Heb 4:12)
8. A blueprint for wise life construction (Matt 7:24–27)

Because It Instructs the Lost in the Way of Salvation

> But as for you, continue in what you have learned and have firmly believed, knowing from whom you learned it and how from childhood you have been acquainted with the sacred writings, *which are able to make you wise for salvation through faith in Christ Jesus.* (2 Tim 3:14–15 ESV, italics added)

Regarding the power of the Word to save souls, John MacArthur writes:

> The Jews used to claim that their children drank in the law of God with their mother's milk and it was so imprinted on their hearts and minds that they would sooner forget their names than forget God's law. The law was the tutor that led to Christ. . . . Bottom line he's saying you know that the Word of God has the power to save. . . . What else would you preach?[7]

Paul told the Romans:

> For "everyone who calls on the name of the Lord will be saved." How then will they call on him in whom they have not believed? And how are they to believe in him of whom they have never heard? And how are they to hear without someone preaching? And how are they to preach unless they are sent? . . . So faith *comes from hearing, and hearing through the word of Christ.* (Rom 10:13–17, italics added)

Because It Teaches the Saints the Way of Righteousness

Because the Bible is the captured words of God, it is sufficient. Paul told Timothy that the Scriptures are profitable for doing all that is necessary in making saints righteous and equipped.

> All Scripture is breathed out by God and *profitable for* teaching, for reproof, for correction, and for training in righteousness, that the man

of God may be competent, equipped for every good work. (2 Tim 3:16, italics added)

Paul tells Timothy that he should stick to preaching the Word because the Word is useful. It is the means whereby people will be directed into lives of righteousness.

Notice the four terms Paul used when he speaks of the benefits of the preaching the Word: *teaching, reproof, correction,* and *training.* He told Timothy that the Bible *teaches,* or shows people they right way to go. It r*eproves,* or tells them when they get off that path. It *corrects* which means that it guides them back on the path. And it *trains,* meaning that the Bible also shows people how to stay on the path. How can you improve on that?

Paul adds to his argument that the Bible ultimately is capable of leading people to a point of *competency and equipment for every good work.* As they learn and apply the Word, people's lives get put together and shaped up for the tasks God has for them.

How to Preach the Word

Preach the Word Urgently

When Paul gave the command to "preach the Word" his use of the aorist verb tense and all of the succeeding imperatives add solemnity and abruptness to the imperative. Timothy was to preach the Word like he never had before.

Preach the Word Persistently

Paul not only told Timothy "preach the Word," but he told him *when* to preach it. He said, "preach the word; **be ready in season and out of season**" (2 Tim 4:2 ESV, italics added).

The command "be ready" is from a verb meaning "to stand by" or "be at hand." It conveys the idea of always being on duty.

The phrase "in season and out of season" answers the question of when should a pastor preach the Word. The answer is that Timothy was to preach the Word whether the opportunity seemed to be favorable or unfavorable, whether it was convenient or inconvenient, whether it was welcome or unwelcome. He was to preach the Word persistently, at all times and all of the time. There should never be a season of life, occasion, or encounter where the pastor does not bring truth to bear upon the situation.

Preach the Word Persuasively

Paul's next command was very simple—"convince." This word implies "proving the point." The pastor should show the reasons behind *why* certain acts are sinful. The preaching should provoke the conviction of sin and point to the confession of sin. Good preaching is not unlike surgery; it cuts in order to expose and remove what is wrong so that ultimately healing can occur.

Preach the Word Boldly

The command to "rebuke" builds on the word "convince." To rebuke is to warn or correct. The wise pastor will use the Word to expose and explain sin (convince), warn of sin's consequences, and call for change (rebuke).

Of course it is not always popular or easy to call out sin and show its price-tag. But such courage is required of the shepherd who loves his flock and wants to protect them.

Preach the Word Encouragingly

The command to "exhort" means to inspire, advise, or motivate. Encouragement is the oxygen of the soul, and exhortation is the call to action. Good preaching afflicts the comfortable, comforts the afflicted, and calls both to obey the Scriptures.

Preach the Word Patiently

Paul commanded Timothy to "preach the word . . . *with complete patience*"—that is, with long-suffering endurance and forbearance. In other words, the pastor should not expect to be able to preach something one time and have everyone who attended the sermon fully understand the teaching and immediately apply it in their lives. The pastor must not get tired of, or give up continually preaching the Word and challenging his people to see it and to live it.

Preach the Word Clearly

Paul reminded Timothy that his preaching was to also include "teaching." The idea is to make truth simple and clear. Good preaching instructs and inspires. It helps people learn, understand, and apply the Bible for themselves.

Ways to Preach the Word

There is a difference between preaching the Word and merely preaching *about* the Word. Preaching the Word is a result of seriously attempting to interpret, understand, explain, and apply God's truth as exposed in the Scripture(s) used. The goal of biblical preaching is to reveal the truth the original author intended his readers to see, to explain it, and to apply it to the hearers.

Solid biblical preaching generally falls into four major categories:

1. *Topical.* A well-done topical/thematic/theological message combines all the significant Scriptures about a particular topic and accurately uses them to reveal God's mind on that subject. The main divisions of the sermon are derived from the topic itself. For example, a message on divorce would look at all the key verses in the Bible on that subject.

2. *Textual.* A biblically solid textual message focuses on one small, yet rich text and accurately interprets it and applies it. The theme of the message and the main points of the outline come directly from the text chosen. Many pastors have preached a textual message on "God's Greatest Gift" using John 3:16 as their text.

3. *Narrative.* A good narrative message does not dissect a biblical story. Instead, it tells the story in a fascinating fashion while highlighting the major theme and yet, paying attention to important historical features. A narrative sermon could be a retelling of the book of Ruth, or the book of Jonah, or the story of the prodigal son.

4. *Expository.* All biblical preaching is essentially expository in nature in that it opens or *exposes* the truths of the Word of God to the hearer. A good expositional message will explain, interpret, and apply the passage selected. Expository messages generally cover a paragraph from the New Testament or a chapter from the Old Testament.

⟶ What Now? ⟵

Starting today, become a Bible lover, if you are not already.

Commit yourself to reading several chapters of the Bible every day for the rest of your life.

While it is often helpful to read good books about the Bible, be certain that above all else, you read the Bible and before all else, you have read the Bible.

Make a serious commitment to always preach the Word. Never get up to speak unless what you have to say is founded in the Word.

⁓ Quotes ⁓

In my own ministry, I have seen what preaching the Word can do in churches and in individual lives; and I affirm that nothing can take its place.

—WARREN WIERSBE[8]

If I could today become king or emperor, I would not give up my office as preacher.

—MARTIN LUTHER[9]

It takes more courage to be a preacher than to be a gladiator, or a stormer of fortresses, because the preacher's battle is ever on, never ceases, and lacks the tonic of visible conquest.

—WILLIAM QUAYLE[10]

Notes

1. Mark Driscoll, *Confessions of a Reformission Rev* (Grand Rapids, MI: Zondervan, 2009), 78.

2. John MacArthur, "Marks of the Faithful Preacher, Part 1," January 10, 1988, http://www.gty.org/Resources/Sermons/55-20_Marks-of-the-Faithful-Preacher -Part-1 (accessed May 11, 2011).

3. John Piper, "Advice to Pastors: Preach the Word," February 4, 1996, http:// www.desiringgod.org/resource-library/sermons/advice-to-pastors-preach-the -word (accessed May 11, 2011).

4. Ibid.

5. J. Vines and J. Shaddix, *Power in the Pulpit* (Chicago, IL: Moody, 1999), 27.

6. Tony Merida, *Faithful Preaching* (Nashville, TN: B&H, 2009), 6.

7. John MacArthur, "5 Reasons to Preach the Word" a sermon given March 8, 1998 at Grace Community Church, http://www.gty.org/resources/Sermons/80-180 (accessed July 4, 2011).

8. Warren Wiersbe, *Be Faithful (1 & 2 Timothy, Titus, Philemon)* (Chicago, IL: Moody, 1983), 19.

9. Martin Luther, quoted on Preachers on Preaching, http://fide-o.com/2005/11/ preachers-on-preaching (accessed May 16, 2011).

10. William Quayle, *The Pastor-Preacher* (Grand Rapids, MI: Baker, 1979), 256.

15

Communicating for Life Change

If you decide to preach for life change you won't be satisfied until the behavior of your audience is transformed; and you will be willing to do just about anything to see that happen.

—ANDY STANLEY[1]

Thunder in the Desert

He exploded out of the wilderness like a thunderbolt and rose to sudden national prominence. God's Word was a fire in his bones and in his mouth. In fulfillment of Isaiah's prediction, John the Baptizer prepared the way of the Lord. His strange personality and strong message of repentance bulldozed spiritual mountains and leveled steep paths. The masses began to flood to him to be baptized in recognition of their need of real righteousness.

His was not a soothing prosperity gospel, but a blunt club of rebuke. He shredded facades and cut through charades. Listen to his message:

> Brood of snakes! What do you think you're doing slithering down here to the river? Do you think a little water on your snakeskins is going to deflect God's judgment? It's your life that must change, not your skin. And don't think you can pull rank by claiming Abraham as "father." Being a child of Abraham is neither here nor there—children of Abraham

are a dime a dozen. God can make children from stones if he wants. What counts is your life. Is it green and blossoming? Because if it's deadwood, it goes on the fire. (Luke 3:7–9 MSG)

Instead of turning John off and walking away, the people were drawn to his honesty and directness. His message was so Spirit-saturated and truth-punctuated that it could not be denied. It was so persuasive, pointed, powerful, and practical, the hearers responded to his message as every preacher hopes their audience responds to their own. The crowd asked him, "Then what are we supposed to do?" (Luke 3:10 MSG).

"What are we supposed to *do*?" Sound familiar? In chapter one of this book, we spoke of Jethro giving Moses three priorities to build his ministry upon. The first priority was prayer. The second was teaching the people how to live the Word of God. Jethro said,

Instruct them about the statutes and laws, and teach them the way to live and *what they must do*. (Exod 18:20, italics added)

The criteria for evaluating a sermon are not the catchiness of the title, the cleverness of the outline, the entertainment value of the bumper video, or the pictures in the Power Point. It is also not the amount of Greek words used, grammatical references made, or historical insights given. Ultimately a sermon is measured by its impact in people's lives. Do they make the changes that will make them more like Jesus?   Impact

Life-Changing Preaching and Teaching

Few persons have ever preached with the transforming power and practicality of John the Baptizer. When he preached, lives were changed. From the sample sermon described by Luke we can learn several significant aspects of teaching the Word with practicality and power.

Listen Attentively to the Word of God

Before John could *give* the powerful message recorded in Luke 3:7–9, he had to *get* the message from somewhere. This section begins with the words, "The word of God came to John son of Zechariah in the desert" (Luke 3:2 NIV).

John had great power in his preaching because he got his message from God. Never underestimate the power of a God-given message. Nothing gives a preacher more God-based confidence and Spirit-anointed boldness than knowing that he has a message from God for his church.

John got his life-changing message from God. Without the Word of the Lord, he did not have anything to say—and neither do we.

John lived in the wilderness eating locust and honey. He was a hermit, a mystic, and a prophet, but not a pastor. He had one basic sermon: *Repent.*

How do pastors get life-changing sermons from God to give to their people week after week? Like John, we must learn to get our messages from the Word of God.

There is only one way to get a Word from God—listening for it. God is a verbal God. He *spoke* the world into existence. One of the primary titles of Jesus is "the *Word* of God." His sheep hear His voice and follow Him. The only way to get a word from God is to listen for it. We must learn to hear God's voice in and through His Word.

This active listening involves two parts—diligent study of the Word of God and active reliance upon the Spirit of God.

Diligent study has two primary aspects. First, it requires digging into the written Word of God with the goal of determining the primary message the original author wanted to communicate to his original audience. We will discuss this process in detail in chapter 17.

Second, studying for a sermon is wrestling with the big idea of the Scripture text with the goal of deciding the best way to communicate it to your audience. We will discuss this process in detail in chapter 18.

Active reliance upon the Spirit of God is expressed by faith and prayer. It only makes sense to seek the help of the Holy Spirit in this process. After all, the Holy Spirit wrote the Bible in the first place (2 Tim 3:16; 2 Pet 1:20–21). His job is to guide us into all truth (John 16:13). Therefore, we can come to Him in prayer expecting Him to reveal to us what He meant by the words contained in the Book He authored.

Listening is the active understanding that He will give a depth of insight that cannot possibly be achieved by raw human intellect. It is a matter of asking God to speak to us and open our eyes so we can see the wonderful truth God has in His Word (Ps 119:18). It is asking God to show us what the Bible portion we are studying means.

Beyond that, cooperating with the Holy Spirit in sermon preparation further involves depending upon Him to show you how He wants you to apply the big idea of the chosen Scripture passage to your audience. After all, He knows everyone who will be there. He knows what they are going through. He knows their preconceived ideas. Therefore, He knows the best way to present the truth of the Word so it will have the maximum impact on the lives of your hearers.

Clarify Memorably the Main Truth

> He went into all the vicinity of the Jordan, preaching a baptism of repentance for the forgiveness of sins. . . . He then said to the crowds who came out to be baptized by him, . . . "Produce fruit consistent with repentance." (Luke 3:3,7–8)

John's message was very simple. *Repent!*

His sermon had one main point—repent; one big idea—repent; and one primary point of application—repent. It does not get any clearer, simpler, and more powerful than that.

Never underestimate the power of simplicity. J. Kent Edwards makes an insightful statement regarding the power of simplicity when he writes,

> An inverse relationship exists between a sermon's effectiveness and the number of ideas it contains. The more ideas you pile into a sermon the less impact it has. . . . Less is more![2]

The life-changing communicator believes and practices the truth that every passage of Scripture has *one* primary theme. The difference between a lecture and a life-changing message is that the latter attempts to persuade the hearer regarding *one* primary issue. Therefore, as we study the text in preparation to preach, we need to identify and clarify the key truth of that text in order to be best able to drill this truth into the minds of our hearers.

As we listen to God while we study the text of Scripture for our upcoming message, we are listening for the dominating theme, the central idea, the big idea, the key truth of the text. Then we listen further with the goal of identifying and clarifying that theme as it relates to our audience.

You can call this big idea *the sermon in a sentence*. John's sermon in a word in Luke 3 is "repent" (Luke 3:3). His sermon in a sentence is, "Produce fruit consistent with repentance" (Luke 3:8). The rest of his message points out the need for it and the ways his listeners could express it. We will talk in more detail about developing this "main truth" or "sermon in a sentence" in chapter 18.

For now, it is enough to realize that doing the hard work to clarify and summarize the scriptural text into one concise, clear, memorable word, phrase, or sentence is a nonnegotiable key to high-impact preaching.

It is very easy to lose the power of a message by cluttering it up with too much other stuff. One of the greatest temptations in preaching is succumbing to the temptation of including interesting, but unnecessary information. When this happens, the clear sound of God's voice in the ear of the hearer is drowned out by other noise. The life-changing message becomes little more than an interesting lecture.

When I started out as a pastor, it was about all I could do to come up with enough stuff to fill a thirty-minute message. But as years of study piled up, I soon learned that the hard part was not trying to figure out what to say, but rather trying to figure out what *not* to say. I learned that to be an effective communicator I needed to "leave a lot of good stuff on my desk." I learned to file that good stuff for future sermons or series. Once you can narrow it down to the one big truth, you can then spend the rest of your study time determining the best way to say it.

Question Convincingly

In his high-impact sermon on repentance, John knifed through the religious clutter in his hearers' lives by asking several convicting, convincing questions. "What do you think you're doing slithering down here to the river? Do you think a little water on your snakeskins is going to deflect God's judgment?" and "What counts is your life. Is it green and blossoming?" God used these probing questions to deeply convict the crowds of their sin and prompt them to action.

Never underestimate the impact of a well-phrased, well-timed question. God Himself used this method in the garden of Eden. When Adam and Eve were hiding in guilt, God asked, "Where are you?" (Gen 3:9). Of course God was not looking for information. Being omniscient, God already knew where they were located. Instead, He used the question to reveal the change in their relationship brought on by their recent sin.

Jesus used the power of a question to help His disciples clarify who He was and what it meant. First, He asked a general question to focus their attention on the issue at hand, "Who do people say that the Son of Man is?" (Matt 16:13). Then He followed it with a specific question designed to cause them to examine their relationship with Him, "But who do you say that I am?" (Matt 16:15 ESV).

I have found that often I can make my point more effectively through the use of a question than through a direct statement. I was preaching a sermon on prayer to a group of well-educated, spiritually mature, solid, Bible-believing Christians. This group could easily fall into the habit of replacing knowledge of truth for practical expression of it.

So at the beginning of my message I asked, "How many of you believe that God can do things bigger than you can?" Every hand was raised.

"How many of you believe that God can do things better than you can?" Again, every hand was raised.

"How many of you believe that God can do things faster than you can?" Again, they shot their hands up

"How many of you believe that God can do things more long lasting than you can?" They smiled skeptically now as they raised their hands a fourth time.

Then I asked, "How many of you have prayer lives that truly reflect those beliefs?"

I had them—nowhere to run, nowhere to hide. You could have cut the conviction with a knife.

As I spoke through that message on the power of prayer, I referred to that set of questions as I transitioned between each of my points. I also concluded my message with that same set of questions.

The response was strong, and lives were changed. The next day, a lady said, "I have been a Christian for fifty years, but after yesterday's message, my prayer life has been completely changed."

Challenge Directly

John gave his audience a direct challenge. He said, "Produce fruit in keeping with repentance" (Luke 3:8 NIV). In other words, "Words won't cut it anymore. You say that you are real God-fearers, prove it." In other words, "Put up or shut up."

This is what separates a sermon from a lecture and a powerful communicator from a boring professor. In the message on prayer that I mentioned above, I actually stopped at one point, asked the audience to one by one look me in the eye and say, "I am challenged to pray more the rest of this year than I ever have in my life."

Never underestimate the power of a direct challenge. *The direct challenge is the whole point of the whole thing*. It is the reason you have studied so hard and prayed so much. It is the reason God has brought these people together to hear from His Word. *Without* the direct challenge, the people might as well stay home and read a commentary on that particular passage of Scripture. *With* a direct challenge, saints are stirred to action, souls are saved, and lives are changed.

The direct challenge moves the message from the head of the hearer to their heart. It pushes beyond the intellect to the will. It drives past a nice thought to a changed life.

This is called *preaching for a verdict*. Robert Coleman writes,

The test of preaching ultimately is what men do about it. The decision is what counts . . . the preacher must do everything possible to make the issue plain, and then call the congregation to account. Eternal destinies are at stake. For this reason, the appeal for commitment is the most decisive point of the message. The wise preacher, thus, should give as much or more consideration to the invitation as to any other part of the sermon. . . . This is the crowning achievement of the message.[3]

W. A. Criswell, the great expository preacher at First Baptist Church of Dallas, said, "Pastor, preach for a verdict and expect it. God will honor your faith with souls."[4]

Andy Stanley offers this pep talk to communicators: "How would you communicate this message to your eighteen-year-old son who had made up his mind to walk away from everything you have taught him morally, ethically, and theologically, unless he has a compelling reason not to? What would you say this [Sunday] morning if you knew this was at stake? Because for somebody's son out there this may be his last chance. Now quit worrying about your outline. Go out there and plead your case."[5]

Apply Specifically

John's message went from really good to great after his challenge. This is because he not only told them what God said—repent; what to do—prove they have repented; he told them *how* to do it. He gave them very specific application.

> "What should we do then?" the crowd asked. John answered, "The man with two tunics should *share with him who has one*, and the one who has food should *do the same*." Tax collectors also came to be baptized. "Teacher," they asked, "what should we do?" *"Don't collect any more than you are required to,"* he told them. Then some soldiers asked him, "And what should we do?" He replied, *"Don't extort money and don't accuse people falsely—be content with your pay."* (Luke 3:10–14 NIV, italics added)

Notice that John's message had several points of application. For the crowd in general, he said to prove real repentance by radical generosity—sharing a tunic and food. This led to some even more specific applications for particular individuals, one for the tax collector and another for the soldier.

Every passage of Scripture has one primary interpretation, yet many applications. Sermons also should have one main point of truth leading to one clear challenge that naturally leads to several points of application.

Effective preaching evokes *change* in the hearer. It is more than giving information. It is a means of *transformation*. Transformation never occurs without *application*.

Pastor James teaches us that *information without application leads to delusion and deception* (Jas 1:22–24), but information *plus application* produces *blessing* (Jas 1:25). Jesus said essentially the same thing at the end of the Sermon on the Mount, except He upped the ante. He said, information without application leads to destruction (Matt 7:26–27).

Nothing is dynamic until it is specific. The more specific the application people make, the more powerful it becomes in changing their lives. Never underestimate the power of a specific application.

In the message on prayer that I referred to earlier, my main truth was "prayer is powerful." My challenge was "to pray more in the rest of this year than you ever have in your life." My application immediately followed the challenge. I said, "I don't know what praying more will look like for you. Maybe it will mean praying every day and not just now and then. Maybe it will be going from fifteen minutes a day to thirty minutes or going from thirty minutes to an hour. It could be committing to being part of a corporate prayer gathering every week, or having a prayer partner, or praying with your mate daily beyond meal time."

I continued, "I don't care how you do it, but I do care *that* you do it. So in just a moment I am going to ask you to use the response card in your bulletin to write down the type of commitment to pray more that you plan to make this year. Then at the end of the service, bring it forward and place it on this altar as you talk this commitment over with God."

Always Ultimately Point to Jesus

John's ministry was primarily about preparing the way of the Lord (Luke 3:4). The bottom line in all gospel-centered preaching is exalting Jesus and pointing people to Him. In fact, at the end of his message, John explicitly and intentionally pointed the crowd back to Jesus, saying, "I baptize you with water, but One is coming who is more powerful than I. I am not worthy to untie the strap of His sandals" (Luke 3:16).

Never underestimate the power of Jesus. You and I *can't* save a soul. We *can't* change a life. We *can't* heal a broken heart. We *can't* fix a marriage. We *can't* deliver someone out of addiction.

But Jesus can.

Powerful, life-changing, high-impact communication is preaching that points people to Jesus.

⌐ What Now? ⌐

Which of the six requirements for life-changing communication most surprised you?

Which resonated most deeply with you?

Which do you need to work on the most?

How life-changing was your last message?

What will you do to apply these principles to your preaching and teaching?

⌐ Quotes ⌐

The sermon itself is a powerful agent of change.

—LEITH ANDERSON[6]

Every time I stand to communicate I want to take one simple truth and lodge it in the heart of the listener. I want them to know that one thing and what to do with it.

—ANDY STANLEY[7]

The way I read it, spiritual maturity is gauged by application, not contemplation.

—ANDY STANLEY[8]

When you commit to preach for life change, your preparation is not complete until you have answered two very important questions: So what? and Now what?

—ANDY STANLEY[9]

Notes

1. Andy Stanley and Lane Jones, *Communicating for a Change* (Colorado Springs, CO: Multnomah, 2006), 97.

2. J. Kent Edwards, *Deep Preaching* (Nashville, TN: B&H, 2009), 60.

3. Robert E. Coleman, "Preaching for a Verdict: Evangelistic Preaching in the Wesleyan Tradition," http://www.preaching.com/resources/articles/11565629/page -2 (accessed 3/29/12).

4. Wallie Amos Criswell, *Criswell's Guidebook for Pastor's* (Nashville, TN: B&H, 1980), 37.

5. Stanley and Jones, *Communicating for a Change*, 99.

6. Leith Anderson, quoted in an interview with Michael Duduit in *Communicate with Power* (Grand Rapids, MI: Baker, 1996), 11.

7. Stanley and Jones, *Communicating for a Change*, 12.

8. Ibid., 95.

9. Ibid., 97.

16

Pastoral Leadership Is . . .

Feeding
God's Sheep

*A shepherd who fails to feed his flock will not have a flock
for long. The sheep will wander off to other fields
or die of starvation.*

—John MacArthur[1]

The Great Re-Commission

We hear a lot about the Great Commission (Matt 28:18–20), as we should. But we often overlook the Great Re-Commission. As you recall, Peter, Jesus' top disciple, had completely fallen on his face soon after Jesus was betrayed and arrested. After boasting that he would never deny Jesus (Matt 26:31–35), Peter had denied Jesus three times (John 18:15–18,25–27)!

Weeks later, even though all of the other disciples were excited about the resurrection of Jesus from the dead, Peter was not so much. He had spent three years at the side of Jesus learning to be a rabbi and disciple-maker, only to choke at crunch time. So in order to restore some dignity, Peter decided that he had better go back to doing something that he knew he was good at—fishing. Being a leader, he recruited several of the other disciples to go along with him.

Yet God is a God of the second chance. Jesus, the resurrected Christ, surprised His disciples as they were fishing on the Sea of Galilee. In their encounter,

Jesus extended to Peter the hope of a second chance and clarity as to what real ministry entailed.

"Feed My Sheep"

> Jesus asked Simon Peter, "Simon, son of John, do you love Me more than
>   these?"
> "Yes, Lord," he said to Him, "You know that I love You."
> *"Feed My lambs,"* He told him.
> A second time He asked him, "Simon, son of John, do you love Me?"
> "Yes, Lord," he said to Him, "You know that I love You."
> *"Shepherd My sheep,"* He told him.
> He asked him the third time, "Simon, son of John, do you love Me?"
> Peter was grieved that He asked him the third time, "Do you love Me?"
> He said, "Lord, You know everything! You know that I love You."
> *"Feed My sheep,"* Jesus said. (John 21:15–17, italics added)

Three times Jesus asked Peter. "Do you love Me?" Three times Peter answered, "You know I love You." Three times Jesus responded by giving Peter a responsibility: "Feed my sheep."

In this interplay Jesus accomplished several things. First, He reminded Peter that *the basic essential of all effective and enduring ministry is to love Jesus above all else.* Real ministry is an overflow of our love relationship with Jesus.[2]

Second, Jesus was *re-commissioning Peter to ministry.* Even though Peter had failed before, Jesus gave him a second chance.

Third, Peter was given the ministry of caring for God's *sheep.* One of Jesus' favorite metaphors for spiritual leadership, one He often used to describe Himself, was that of a shepherd—a person who tends God's flock. A shepherd leads, feeds, nurtures, comforts, corrects, and protects—responsibilities that belong to every church leader. In fact, the word "pastor" means "shepherd."

Fourth, for the pastor, *shepherding the flock is primarily the result of good teaching and preaching.* When Jesus re-commissioned Peter, He drove home to Peter the importance of *feeding* the sheep. Twice in His command to Peter, Jesus used the Greek term *bosko,* which means "to feed or nourish the flock" (John 21:15,17). Jesus wanted Peter to understand that pastoral leadership is feeding God's flock.

God Loves His Flock

When Jesus commissioned Peter to feed His sheep, this was a not a menial task. God loves His flock and views shepherding as the ultimate in leadership.

Consider David, the man after God's own heart and the boy He elevated to kingship. David was a faithful shepherd boy. His heart for the flock was such that God elevated him to king *because* he was a trustworthy shepherd (Ps 78:70–72; Ezek 34:23; 37:24).

God views His ministry to His flock as *shepherding* (Isa 40:11; Jer 31:10; Ezek 34:11–16). The author of Hebrews called Jesus the Great *Shepherd* of the sheep (Heb 13:20). Jesus is referred to as the Lamb who will *shepherd* the multitude saved during the Great Tribulation (Rev 7:17).

Peter obviously walked away from his re-commissioning with a clear understanding of the significance of being tasked to feed God's flock. He called Jesus the *Shepherd* and Guardian of our souls (1 Pet 2:25), and the Chief *Shepherd* who will reward His faithful, human under-shepherds (1 Pet 5:4).

Three Primary Elements of Feeding God's Sheep

1. Guide the Flock through Gospel Preaching

Unlike some animals, sheep have no internal guidance system. Even close to home, a sheep can be hopelessly lost. With no sense of direction and no instinct for finding the fold, a lost sheep will continue to wander in confusion and anxiety. It needs a shepherd to bring it home.

When Jesus looked out at the masses of people gathered in Jerusalem over Passover, He felt compassion for them. In His eyes, they were harassed, hurting, hopeless and helpless, weary and worn, as sheep without a shepherd (Matt 9:36). The prophet Isaiah described Israel as lost and needing guidance. In his eyes they were like sheep, having gone astray—each one turning to his own way (Isa 53:6).

People, like lost sheep, need a shepherd to lead them to the safety of the fold. A pastor does that by faithfully pointing people to Jesus, the Good Shepherd who lays down His life for the sheep (John 10:11,14). The focal point of the apostle Paul's preaching was guiding sheep to Jesus. He stated, "but we preach Christ crucified" (1 Cor 1:23–24); "For I determined to know nothing among you except Jesus Christ and Him crucified" (1 Cor 2:2); and "But as for me, I will never boast about anything except the cross of our Lord Jesus Christ" (Gal 6:14).

Charles Spurgeon has often been referred to as the prince of preachers. Large crowds numbering in the thousands crowded into his church on both Sunday morning and Sunday evening to hear him preach. Regarding guiding lost sheep to the Good Shepherd and Savior of their souls through preaching, he said,

> Let your sermons be full of Christ, from beginning to end crammed full of the gospel. . . . People have often asked me, "What is the secret of your success?" I always answer that I have no other secret but this, that I have preached the gospel,—not about the gospel, but the gospel,—the full, free, glorious gospel of the living Christ who is the incarnation of the good news. Preach Jesus Christ, brethren, always and everywhere; and every time you preach be sure to have much of Jesus Christ in the sermon.[3]

When someone commented to him that all of his sermons sounded alike, Spurgeon replied, "That is correct. Wherever I take my text, I make a bee-line to the cross."[4]

2. Protect the Flock through Doctrinal Teaching

What picture comes into your mind when I say the word "sheep?"

Large pointed fangs? Razor sharp claws? Camouflaged skin? Cunning mind? Blazing speed? Or a blood-curdling growl?

Of course not! Sheep are not ferocious predators. They are harmless, helpless prey. Not only are they incapable of attacking others, they cannot even defend themselves. They are slow and dull-witted beasts who can't bite, scratch, scare, poison, hide from or outrun predators. When attacked, they huddle together making them easier prey. When alone and attacked, their only defense is to lie on their backs with their feet in the air, crying.

Christians, like sheep, need protection from error and those who spread it. Pastors guard their spiritual sheep from going astray and defend them against the savage wolves that would ravage them. Paul admonished the pastors at Ephesus to stay alert and to protect the churches under their care through sound teaching.

> Be on guard for yourselves and for all *the flock*, among whom the Holy Spirit has appointed you as overseers, to *shepherd the church of God*, which He purchased with His own blood. I know that after my departure *savage wolves* will come in among you, not sparing the flock. And *men from among yourselves* will rise up with deviant doctrines to lure the disciples into following them. (Acts 20:28–30, italics added)

Paul likened false teachers to *savage wolves*. Wolves are apex predators with no predators of their own, residing at the top of their food chain. They are slender, powerfully-built animals with long limbs. Wolves are extremely strong for their size and very fast. They are also capable of running at speeds of 25–35 miles per hour. Wolves are keen of hearing. They have strong jaws and their teeth are heavy and large, suited for bone crushing.

Sheep are no match for a hungry wolf. Sheep need protection from these false teachers.

When Paul warned of savage wolves, he was referring to false teachers who are outside the flock and do not pretend to be Christians. They are popular in the world and powerfully persuasive. Their deceptive doctrines undermine cardinal truths such as creation, the existence of God, the inerrancy of Scripture, the deity of Jesus Christ, the necessity of salvation, and the reality of heaven and hell.

Yet, Paul not only warned about wolves, he also warned of *men rising up from among them who would teach deviant doctrines.*

Sometimes the threat to the flock comes from *within* the flock. Within large commercial herds of sheep are special castrated males whose purpose is to lead the flock to slaughter. They are called the "Judas sheep."

When the rancher decides it is time to slaughter a flock for the meat, he has the "Judas sheep" lead the unsuspecting flock to a killing floor. Thinking he is leading them to food and rest, they blindly follow him to their death. As they approach the killing floor, a trap door opens and the "Judas sheep" slides down a ramp to go back down to the pen and lead another group of sheep to slaughter.

The shepherding pastor-teacher must faithfully teach His flock sound doctrine so they can discern when false teachers arise. His sheep are not led astray through "Judas sheep."

I had a friend who trained bank tellers. "How do you train them to spot counterfeit bills?" I asked her, "Do you give them samples of fake bills to test them?"

"That is not necessary," she said. "We really don't need to teach them to spot the fakes. We spend our time getting them keenly aware and deeply familiar with the real thing, then they can always tell the difference," she said.

The best way for the shepherding pastor to protect his flock from counterfeit truth is to teach them the real thing consistently. This means our preaching should be grounded upon and seasoned with a healthy understanding of the great doctrines of the Bible: theology (the study of God), bibliology (the study of the Bible), Christology (the study of Christ), pneumatology (the study of the Holy Spirit), anthropology (the study of Man), hamartiology (the study of sin), soteriology (the study of salvation), ecclesiology (the study of the church), and angelology (the study of angels, good and bad).

A pastor may choose to take at least one of these doctrines and teach through it in depth every year. He also should refer to the main truths of each doctrine as it comes up in his teaching through books of the Bible.

3. Nourish the Flock through Balanced Teaching

Even though sheep spend most of their lives eating and drinking, they are indiscriminate about their diet. They do not know the difference between poisonous and nonpoisonous plants. Therefore, it is the responsibility of the shepherd to guard their diet carefully and provide them with a pasture rich with nutrients.

In his farewell address to the elders of the church of Ephesus, Paul made an interesting summary of his ministry,

> You know, from the first day I set foot in Asia, how I was with you the whole time . . . and that *I did not shrink back from proclaiming to you anything that was profitable*, or from teaching it to you in public and from house to house. (Acts 20:18–20, italics added)

> Therefore I testify to you this day that I am innocent of everyone's blood, for *I did not shrink back from declaring to you the whole plan of God*. (Acts 20:26–27, italics added)

Too often pastors get caught in the rut of taking shortcuts and of preaching the same things over and over; yet, sheep need a balanced diet. Therefore, the good pastor will preach the whole Bible.

Noted pastor, professor, and author Dr. Steven Olford said,

> At the end of one's ministry in any given place, the preacher should be able to say that he did not shun, he never hesitated, to proclaim the whole counsel of God, that Christ-centered, biblical agenda was evident throughout his preaching ministry; that preaching was not deceptively selective, nor was there negligence in this matter; and from center to circumference, the truths of the Word of God were declared.[5]

Planning for Feeding the Flock

It is a given that a pastor must preach the Word (2 Tim 4:2). His goal should be to preach for life change (Luke 3:1–18). As we have seen in this chapter, he must feed the flock a well-balanced (Acts 20:26–27), Christ-focused (1 Cor 2:2), gospel-centered diet.

This brings us to the question: What part of the Word shall be taught?

When deciding the primary content for a message, the answer lies in your teaching calendar. A teaching calendar is a tentative plan covering the text and tentative title for every sermon and/or series of sermons you plan on giving in the coming year(s).

Benefits of a Teaching Calendar

The benefits of planning ahead are many. First, if you know you are preaching on Matthew 5–7 a year from now, you can begin reading it, gathering information on it, looking for illustrations for it now. That way, when the time comes to prepare the message, you will not be starting from scratch.

Second, a plan allows stage construction crews, worship bands, and media teams to be preparing ahead. They will have the best sets, songs, graphics, and videos to match the sermon series when it comes.

Third, it allows you to promote the series most effectively. This may mean preparing banners and other pieces to help your members strategically invite guests, or your marketing team may purchase ads to promote it to the community when it is appropriate.

Fourth, knowing what you are doing ahead of time allows you to strategically invite guest speakers. For example, when we did a series on creation, we were able to get a top-flight speaker because we booked him a year in advance.

Ingredients of a Teaching Calendar

The simplest preaching calendar would be one based on an extended series through a lengthy book of the Bible. One book of the Bible could dominate all fifty-two weeks of Sunday-morning messages as you preach through the Old Testament chapter by chapter or the New Testament paragraph by paragraph.

While there are many benefits of this style of preaching, you may find it difficult to sustain a Sunday-morning series that lasts more than twelve weeks. I have a short attention span and so do most people. After several weeks, I am ready to move on to something different. If I do preach through a lengthy book of the Bible, I break it up into smaller miniseries.

As you develop your preaching plan, try to think like a chef. The goal is to provide a balanced, healthy, yet also attractive diet for the flock. A good preaching plan covers both Old and New Testaments, surveys major doctrines, hits apologetic issues, and addresses key issues and felt needs.

Every year, consider doing a four-to eight-week series on a major doctrine. One year it could be a series on the Holy Spirit (*The Most Important Person in Your Spiritual Life*). Another year the doctrinal series could be on the Bible itself (*Everything You Need to Know about the Bible*).

It is also wise to mix in an apologetics series every year. Your people's faith is constantly being challenged by an increasingly post-Christian culture. They need their faith strengthened and to be supplied with good arguments they can use in sharing with others. Give your people a biblical defense for classic Christian beliefs regarding the existence of God, creationism, the deity of Jesus, the exclusivity of salvation, and the superiority of Christianity compared with other religions.

The staple in any preaching plan is the New Testament. It is easy to preach all the way through smaller books like Philippians or Colossians in eight to twelve weeks. I suggest breaking up a longer book like Romans or Hebrews into smaller sections.

More Suggestions

The key to maintaining interest and urgency as you preach through books of the Bible is selecting a passage that can stand alone each week, yet function within the series. It is impossible and unnecessary to address every phrase and every issue raised by every verse. Some verses are more significant to your congregation than others.

It is beneficial to craft series around felt needs. People deal with money, sex, and relationships all the time. They also struggle with anger, stress, depression, worry, and bitterness.

It is wise to be sensitive to special days and seasons. For example, in late December talk about Jesus. On Easter the subject should someway be linked to the Resurrection.

You will find it very beneficial to use short series to preach on your church's core values in order to build up your church life. For example, when launching a battery of new small groups, consider doing a series on the value of community. Prior to a giant neighborhood servant-evangelism outreach, teach on servanthood for several weeks.

You can involve your elders and pastoral staff in the process of planning the teaching calendar. Poll them annually for suggestions as you gather input regarding the teaching calendar for the year.

When the schedule is complete, distribute it throughout the church leadership three months in advance so they can coordinate children's ministry; student ministry; worship, media, and adult ministries with the central teaching plan of the church.

Review the plan halfway through and make any necessary adjustments for the following months.

Of course the primary issue in sermon calendar preparation and text selection is Holy Spirit sensitivity and listening prayer. Also, everyone involved needs to be willing to be flexible as the Lord might want to change our plans.

⏤ What Now? ⏤

I challenge you to create a one-year preaching calendar. In it, show how you will provide a balanced diet for your flock. Show how you plan to teach through key sections of the New Testament, important parts of the Old Testament, and the major Bible doctrines.

⏤ Quotes ⏤

Christ is the one great theme of the pulpit and around this all other themes gather to their center and end. . . . All true preaching, whatever its range of topics, is the preaching of the Christ. No topic is fit for the pulpit that does not lead to him.
—W. A. CRISWELL[6]

I prepare my preaching a year in advance. I know where I'm headed—I know what specific subject, topic, and text that I'm going to be addressing on a given Sunday a year in advance.
—FRANK HARRINGTON[7]

Notes

1. John MacArthur, *Pastoral Ministry* (Nashville, TN: Thomas Nelson, 2002), 23.
2. For an entire chapter on this passage and ministering out of the overflow of our relationship with Jesus, see Dave Earley and Ben Guterriez, *Ministry Is . . .* (Nashville, TN: B&H, 2010), 74–83.
3. Charles Haddon Spurgeon, *The Soul Winner* (New Kensington, PA: Whitaker House, 2001), 86.
4. Spurgeon, quoted in W. A. Criswell, *Criswell's Guidebook for Pastors* (Nashville, TN: B&H, 1980), 41.
5. Steven Olford, *Anointed Expository Preaching* (Nashville, TN: B&H, 1998), 91.
6. Criswell, *Criswell's Guidebook for Pastors*, 40.
7. Frank Harrington, quoted in an interview with Michael Duduit in *Communicate with Power* (Grand Rapids, MI: Baker Books, 1996), 41.

17

Studying
the Bible

*If this book is indeed the Word of God, then away with
slovenly, slipshod, exegesis. . . . Only when we have ourselves
absorbed its message, can we confidently share it with others.*

—JOHN STOTT[1]

Master Craftsman

Ephesus was the most strategic city in Roman Asia. When it was made the
capital of Roman Asia, it quickly grew into an ancient metropolis of nearly
half a million people. A pagan outpost, city life was dominated by the temple
to the sex goddess Diana. Violence was common as the gladiator fights drew
crowds numbering more than twenty-five thousand.

The church at Ephesus had enjoyed a wonderful beginning, but became
the victim of false teaching, false prophets, false apostles, and even a few false
elders and pastors. They had bought into false doctrine and as a result were
living an ungodly lifestyle. Paul set Timothy in that congregation at Ephesus
to straighten them out. In the process, Paul sent Timothy two letters to guide
him, to strengthen his hand, and to remind him to stick with the things that are
most needful.

One of the priorities was for Timothy to give himself to diligent study of the Word of God. It would only be through the word of truth that Timothy would be able to correct the issues. But in order to do so, it would require hard work.

> Be diligent to present yourself approved to God, a worker who doesn't need to be ashamed, correctly teaching the word of truth. (2 Tim 2:15)

According to Paul, the goal of the pastoral Bible teacher is preparation of himself for the day he will stand before God. There are two sides to being well-prepared for that day. First, on the negative side, the goal is to avoid being a worker who is *ashamed.* Shame is the painful feeling arising from the consciousness of having done something dishonorably. In this verse, it refers to the shame that a pastor could have for the work he has done when it is inspected by God.

On the flip side, the goal of the pastoral preacher is to be able to be presented as approved by God. The word "present" means "to stand alongside, to be parallel to." The word "approved" means "proven to be worthy after testing."

So, what is the goal of the teacher? It is to make a maximum effort so that he may someday stand alongside of God unashamed because he has proven himself to be a worthy teacher of His truth.

Notice that the key to being unashamed is working hard at *accurately handling the word of truth.* This requires *diligence.* The word means "to work hard, to give maximum effort, to give persistent zeal, to do your best." Paul told Timothy to give his maximum effort so he could stand before God as approved. He uses the image of a "worker"—a hired hand, one who labors for a day's wage.

Paul also used the language of being a craftsman. The phrase "correctly teaching" was used in Greek literature for a variety of tasks, such as for plowing a straight furrow through a field, making a straight path through the woods as you built a road, cutting and squaring a stone so that it fit into the correct place in the structure of the building, cutting a board accurately, and cutting cloth and sewing a straight seam.

Paul is saying that a pastor is to be a master craftsman in the Word. Like the master mason, the Word is his tool for measuring, cutting, and placing the people of God together so as to build a strong church. Like the master carpenter, the Word is his tool for measuring the wood and cutting it straight in order to build objects of beauty. Like the master tentmaker, the Word is his tool for measuring, cutting, and stitching together the people of God to make a tabernacle for God's glory.

Therefore, if you as a pastor hope to stand alongside God unashamed, you need to learn how to handle God's Word skillfully in order to silence heresy and build up the church. This requires a serious commitment to study the Word so you can communicate it like a master craftsman.

Steps for Studying the Passage of Scripture

The key to handling the Word of truth accurately is diligently studying the Word of truth. As you diligently study the Word of truth, there is one big question that must be answered: What did the original author intend for *his* audience to hear from this passage?

Effectively answering the big question comes as the result of asking and answering two other questions: What does this text say, and What does the text mean?

Step 1: Observation—What Does This Text Say?

Observation begins by *reading and re-reading the text*. I also like to listen to it on CD in my car on the way to work. Read a chapter ahead and a chapter behind the one you are teaching from so you can gain the context. Notice natural divisions in the text based on sentence structure. Highlight key verbs. Is there a word or words that are repeated frequently in the text? Does one particular phrase stand out?

I usually read it in one translation until that feels a bit stale, then I read it in a different translation. The goal is to marinate in it. As you do, the Holy Spirit will surface themes and concepts that He wants you to address in your own life and the lives of your people.

Read with the awareness that you are listening to what God is saying through this portion of Scripture. Also, as you read, look for surprises. Ask yourself why the author might have inserted *that* phrase, choosen *that* word, or omitted something you would have expected him to say. Read while looking beneath the surface, trying to see the original author's purpose.

Next, *observation requires doing some background work*. You can use a good study Bible to find out about the author, the place of writing, the date, the audience, the occasion, and the genre. Obviously, if you are preaching a lengthy series through a book of the Bible or spending several weeks in a lengthy section of the same Scripture, you will not need to spend much time here after the first few weeks.

As you are in the observation phase, it is also helpful to *ask the basic questions*: Who? What? When? Where? Why? and How? Answer each of these questions with no more than one sentence each.

The last aspect of observation is *summarizing and paraphrasing* the text into your own words. First, rewrite all of the passage into your own words covering several sentences. Then see if you can summarize and paraphrase the entire text into one sentence.

Step 2: Interpretation—What Does It Mean?

This is an extremely important issue. When you preach a text of Scripture, you must be careful that you discern accurately the truth that is in that text. The question you want to nail down is: What did the original author intend for the *original* readers to understand from this text?

First, *examine the specifics*. Depending on the length of the passage chosen, careful attention must be given to sentence structure, transitions between paragraphs, and transitions between sentences. An understanding of the original languages is obviously valuable as you wrestle with verb tenses and the meaning of salient words.

Start by doing your own work. Then it is at this stage of preparation that commentaries become helpful. The thoughts and insights of a scholar can shed light on a tricky issue or clarify a confusing element. Every commentary has its own set of strengths and weaknesses. Some are great on word studies, but weak on historical issues. Others are great on explaining the biblical author's flow and structure, but avoid tough issues. It is best to look at more than one commentary so as to get a few different angles on the meaning of the text.

It is also wise to see how key words, phrases, or concepts are referenced elsewhere in the Bible. Use the Bible to interpret the Bible. There is much more we could say about accurate interpretation of the Word, but that is best left for a book dedicated to hermeneutics.

The second part of interpretation is to *determine and define the central truth*. Too often a young exegete will lose the big picture as he surfaces interesting details. Remember, the goal is to get to the dominating theme that God wanted the original author to convey to the original hearers.

Try to state in rough fashion what you think the writer is talking about—his subject—and what major assertions he is making about the subject—his complement. The exegetical idea is reached when you can come up with the subject and complement.[2] Try to write this exegetical idea out in a word, phrase, or sentence. Then write additional words, phrases, or sentences that arise from the text to modify this big truth.

Third, *make a simple diagram or outline of the text*. This outline or grammatical diagram should note the major, minor, and modifying aspects of the text. The goal is to see the text and define the details as clearly as possible.

I am a visual person. I work hard at studying a text so I can reach the point where I "see" the text as unfolding in my outline or diagram. After that, everything else flows much more easily.

Step 3: Personal Application—What Does It Mean to Me?

As you wrestle with the text, consider how it relates to you. Did reading and studying this passage make you feel guilty about anything? Does it provoke praise to God? Did it take you back to a point in your past? Does it strengthen your faith? Does it raise more questions than you had when you started? Does it answer questions you had when you started? Does it offer guidance that you needed?

The goal here is to determine what this passage or Scripture has meant to you or means to you. For example, I spoke to several hundred young adults from 1 Cor 6:9–18 on the subject of the high cost of sexual immorality. While the subject matter had already captured their attention, they leaned in with greater interest when I personally applied the text. The truth hit home as I shared how one of my closest family members had paid a steep price for the immorality committed while in high school.

The other day, my wife, Cathy, was speaking to a group of women. She spoke from Psalm 127 in a message titled "What to Do When You Find Yourself at Wit's End." From the feedback I heard afterward, what caused her talk to go from good to great was when she applied the text to an incredibly difficult week our family had endured a few years earlier. Her carefully worded story of our experience breathed life into her message and gave her a high level of credibility with her hearers.

Calvin Miller writes, "People discover who they are in the context of a preacher's honesty. . . . Transparency paves the way to the Spirit's advance. And Christ always visits us on the runways of openness."[3]

Miller goes on to give several rules to govern how far a pastor should go in confessional preaching. First, never betray any member of your family or any members of your church with your openness. Second, any confession that injures the church goes too far. Third, when our confession begins to embarrass our audience, we are on shaky ground.[4]

I do not think I have a right to preach a passage of Scripture and call my hearers to obey it if I am not willing to obey it first. If I am too apathetic or cowardly to apply it, why should I expect them to?

Great biblical communicators apply the Bible to themselves. The goal at this step is to write at least one sentence, if not a whole story, in reference to how this passage of Scripture impacted your life.

Start to Put It All Together

At this point in your sermon preparation process, you have decided to be a preacher of the Word (2 Tim 4:2 and addressed in chap. 14). You have purposed to communicate for life change (Luke 3 and addressed in chap. 15). You have planned to feed your flock a balanced, Christ-focused, gospel-centered diet; determined what portion of God's Word it is that He wants you to preach; and created a tentative sermon calendar (John 21:15–17 and addressed in chap. 16).

You have also completed the Bible study aspect of your sermon preparation. At this stage you should be able to state the idea of the passage in a simple, clear sentence. You should also have a rough outline or diagram of how the rest of the passage relates to the central truth. And you should have a sentence or more describing how this passage applied or applies to your life.

I suggest that you record the summary of your insights on an Exegetical Worksheet. Below is a sample of such a worksheet.

Sample Exegetical Worksheet

Scripture Text: *Ephesians 6:18–20*

Central Exegetical Truth: (summarize this text in one sentence that is accurate to the intent of the original author)
   When it comes to spiritual warfare, prayer is the battle.

Rough Outline of the Text or Passage to Be Preached: (create an outline of this passage that is accurate to the intent of the original author)

WHAT? Praying — Prayer is the climax of all Paul has been discussing in verses 10–17 about spiritual warfare.

HOW?

1. *at all times*
2. *in the Spirit*—(Rom 8:26–27)
3. *with all prayer*—all types of prayer: adoration, confession, thanksgiving
4. *supplication*—asking God to "supply" *specific* needs (example: Luke 11:5 "three loaves," and Gen 24:12 "let her offer my camels water as well")
5. *keep alert with all perseverance/persistence/endurance* (see Luke 11:9–10, *keep on* praying, *keep on* asking, *keep on* seeking)
6. *making supplication for all the saints*—intercessory prayer
7. *and also for me.* Paul frequently requested prayer (see 1 Thess 5:25—Brothers, *pray for us*; 2 Thess 3:1—Finally, brothers, *pray for us* that the message of the Lord may spread rapidly and be honored, just as it was with you; Rom 15:30—I urge you, brothers, by our Lord Jesus Christ and by the love of the Spirit, to join me in my struggle by *praying to God for me*; Col 4:3—And *pray for* us, too, that God may open a door for our message, so that we may proclaim the mystery of Christ.)

Personal Application: Reading and studying this passage made me or makes me . . .

Even though the church in Asia, Africa, and South America is growing, the church in North America is declining. As I have come to understand this passage, I have become convinced that the church in the West is declining because we are losing the battle on our knees. We not only do not have strong enough prayer lives to push the enemy back, we don't even have potent enough prayer lives to keep the enemy from taking more ground. But the question is not when will we have more potent and militant prayer lives. The question is when will I have a more potent and militant prayer life and what steps will I take to get there.

⟶ What Now? ⟵

Select a verse or passage of Scripture. Use the three steps given in this chapter for studying it out. Work until you can create an exegetical worksheet for that passage.

Sample Exegetical Worksheet

Scripture Text:

Central Exegetical Truth:

Rough Outline of the Text or Passage to Be Preached:

Personal Application(s):

~ Quote ~

*Billy Graham said that if he had his ministry to do over
again, he would make two changes. First, he would study
three times as much. "I have preached too much and studied
too little." Second, he would give more time to prayer.*

—JOHN STOTT[5]

Notes

1. John Stott, *Between Two Worlds* (Grand Rapids, MI: Eerdman, 1982), 182.
2. Haddon Robinson, *Biblical Preaching* (Grand Rapids, MI: Baker, 1980), 67.
3. Calvin Miller, *Preaching* (Grand Rapids, MI: Baker, 2006), 130–32.
4. Ibid., 131–32.
5. Stott, *Between Two Worlds*, 181.

18

Pastoral Leadership Is . . .

Preparing
the Message

*Don't complain about the hours you are spending
and the agony you experience. The people deserve all
you can give them.*

—HADDON ROBINSON[1]

Work Hard at Preaching and Teaching

The elders who are good leaders should be considered worthy of an
ample honorarium, especially those who *work hard at preaching and
teaching*. (1 Tim 5:17, italics added)

In this passage Paul is obviously addressing the compensation of elders. Note
that he distinguishes between regular elders and those who labor at preaching
and teaching. The assumption, is teaching elders should literally "wear themselves out" at preaching and teaching because doing it well requires hard work.

John MacArthur is one of the best-known Bible teachers alive today. His
expansive ministry and church is founded on the preaching of the Word of
God. Regarding the time required for effective study, he writes, "Though I may
preach only three hours a week, I study thirty."[2]

John Stott, the lauded English Bible preacher comments that beginning preachers need twelve hours to construct a sermon.[3] Tony Merida writes, "The call to preach is a call to enter God's gym, for God's glory. We must train personally, daily, and faithfully."[4] Communicating God's Word effectively is hard work.

Eight Steps to Preparing the Message

At this point in your sermon preparation process, you have decided to be a preacher of the Word (2 Tim 4:2, addressed in chap. 14). You have purposed to communicate for life change (Luke 3, addressed in chap. 15). You have planned to feed your flock a balanced, Christ-focused, gospel-centered diet and determined what portion of God's Word it is that He wants you to preach and created a tentative sermon calendar (John 21:15–17, addressed in chap. 16).

You have also completed the Bible study aspect of your sermon preparation (2 Tim 2:15, addressed chap. 17). You have clearly stated the idea of the passage in a simple, clear sentence. You have crafted a rough outline or diagram of how the rest of the passage relates to the central truth. And you have a sentence or more describing how this passage applied or applies to your life. The summary of these Bible study insights is recorded on an Exegetical Worksheet.

At this point, the sermon preparation process is only half done. You have a nice Bible study, but not a powerful sermon. The trick here is to move from the exegetical idea and diagram or outline to the homiletic idea and outline. The pastor must take what the Bible says and relate it to his audience in an effective manner.

The issue is twofold: discerning what God wants to say to your people through this passage of Scripture and determining the most effective way to say it. In the rest of this chapter I am going to offer you an eight-step plan for creating a strong message.

Step 1: Decide the Main Truth

At this point, you first want to be able to tell your audience succinctly what God wants them to hear from this text. You will take your central exegetical idea and reword it to relate to your people in a memorable, homiletic truth. This is your sermon in a sentence.

For example, you might determine that the central exegetical idea of Eph 1:3–12 is: *Believers have been given a lofty position in Christ.* However, the big homiletic truth is: *You have got the power!* Or you might have decided that the central exegetic idea of Rom 8:35–39 is: *The love of Christ gives the believer victory and confidence through trials.* But the big homiletic truth is: *You are inseparable from and invincible through Christ's love.*

One way to turn the exegetical truth into your homiletic truth is to ask yourself this question: When someone walks out of the gathering this Sunday and someone stops them in a restaurant later in the day and asks, "What was the sermon about?" What do you want them say?

By answering this question you have to focus only on the essential aspect of the message. It also keeps your "sermon in a sentence" short. It further causes you to craft it in such a way that it will be remembered later.

If I get stumped on the main truth, I ask myself this question: If the hearer remembers only one thing, what do I want them to remember? When I can answer that question, I am ready to move to step 2.

Step 2: Choose the Target

The next step is determining the aim of your sermon. Nothing could be more significant. Haddon Robinson makes a powerful insight when he declares, "No matter how brilliant or biblical a sermon is, without a definite purpose it is not worth preaching."[5]

Determining your purpose is answering the question: What does God want to *do* in the lives of my people through this passage of Scripture? This is the target of the message. It is the reason you are standing up, opening your Bible, and talking. It is the measuring stick that determines every other aspect of sermon preparation.

It is pointless to wrestle through a text of Scripture if we do not carry it to the next step and turn our findings into a clear target for transformation in the lives of the hearers. This target would become the basis of the direct challenge we should offer the congregation in every message. It would set up the nature of the invitation we give at the end of the message.

It is important to put in the time to craft a good target. The "smarter" the target, the greater impact it has. Leadership guru Peter Drucker, in his seminal work *The Practice of Management*, coined the usage of the acronym for SMART objectives.[6] A SMART objective is one that is *specific, measurable, achievable, relevant*, and *time-bound.*

Your goal at this point in the sermon preparation process is to turn your exegetical study into a SMART target. Hone your target into a statement that is as *specific, measurable, achievable, relevant*, and *time-bound* as possible. Below are some samples of both non-SMART and SMART targets.

Non-specific target: *Feel more confident that the Bible is God's Word.*

Non-measurable target: *Love the Word of God and want to read the Bible more.*

Non-attainable: *Pledge to read the entire Bible this week.*

Non-relevant: *Read more comic books.*

Non-time oriented: *Read the Bible more.*

SMART (specific, measurable, attainable, relevant, time-based) target: *Make a commitment to read at least one chapter of the Bible each day for the next thirty days.*

When I get stumped crafting a target, I complete the following sentence: "My goal in preaching this sermon is that the hearer would . . ."

Step 3: Construct the Outline

The next step in sermon development is organizing your thoughts for the message. Organization is the plan or the map of the sermon. Without a map, a traveler will easily get lost and never arrive at his destination. Without organization, your sermon will never reach its target.

An effective sermon has *unity*. Unity keeps the message from veering off course. All of the parts are organized to fit together into a whole. Those parts that do not fit with the rest are discarded. The key to unity is making sure that everything in the message fits under the dominating theme.

The effective message also has *progression.* The sermon must continually be moving toward its goal. Once you have determined the target, be certain that everything else moves the message in the direction of the target.

To achieve progression, the message generally follows a track of five phases:

1. Arrest the *attention* of the audience.
2. Establish the *need.*
3. *Satisfy* the need.
4. *Visualize* the results of the satisfaction step.
5. Lead the hearer to take *action.*[7]

The easiest way to organize a sermon with both unity and progression is through the use of an *outline.* Having an outline makes it easier for the preacher to stay on track and reach his final destination. It also helps him remember it and deliver it more effectively.

Having an outline also makes it easier for the congregation to follow the message. Beyond that, it helps the hearers remember and apply it.

Dr. Woodrow Kroll is a master Bible teacher. He has served as a pastor, professor, and college president. Since 1990 he has been the president and principle Bible teacher on *Back to the Bible*, an international radio and television ministry that has a listenership of millions in various countries around the world. He has authored more than fifty books and has ministered in more than one hundred countries. He writes, "A good sermon needs an outline just as a man needs a skeleton. . . . Lack of arrangement is probably the single most common fault of preaching today."[8]

In his book on preaching, Kroll acknowledges the late Dr. Gordon Davis, of the Davis Bible College in Binghamton, New York, for developing a system of mechanical devices that unlock a passage into a helpful outline.[9] It is based on grouping all of the sub-points of the outline under a particular approach. I have often used this method when I get stuck while trying to prepare a message.

Outline Approaches

There are a number of different methods for outlining:

Advantages in/Benefits of/Blessings of /Rewards of approach
Advisability of approach
Aspects of/Characteristics of/Elements of approach
Commands of approach
Consequences of approach
Dynamics of approach
Evidences for/Proofs of approach
Examples of approach
Necessities for/Requirements for approach
Paths of approach
Phases of approach
Possessions of/Riches of approach
Results of approach
Steps to approach
Types of approach

The listing above is just a sample of some you can use. No matter whether your message is expositional, topical, textual, or a combination, the above mechanical devices can help unlock your message and give you an outline that works.

Below is a sample expositor outline covering Eph 6:18–20. This outline was the seventh message in a series on spiritual warfare from Eph 6:10–20. It uses a "requirements for" approach based on the idea of revealing the requirements for warfare prayer by answering the heading How to Wage Spiritual Warfare.

Series: *This Is War! Ephesians 6:10–20*

Text: *Ephesians 6:18–20*

Title: *Fighting from Our Knees*

Truth: *We must wage prayer warfare*

Target: *The goal in this message is that the hearer would make a commitment to make prayer more central in their life by praying fifteen extra minutes each day this month for themselves, the church, the pastors, and one other believer.*

Outline: *Preaching outline of the text or passage to be preached using the "requirements for" approach—The Requirements for Waging Prayer Warfare.*

How to Wage Prayer Warfare

1. PRAY CONSISTENTLY — *praying at all times*
2. PRAY SPIRITUALLY — *praying . . . in the Spirit*
3. PRAY THROUOUGHLY — *praying . . . with all prayer*
4. PRAY SPECIFICALLY — *praying . . . with . . . all supplication*
5. PRAY ALERTLY — *praying . . . keep[ing] alert*
6. PRAY PERSISTENTLY — *praying . . . with all perseverance*
7. PRAY UNSELFISHLY — *praying . . . making supplication for all the saints*
8. PRAY SUBMISSIVELY — *praying . . . making supplication . . . also for me*
9. PRAY EVANGELISTICALLY — *praying . . . to proclaim the mystery of the gospel*

On the other hand, if you are preaching a textual expository message on John 3:16, your approach could be the "characteristics of" approach. It might look like this:

The Great Love of God

1. Love's Great Source—*God*
2. Love's Great Object—*The World*
3. Love's Great Expression—*He Gave*
4. Love's Great Price—*His Only Son*
5. Love's Great Reward—*Everlasting Life*
6. Love's Great Demand—*Believe in Him*

Another basic way to outline a message is to take a subject and answer three questions: What, Why, and How. For example:

Tapping into the Power of Prayer

What?   Pray
Why?   Prayer connects us with Omnipotence
        Prayer connects us with Omniscience
        Prayer connects us with Eternity
How?   Talk with God
        . . . everyday
        . . . about everything that is on your mind
        . . . about everyone who is on your heart

Step 4: Fill in the Content

If the outline is the skeleton, the content is the meat on the bones of your sermon. According to Tony Merida, the content is made up of three functional elements: explanation, application, and illustration.[10]

Explanation involves making a particular truth clear and understandable. The idea is that you want it to be so plain that a sixth grader will understand it. To do this you might need to explain key words or phrases. Maybe the context will require some explanation. You should point out key doctrines that are unearthed by the passage.

Explanation may occur as you simply present the facts required for understanding. It may be a matter of interpreting one Scripture by using another. It could involve linking an ancient concept with a contemporary one. Maybe it is paraphrasing a verse in your own words, or retelling the story in twenty-first-century language.

Application answers the question, What does this passage say to these hearers? Here you refer to the basic Bible study questions: Does this text contain any: (1) actions to take, (2) commands to keep, (3) convictions to hold, (4) errors to avoid, (5) praises to offer, (6) promises to claim, (7) sins to confess and forsake, or (8) questions to answer?

You can supply applications for each of the main points of your outline or weave one primary application throughout your message. It is important to be sure to apply the text at the end of your message.

You can state the application by use of personal pronouns. You may also want to bring the application through use of a penetrating question or series of questions.

If you study the sermons of Jesus and read the letters of Paul you will see the value of application. In some cases they spent up to 50 percent of their teachings applying the truth.

Illustration is the act of showing the hearers what a particular truth looks like when brought into their daily lives. Good illustrations shed light on the truth.

An illustration can also be used as a way to make truth more compelling. It can inspire action. An illustration may be very helpful in making an argument and proving your point.

Step 5: Write the Introduction

Seven seconds. That's it. Seven seconds. Within the first seven seconds of meeting, people form opinions about each other that will influence the rest of the relationship. The same thing happens with a sermon. Within a very brief moment the hearers silently determine if and how they will listen to what follows.

Never underestimate the power of the introduction. John Stott writes:

> A good introduction serves two purposes. First, it arouses interest, stimulates curiosity, and whets the appetite for more. Secondly, it genuinely "introduces" the theme by leading the hearers to it.[11]

Beyond those two purposes, a good introduction also connects the listeners with the speaker. They decide if you are knowledgeable, likeable, and trustworthy. On top of that, a good introduction surfaces felt-needs and causes the hearer to listen because they feel the need to pay attention.

Paul O'Neil was a noted magazine writer. His advice for compelling writing fits well with a great introduction.

> Always grab the reader by the throat in the first paragraph, sink your thumbs in their windpipe in the second and hold him against the wall until the tag line.[12]

Kent Edwards suggests the following principles for crafting compelling introductions.

> 1. *Begin with a clear understanding of the big idea of the sermon.*
> 2. *Develop interest.* Show listeners why it is in their best interest to listen. Remember, the more abstract the idea, the more time is needed to help people understand its relevance to their lives.
> 3. *Write it well so that it is striking, specific, and direct.* A good first statement can be a paradoxical statement, a twist on a familiar quote, or a rhetorical question.
> 4. *Match the mood of the introduction with the mood of the sermon.*
> 5. *Adapt it to fit the style of your message.* Either show the big idea and the way it will be developed in a deductive sermon, or build tension for an inductive sermon.
> 6. *Prepare to deliver it well.*
> 7. *Be yourself.*[13]

I would add five additional important principles to Edwards' list. First, *bring energy*. Energy naturally attracts attention. Second, *be confident*. Confident speakers also attract attention and interest. Third, *use eye contact*. Memorize your first few sentences so the first words out of your mouth will be delivered with you looking the audience in the eye instead of you looking down at a sheet of paper.

Fourth, *change it up*. There is more than one way to introduce a talk. You could start with a startling fact. (*Forty percent of the people in this room have seriously contemplated suicide at one time or another.*) You could tell a ministory. You could ask a compelling question (*How many of you actually believe that God can do things bigger and better than you can?*)

Fifth, use the introduction to *expose felt needs*. Haddon Robinson observes,

> Sermons catch fire when flint strikes steel. When the flint of a person's problems strikes the steel of the Word of God, a spark ignites that burns in the mind. Directing our preaching at people's needs is not a mere persuasive technique; it is the task of ministry.[14]

He further notes,

> Should a preacher of even limited ability bring to the surface people's questions, problems, hurts, and desires and deal with them from the Bible, he will be acclaimed a genius.[15]

Step 6: Form the Conclusion

A good introduction and a great conclusion can make a mediocre sermon great. In fact, some preachers see the conclusion as being of such import that they prepare it first and point the rest of the message toward it.

The conclusion is where the effective preacher, like a successful prosecuting attorney, makes his final appeal by calling for a verdict. It can stir the hearer from merely leaving with good intentions to making significant life changes.

Conclusions take various forms depending on the message, the audience, and the occasion. These include:

- a summary
- an illustration
- a quotation
- a question
- a direct challenge
- a prayer

Step 7: Determine the Invitation

The invitation is a logical extension of the conclusion. It is the direct, personal, practical, and specific call to action that naturally flows from the rest of the message.

Just as every text is different and every message is unique, every invitation should be distinct. For example, an evangelistic message centered on the cross would naturally lead to an invitation to call upon the name of the Lord to be saved. A teaching message on the credibility of the Bible would have a call to make a commitment to read the Bible daily for a month. A challenging message on Christian service might end with an appeal to sign up to serve in children's ministry.

I like to employ a variety of potential expressions to offer the hearer by way of invitation. For example, after a compelling message on the value of community, the invitation would be to get up, walk to the lobby, and sign up to join a small group.

Following a message on the power of Jesus to heal broken hearts, the invitation might be to come to an altar and kneel as an act of bringing your broken heart to the cross. There, prayer partners would kneel next to the responders and pray for them.

A message on salvation might have the invitation of asking the audience to bow their heads, then leading a sinner's prayer for all who desire to repent and believe in the Lord Jesus Christ. Afterward, those who prayed are directed to drop a card in the offering plate indicating their decision to pursue Christ and seek further instruction.

I rarely have music play while I am asking people to respond, but I do love to have a few appropriate songs of worship and praise as a way of allowing the congregation to express their response to the truth of the Word given in the sermon.

A few invitation pointers are as follows:

- Never offer an invitation without first proclaiming truth.
- Make sure the invitation matches the mood and content of the message.
- Use a variety of invitation styles to match the nature of the challenge given.
- As you prepare your sermon, prayerfully ask God what response He wants you to offer the hearers after this message.

Expect people to respond. If you have done your job well and the Lord has worked through the message, they will respond.

- Never badger or belittle people into responding.
- Make the invitation brief, simple, clear, and compelling.

Step 8: Craft the Title

I am an author who has had twenty of my books published. One book I wrote was rejected by twenty-one publishers. But after I changed the title, three publishers quickly got in a bidding war for it. In the last few years, it has sold nearly two hundred thousand copies and has been translated into numerous languages.

What made the big difference?

All I did was change the title.

Never underestimate the power of the title.

The title captures interest and gives people an idea of what the message is about. It should also encourage them to want to hear the message.

One of the best ways to come up with a good title is to tweak the titles of current movies, or play off the titles of popular television series. Go to secular book stores and note the titles of the best sellers. Consider phrases that are hot in popular culture.

One of the most important aspects of title making is knowing your audience. Are they primarily baby boomers or millennials? Believers or nonbelievers? Married or single? Modern or postmodern? Churched or nonchurched? What is appealing to one audience may be repulsive to another.

— What Now? —

The best way to learn to write good sermons is to practice writing sermons. The only way to learn to do it is to do it.

Take the exegetical worksheet that you prepared at the end of the last chapter. Now use the eight-step process described in this chapter to craft your message. Over time you will tweak and adjust your plan to fit your own style and personality, but use this as a starting point.

Notes

1. Haddon Robinson, *Biblical Preaching* (Grand Rapids, MI: Baker, 1980), 44.
2. John MacArthur, *Pastoral Ministry* (Nashville, TN: Thomas Nelson, 2002), xiii.
3. John Stott, *Between Two Worlds* (Grand Rapids, MI: Eerdmans, 1982), 259.
4. Tony Merida, *Faithful Preaching: Declaring Scripture with Responsibility, Passion, and Authenticity* (Nashville, TN: B&H, 2009), 125.
5. Robinson, *Biblical Preaching*, 107
6. Peter Drucker, *The Practice of Management* (New York: Harper Collins, 1954).
7. Alan Monroe, *Principles and Types of Speech* (Chicago, IL: Scott, Foresman and Co., 1949), ix.
8. Woodrow Kroll, *Prescription for Preaching* (Grand Rapids, MI: Baker, 1980), 153.
9. Kroll, *Prescription for Preaching*, 189.
10. Merida, *Faithful Preaching*, 100.
11. John Stott, *Between Two Worlds*, 244.
12. Paul O'Neil, quoted in George Hunt, "Editor's Note: Attila the Hun in a Tattered Sweater," *Life*, 13 November 1964, 3.
13. Kent Edwards, "Why Should I Listen?" in *The Art and Craft of Preaching*, ed. Haddon Robinson and Craig Larson (Grand Rapids, MI: Zondervan, 2006), 372.
14. Robinson, *Biblical Preaching*, 163.
15. Ibid., 164.

19

Living and Giving the Message

*I preached as never sure to preach again and as
a dying man to dying men.*

— Richard Baxter[1]

Study, Obey, Teach

Ezra was handed a nearly impossible job. He was sent by God to a city that was in chaos, to a people who were in defeat, to rebuild a temple that had been ruined.

Yet God's hand of blessing was evident on Ezra's life and ministry. Soon the temple was rebuilt and the people of Jerusalem were eventually led into a powerful season of revival (see Nehemiah 8).

The favor of God on Ezra was the result of a simple, three-fold commitment he had made.

> Ezra came to Jerusalem in the fifth month, during the seventh year of the king. He began the journey from Babylon on the first day of the first month and arrived in Jerusalem on the first day of the fifth month. The gracious hand of his God was on him, *because Ezra had determined in his heart to study the law of the LORD, obey [it], and teach [its] statutes and ordinances in Israel.* (Ezra 7:8–10, italics added)

Study, obey, and teach the Word of God. It is so simple. It is necessary.

In the last couple of chapters we have talked about studying the Word and crafting the sermon, both of which are very important. But in order for your message to be powerful and transformational, you also need to live it and deliver it.

Do and Teach

I wrote the first narrative, Theophilus, about all that Jesus began to *do and teach*. (Acts 1:1, italics added)

Jesus was a great preacher. Crowds numbering in the multiple thousands flocked to hear Him teach. His words are so significant that they are recorded in leather books and are printed in red ink. Countless books have been written and lectures given about His words.

Yet Jesus' ministry was more than mighty words. His words were backed by an exceptional life. He *did* astounding things; therefore, He was able to say powerfully impacting words.

Luke, the author of the Gospel bearing his name, began the book of Acts with an interesting comment. He described his Gospel as an account of "all that Jesus began to *do and teach*."

"Do and teach." That should be a motto for every communicator. A pastor is known by his flock. If his life fails to back up his words, no one will listen. John MacArthur observes, "Behind the content of his message is the character of the expositor."[2]

A great sermon is born out of a great life. Someone noted that a message prepared in the head, reaches the head. A message prepared in the heart, reaches the heart, but only the message prepared in the life, reaches and changes other lives.

The most powerful sermons are often those that are, in a sense, the preacher's life message. His story has intersected with the story of the Scriptures. His sermon is not merely theoretical. It is not something he simply read out of a book or listened to somebody else discuss on a podcast. The pain, the joy, the questions, and the struggle are owned by the preacher. They lend weight to his words.

Be an Example

In his first letter to Timothy, Paul gave the young pastor suggestions and admonitions about preaching. Yet each command to preach is given in the context of equally weighty command to be an example of what was being taught.

Notice that in Paul's words there is a back and forth flow addressing Timothy's preaching and his living.

> *Command and teach* these things. No one should despise your youth; instead, you should *be an example* to the believers in speech, in conduct, in love, in faith, in purity. Until I come, *give your attention to public reading, exhortation, and teaching.* Do not neglect the gift that is in you; it was given to you through prophecy, with the laying on of hands by the council of elders. *Practice these things;* be committed to them, so that *your progress* may be evident to all. *Be conscientious about yourself and your teaching;* persevere in these things, for by doing this you will save both yourself and your hearers. (1 Tim 4:11–16, italics added)

Living the Message

Great communicators not only live *in* the Word as they study it, but they also live *out* the Word in their lives. It is as we live the message that the Lord will accompany the message with His presence and with fresh power.

We will discuss what it means to live your message from two angles: macro and micro. On the macro level, living the message involves the big picture of your life. Is the overall course of your life being lived in obedience to the message of the Bible? Is it a magnet that consistently draws others to Christ? On the micro level, living the message is a matter of trying to obey everything that is in the passage of Scripture you have been called to preach that week. Are you living the message you are about to stand up and give?

Let me offer three reminders regarding the importance of living the message.

1. Remember, You Are Your Tools

While it is true that the preacher has books, computer programs, the Internet, and media to aid him in the sermon-making and sermon-giving process, they are not his primary tools. Spurgeon writes, "We are, in a sense, our own tools, and therefore must keep ourselves in order . . . my own spirit, soul, and body are my nearest machinery for sacred service; my spiritual faculties and my inner life are my battle axe and weapons of war."[3]

Robert McCheyne wrote to a pastor expressing the same notion.

> Remember you are God's instrument—I trust, a chosen vessel unto Him to bear His name. In great measure, according to the purity and perfection of the instrument, will be the success. It is not great talents

God blesses so much as great likeness to Jesus. A holy minister is an awful weapon in the hand of God.[4]

2. Remember, You Only Have One Shot

Several months ago, Cathy and I were in the ancient city of Corinth. Standing out in the middle of the agora was a large, square, rock platform. A sign on the side said "BEMA." The guide told us how legal decisions were handed out from this Bema, or judgment seat. Also, victorious athletes from the nearby games were awarded their victory wreathes from that platform.

As I stood there, my mind went to the words Paul later wrote the people who walked by that judgment seat every day: "For we must all appear before the judgment seat of Christ" (2 Cor 5:10). He later wrote similar words to the Romans: "For we will all stand before the judgment seat of God. . . . So then, each of us will give an account of himself to God" (Rom 14:10–12).

One day all of us will give an account of what we have done with what we have been given. Our thoughts, words, deeds, and motives will be meticulously and thoroughly examined as Jesus looks to give us rewards.

Pastor James reminds us that pastors are not exempt from evaluation. In fact, he points out that pastors experience stricter judgment: "Not many should become teachers, my brothers, knowing that we will receive a stricter judgment" (Jas 3:1). As a pastor, you will not only give an accounting of the words you have spoken, but also of the life you have lived. Did your life back up your words?

You only have one shot at this life (Heb 9:27). There will be no do-overs, no second chance. You must make this life count. Determine today to preach everything God says and to live everything you preach.

3. Remember, You Should Be Giving Hell Fits

Every pastor should live such a life that he causes hell to shiver. Make up your mind that you will not be content to live anything less than a sold-out, on-fire, radically righteous, ridiculously loving, God-centered, Word-filled, Christ-exalting, Satan-stomping life. Decide that you will be a pastor who God uses to the absolute maximum of your abilities. Become a spiritual gate-kicker and one who snatches souls from the flames of hell. Be such a holy warrior that your life gives headaches to hell itself.

Paul was such a man. Luke records the sad account of Jewish exorcists trying to cast out demons in the name of Jesus and Paul. As you recall, the demons were unimpressed and pummeled them, claiming, "Jesus I know, and Paul I recognize—but who are you?" (Acts 19:14–16).

In his classic book *Why Revival Tarries*, Leonard Ravenhill explains why Paul was well known in hell. Building on the theme of Paul viewing himself as crucified with Christ, Ravenhill writes,

> He had no ambitions—and so had nothing to be jealous about. He had no reputation—and so had nothing to fight about. He had no possessions—and therefore nothing to worry about. He had no "rights"—so therefore he could not suffer wrong. He was already broken—so no one could break him. He was "dead"—so none could kill him. He was less than the least of the least—so who could humble him? He had suffered the loss of all things—so who could defraud him? Does this throw any light on why the demon said, "Paul I know?" Over this God intoxicated man, hell suffered headaches.[5]

Giving the Message

The faithful pastor should study the Word, obey the Word, and also *teach* the Word. As we discussed in chap. 15, the goal of this teaching is significant change in the lives of the listeners. In order for this to occur there needs to be genuine spiritual power. The Holy Spirit must work and move in the hearts of the hearers in a way no human could.

Old-time preachers call preaching with power "divine unction." Lee Eclov defines divine unction as "the anointing of the Holy Spirit on a sermon so that something holy and powerful is added to the message that no preacher can generate, no matter how great his skills . . . the sermon and the Spirit meet to form a spiritual torrent."[6]

Keys to Unleashing Divine Unction in Your Preaching

1. Pray

I have a friend who took over a young church shortly after he graduated from university. After a few years of pastoral ministry, he felt the need to get a seminary education. While seminary gave him a deeper, broader well from which to draw living water, all of the study left him rather spiritually dry. He felt as if he had lost the power in his preaching.

I suggested that the next two weeks he try to spend one hour praying for every hour he spent studying for his sermon. He decided to try it.

When I saw him two weeks later he greeted me with a big smile. "Wow!" he said. "The last two Sundays were the best we have had in a long time. I had forgotten the power of prayer in preaching."

Charles Spurgeon was a powerful communicator. He told his students, "Prayer will singularly assist you in the delivery of your sermon. . . . None are so able to plead with men as those who have been wrestling with God on their behalf."[7]

Below I have listed several requests you may offer regarding your preaching:

- Pray for guidance as to what it is God wants you to preach.
- Pray for illumination as you repeatedly read the text.
- Pray for insight as you study the text.
- Pray for direction as you begin to craft the sermon.
- Pray for success (Gen 24:12), blessing (Gen 32:26), divine Presence (Exod 33:15), wisdom, (2 Chr 1:10), favor (Neh 1:11), energy and endurance (Neh 6:9), and especially power from on high (Luke 24:49).
- Pray Paul's prayers over your flock (see chap. 10).

I also suggest that you ask your people to pray for you as you prepare and as you preach each week (1 Thess 5:25; 2 Thess 3:1; Rom 15:30; Eph 6:19; Col 4:3). I recruited a team of twelve men who prayed for me every day. They also divided into four teams that each prayed during the worship service once a month. Their prayers powered my preaching.

2. Be Real

People connect most quickly and deeply with your struggles, not your successes. Fearlessly expose your hurts and your heart. Dan Baty said, "Lives change only when hearts have been affected, and hearts are most deeply affected when the speaker exposes his own."[8]

3. Be Passionate

Jeremiah was the passionate prophet of God. For him preaching was not a mere intellectual exercise. His was a gut-wrenching, soul-convicting endeavor. He took the Word of God literally and viewed it as powerful. It is no wonder he wrote, "Is not My word like fire"—the LORD's declaration—"and like a sledgehammer that pulverizes rock?" (Jer 23:29).

Passion in preaching is that glorious mixture of the power of God's Word, the might of God's Spirit, and the preacher whose heart is on fire. Passion is the difference between a nice talk and a changed life. Genuine passion makes up for a multitude of inadequacies. Godly zeal draws a crowd and impacts lives.

John Wesley is said to have been visited by a young pastor. "I am greatly impressed with the popularity and impact of your ministry," the young man said. "What do you suggest I can do to attain such a following?"

Wesley looked him in the eye and replied, "Catch yourself on fire and people will come to see you burn."[9]

When I speak of a preacher's passion, I am talking about an intense, driving, overmastering feeling or conviction. I am talking about holy "heart burn" and having a fire in the belly that refuses to be quenched.

Passion is that which stirs the emotions, affections, devotions, and decisions of the speaker and the hearer. Passion flows from an unrelenting, overwhelming sense that what God has given you to say is vitally significant. It is the burning heart of the effective communicator.

Effective speakers pour out their hearts. They put all of themselves into what they are doing. They are not distracted, but are focused on the moment, seizing the opportunity.

I have a simple rule of thumb: If I am not passionate about a sermon, I will not preach it. Therefore, I must do whatever it takes to get my heart in the place where I am passionate about it.

As a communicator of the Word of God you have the incredible privilege of standing up and representing God before people. You have the immense responsibility of saying words that could impact the eternal destiny of your listeners. You have the intense joy of speaking of things that truly matter. You get to speak of heaven, hell, the cross, sin, and salvation. You are honored to lift high the name of Jesus! If that does not fire you up, you should forget about being a preacher and get another job.

4. Use Stories with a Purpose

Few things can open or close a message more effectively than a good, well-told story. Dan Baty gives four keys to telling a story so as to unleash greater power into your message.

Describe the story with sensory detail. Try to let your audience see, hear, smell, touch, and taste the scene and setting of the story.

Attach a specific emotion. Take the risk to tell how you felt or feel about what happened. Connection is made with the audience as they experience your feelings.

Reveal why you felt of feel that way. Give enough information so the audience can adequately comprehend the depth of your feelings.

Explain what it all means. Tell the audience the point of the story. Give them that one-sentence explanation that ties the emotions together and drives truth into their hearts and minds.[10]

5. Cooperate with the Holy Spirit

The older I get, the more convinced I become that real, lasting, deep, life-changing ministry is primarily a matter of cooperating with the Holy Spirit. The Holy Spirit is already committed to glorifying Jesus by convicting and regenerating the lost and to glorify Jesus by sanctifying the saints. Our job is to get in on the work He already longs to do.

Cooperating with the Spirit begins as you select the text, continues as you study it, and must be maintained as you craft it into a sermon. But it does not stop there. I have found my most powerful moments in the pulpit have occurred as I have sensed the Spirit prompting me to go in a direction and I have obeyed.

I was speaking at a Bible conference. I got up, looked the people in the eye, and poured out my heart. I gave them a stiff rebuke and a strong challenge. Then I went into my message. The response was significant.

Afterward, Cathy asked me, "Did you plan to say all that at the beginning?"

"No," I said, "God hit me with it during the song before the message, and I decided to scrap my introduction and go with it."

"Well it sure got their attention," she said. "The response was rather amazing."

While cooperating with the Spirit may mean talking in some instances, it means to stop talking in others. If you pay attention, you can tell when God is speaking during your message. No one is coughing. No one is fidgeting. There is a holy hush.

I have learned that in those moments, the Spirit-filled communicator should stop talking. Let God speak. During that minute or two of silence, God is thundering His message into hearts.

6. Urgency

Sunday night at 8:00 p.m. on Oct. 8, 1871, an incident occurred that forever changed the life and ministry of Dwight L. Moody. That Sunday, Moody preached to the largest congregation he had ever addressed in Chicago. After preaching his heart out and presenting Jesus as redeemer, he asked his congregation to return the next week to make their decision for Christ.

They never did.

As hundreds filed out of church that evening, the closing song was interrupted by the din of fire trucks and the crowd was scattered forever—Chicago was on fire. In the next two and a half days, hundreds of people were killed as the Great Chicago Fire destroyed more than four square miles of the city, including burning to the ground the Illinois Street Church.

"What a mistake!" he said, in relating the story to a large audience in Chicago on the twenty-second anniversary of the great fire. "I have never dared to give an audience a week to think of their salvation since. If they were lost they might rise up in judgment against me."[11]

When you prepare to preach, realize these two sobering truths: (1) This could be the last sermon your audience may ever hear, (2) This could be the last sermon you ever give. Richard Baxter summed it up well when he said, "I preached as never sure to preach again and as a dying man to dying men."[12]

— What Now? —

Look back over the six characteristics of life-changing communication. Which one most deeply resonated with you? What can you do to better apply it into your own communication ministry?

— Quote —

Would ministers preach for eternity! They would then act the part of true Christian orators, and not only calmly and cooly inform the understanding, but, by persuasive, pathetic address, endeavour to move the affections and warm the heart.

—George Whitefield[13]

Notes

1. Richard Baxter, quoted in Mark Galli and Ted Olsen, *131 Christians Everyone Should Know* (Nashville, TN: B&H, 2000), 86.

2. John MacArthur, *Preaching* (Nashville, TN: Thomas Nelson, 2005), 63.

3. Charles Spurgeon, *Lectures to My Students* (Grand Rapids, MI: Zondervan, 1954), 7–8.

4. Robert McCheyne, quoted in Spurgeon, *Lectures to My Students*, 8.

5. Leonard Ravenhill, *Why Revival Tarries* (Minneapolis, MN: Bethany House, 1986), 186.

6. Lee Eclov, "How Does Unction Function?" in *The Art and Craft of Biblical Preaching*, ed. Haddon Robinson and Craig Larson (Grand Rapids, MI: Zondervan, 2005), 81.

7. Spurgeon, *Lectures to My Students*, 45.

8. Dan Baty, "Heart-to-Heart Preaching," in *The Art and Craft of Preaching*, 959.

9. John Wesley, http://thinkexist.com/quotation/catch_on_fire_with_enthusiasm _and_people_will/212431.html (accessed July 4, 2011).

10. Baty, "Heart-to-Heart Preaching," 560–61.

11. William R. Moody, *The Life of Dwight L. Moody by His Son* (Murfreesboro, TN: Sword of the Lord Publishers, 1930), 125.

12. Richard Baxter, quoted in Mark Galli and Ted Olsen, *131 Christians Everyone Should Know* (Nashville, TN: B&H, 2000), 86.

13. J. B. Wakeley, *Anecdotes of George Whitefield* (Shropshire, England: Quinta, 2000), 275.

Part 4

Equipping and Leading Others

20

Pastoral Leadership Is . . .

Equipping Saints to Do the Work of Ministry

Dead Sea Christianity

When Cathy and I graduated from college, my parents gave us one of the greatest presents we have ever received. They helped us take an economy trip to the Holy Land. We spent about ten days with a group from my seminary walking where Jesus walked.

The trip was eye opening in many ways. After actually being in the land of the Bible and seeing it with my own eyes, the Bible changed from reading like a black-and-white book to a full-color experience.

One of the images I cannot forget is that of the Dead Sea. It is a bizarre place close to where Sodom and Gomorra are believed to have been. The Dead Sea is actually a large lake fed primarily by the Jordan River. It is surrounded by cliffs and is the deepest body of water on earth. It is so dark it is almost black in color. It is saltier than the ocean. The reason it is called the Dead Sea is because there is no organic life in its waters—none! There are no plants, no fish, nothing.

I will never forget trying to go for a dip in the Dead Sea. The water was so thick it was like wearing a life jacket. I could practically sit on its surface. When I got out of the water, I was covered with a greasy, salty film.

Why?

The reason the Dead Sea is dead is simple: it has no outlet. All sorts of rich minerals flow in, but nothing flows out. Yes it is deep, but it's also dead because it has no outlet.

Many Christians are like the Dead Sea. They take in rich deposits of truth and are deep. Yet, they are not healthy.

Why?

They have no outlet. They never get involved in ministry. This was not God's intent. In fact, God has given instructions that guarantee that a church will never become like the Dead Sea. Paul wrote them out and sent them to Timothy and the church he was leading in Ephesus. They all center on the pastor-teacher carrying out one of the three responsibilities that Jethro had told Moses he needed to do—put day-to-day ministry into the hands of capable people (Exod 18:21–22). In Eph 4:11–16, Paul told the church and Timothy that when pastors equip the saints for ministry, the church will grow and flourish.

It Works!

After graduating from seminary, Cathy and I took a team of four other young men and their wives to Columbus, Ohio, to pioneer a parachute-drop church from scratch. We had no one there waiting to join our church. We did not have a mother church. We did not receive any money or people from any of the local associations.

We all moved together in two U-Haul trucks on a Saturday and the twelve of us (eleven adults and a baby) met the next morning on folding chairs for "church" in the basement of my apartment. We were very young and inexperienced.

Twenty years later, however, our church had an average of nearly two thousand people a week joining us for worship. We consistently grew in quality and quantity.

We never experienced a church split or even a splinter. Five young men had been raised up to plant daughter churches in the community. One hundred twenty five small groups for adults and teens met throughout the community. Our church received a national award recognizing us as one of the healthiest churches in America.

Why?

Apart from the sovereign blessing of God, the growth of our community, and the prayers of our people, the answer goes back to Ephesians 4. We viewed the primary responsibility of a pastor as that of equipping saints for ministry.

As a result, 70 percent of our members served every week in and through our church. To the extent that we obeyed Eph 4:12a (pastors equip saints) and verse 12b (saints do ministry), we experienced the blessings of verses 12c–16 (perpetual church growth and health).

When Pastors Equip Saints for Ministry, the Church Will Grow

You have to love the book of Ephesians. In it, Paul gives an amazing exposition of the Christian life. In the first few chapters he tells us of our position in Christ. In the last few chapters he tells us how to live for Christ. In chapter 4, Paul gives one of his classic, run-on sentences to show the church how to fulfill its destiny and experience continual growth, maturity, unity, and fulfillment as the body of Christ.

> And He Himself gave some to be apostles, some prophets, some evangelists, and some pastors and teachers, for the equipping of the saints for the work of ministry, for the edifying of the body of Christ, till we all come to the unity of the faith and of the knowledge of the Son of God, to a perfect man, to the measure of the stature of the fullness of Christ; that we should no longer be children, tossed to and fro and carried about with every wind of doctrine, by the trickery of men, in the cunning craftiness of deceitful plotting, but, speaking the truth in love, may grow up in all things into Him who is the head—Christ—from whom the whole body, joined and knit together by what every joint supplies, according to the effective working by which every part does its share, causes growth of the body for the edifying of itself in love. (Eph 4:11–16 NKJV)

The key part of this passage is found in verses 11 and 12. Everything else supports the last phrase in verse 12. Let's look more closely at the process for becoming a healthy, growing church.

> And He Himself gave some to be . . . pastors and teachers, for the equipping of the saints for the work of ministry, for the edifying of the body of Christ. (Eph 4:11–12 NKJV)

I used the New King James Version in this chapter because it most clearly displays the process Paul gave for having a perpetually healthy, growing church. If you reprint the verses vertically, the process becomes clear.

> He gave some to be . . . pastors and teachers
> for the equipping of the saints
> for the work of ministry,
> for the edifying of the body of Christ.

In other words:

Christ gave the church pastors.

Why?

So the pastors might equip the saints.

Why?

So the saints will do the work of the ministry.

Why?

So the body will grow.

Therefore, if the church is not growing, it is because the saints are not doing ministry. If the saints are not doing ministry, it is because the pastors have failed to equip them to do so.

The role of the pastor-teachers is not to do the ministry; the role of the pastor-teachers is to equip the saints to do the ministry.

One of the biggest reasons why the traditional church in America is ineffective, unhealthy, declining, and dysfunctional is that we have this process exactly backwards. In most traditional churches the church hires a "minister" to do the ministry while the members sit on the sideline and critique his efforts.

One of the largest oversights of seminaries is that they are training God-called and gifted people to have careers as ministers when they need to be training them to equip saints to do the ministry.

As the church has neglected Ephesians 4, church members no longer live on mission and in ministry. Instead, they have become whining consumers complaining because their hired, seminary-trained, designated "minister" failed to visit them in the hospital.

Most of the pastors of most churches in America are chaplains. Most members of most churches in America are spectators.

It is only as pastors get serious about equipping saints to do the work of the ministry that the church will ever be what Christ died for her to be. Pastors must equip the saints for ministry.

When Pastors *Equip Saints for Ministry,* the Church Will Grow

> And He Himself gave some to be . . . pastors and teachers, for the equipping of *the saints* for *the work of ministry*, for the edifying of the body of Christ. (Eph 4:11–12 NKJV, italics added)

Saints or Ain'ts

I once heard a pastor say, "There are only two types of people in this world. Saints or ain'ts." It is kind of corny, but true. In American churches we tend to view people as either saved or lost, Christian or pagan, believers or nonbelievers. Because of the Roman Catholic perversion of the notion of sainthood, we tend to shy away from the term "saint."

But Paul loved the term.

In fact, "saint" was Paul's favorite term for born-again followers of Jesus. More than sixty times, Paul refers to the saved as "saints" (nine times alone in the book of Ephesians).

He began most of his letters to the churches by addressing them to the "saints."

> To all who are in Rome, beloved of God, called to be *saints*. (Rom 1:7 NKJV, italics added)

> To the church of God which is at Corinth, to those who are sanctified in Christ Jesus, called to be *saints*. (1 Cor 1:2 NKJV, italics added)

> Paul, an apostle of Jesus Christ by the will of God, and Timothy our brother, To the church of God which is at Corinth, with all the *saints* who are in all Achaia. (2 Cor 1:1 NKJV, italics added)

> Paul and Timothy, bondservants of Jesus Christ, To all the *saints* in Christ Jesus who are in Philippi. (Phil 1:1 NKJV, italics added)

> To the *saints* and faithful brethren in Christ who are in Colosse. (Col 1:2 NKJV, italics added)

> Paul, an apostle of Jesus Christ by the will of God, To the *saints* who are in Ephesus, and faithful in Christ Jesus. (Eph 1:1 NKJV, italics added)

The word translated "saints" means "holy" or "set apart." When Paul calls someone a "saint," he is describing who they are "in Christ." He is speaking of their positional standing. When a person is saved by faith in Jesus Christ, their legal, spiritual status changes and they are viewed by God as righteous and holy, set apart for himself.

One reason we have so few church members serve in a ministry is because pastors have failed to teach their people who they are—saints. As a result, if I was to go into your church and ask all the saints to raise their hands, few would do it. They would be embarrassed to lift their hands. Why? Because they do not think of themselves as saints, they do not call themselves saints, and therefore, they do not live or minister like saints. As a result they lose out on living the level of life Jesus purchased for them through His blood, and the church fails to become all it could be.

The Work of the Ministry

Paul told the Ephesians that the responsibility of pastors was to equip saints for the work of the ministry. Somehow we have drifted away from understanding that every believer is a saint and that every saint can and should do ministry.

When he uses the phrase "the work of the ministry," Paul is saying that every saint should make active service a lifestyle. They may have a day job as a policeman, or nurse, or lawyer, but their real occupation is serving the Lord through the church.

One of the most important aspects of the Protestant Reformation was the awakening to the biblical teachings regarding the priesthood of the believer. The point was that every believer had access to God, could read the Bible for themselves, and could serve God. It was an attempt to tear down the nonbiblical gap between clergy and laity.

Putting the ministry in the hands of a few specialists is incredibly ineffective. For example, using the traditional model, a church with seventy members and one pastor would have *one* minister. On the other hand, by using the Ephesians 4 model, the same church would have *seventy* ministers. Seventy times more ministry would get done! It would not remain a church of seventy for long as the members would be equipped and sent out to serve the community.

When Pastors Equip Saints for Ministry, *the Church Will Grow*

> And He Himself gave some to be . . . pastors and teachers, for the equipping of the saints for the work of ministry, for *the edifying of the body of Christ.* (Eph 4:11–12 NKJV, italics added)

Paul encouraged Timothy that as he and the other pastors in Ephesus focused on equipping the saints to do the work of the ministry, the result would be "the edifying of the body of Christ." Edifying is a broad term that in this context speaks of the church growing in quality and quantity. It gets bigger and stronger.

More Disciples

God wants His church growing with *more* disciples. The Great Commission is to make disciples out of people who are not disciples yet. The church is to be joined with Jesus on the mission of continually loving "sinners" (Luke 15:1–10) and seeking the lost (Luke 19:10). We must go out to the alleys, streets, and highways in order to compel people to come into the kingdom (Luke

14:21–23). The church is to glorify God by bringing more people to join in lifestyles of worshipping Him.

Although the popularity of the church growth trend has subsided, do not let the pendulum swing too far. God still wants His church to increase in numbers.

Obviously, God is not opposed to numbers. With *five* loaves and *two* fishes Jesus fed *five thousand* men. After His resurrection, Jesus was seen by *five hundred* brethren at once (1 Cor 15:6).

Read the book of Acts. Luke says in Acts 1:15 that *120* met in the upper room to pray. In Acts 2:41, Luke states that *3,000* were saved and baptized on the day of Pentecost. In Acts 4:4, he says that the number of men who believed grew to *5,000*.

Now I do not think God gets overly excited when one church grows in numbers primarily at the expense of another by taking its members. In Ephesians 4, Paul was not giving a secret to *transfer* growth. Paul is telling the church how it can experience greater *conversion* growth.

Eighty-five percent of the churches in the United States are plateaued or declining in attendance. Yet, of those that are growing, only 1 percent are growing primarily through conversion growth![1]

God's church is not built up when we merely swap people from one church to another. It is built up when we love, serve, and share the gospel with lost people, snatch them out of the kingdom of darkness, and see them born again by the Spirit of God into the kingdom of light.

The bottom line for measuring the success of a church is not primarily the size of the budget or the number and quality of programs it runs. The success of a church is measured by how many lost people are becoming followers of Jesus. In part, the success is measured in the baptistry.

Who would not want to be a part of a church that is perpetually growing through reaching the lost? When pastors equip the saints for ministry, the church will grow and reach the lost.

Better Disciples

There were no church buildings when Paul wrote Ephesians. When Paul speaks of the *edifying* of the body of Christ and experiencing *growth*, he is not talking about the expansion of the church facilities, although that often happens. He is talking about the growth of the people.

God not only wants His church to have *more* disciples, He wants *better* disciples. Biblically, a church is not a building; it is the people. God is interested in the church, the body of Christ, being built up. When a church follows God's plan, the church will grow in quantity *and* qualtity.

In Ephesians 4, Paul describes the quality growth of the church occurring on several directions and areas of church life.

1. *Unity (4:13a)*—"Till we all come to *the unity of the faith* and in the knowledge of the Son of God." When pastors focus their energy on equipping saints to do ministry, the people will get too focused on doing their ministry to fight about anything. The church will grow in unity.

2. *Maturity (4:13b)*—"Till we all come . . . to a *perfect man*, to the *measure of the stature of the fullness of Christ*." Spiritual maturity is measured by Christlikeness, and maturity cannot be attained without serving.

We had a small group of seekers who met in our home weekly for Bible study. After they all got saved, they grew in maturity for a while and then slowed. I realized that our group was beginning to violate Ephesians 4. They were becoming Dead Sea Christians, sponging their spiritual life off of me. None of them were serving.

So I gave them three weeks to find a weekly ministry in our church before I shut down the group and sent them out to serve. They all got plugged in.

One of the men, an engineer who had been an atheist prior to giving his life to Christ, started serving in our midweek children's ministry, helping boys memorize Scripture.

Several weeks later, I saw him in the hallway after a worship gathering.

"How is your ministry going?" I asked.

"Great," he said. "I've grown more in the last three weeks with these boys than I did in my last three months with you."

3. *Stability (4:14)*—"Then we will *no longer be infants*, tossed back and forth by the waves, and blown here and there by every wind of teaching and by the cunning and craftiness of men in their deceitful scheming" (NIV). When people are not serving, they remain spiritual infants. They lose their spiritual appetite. They get mentally lazy and become prey for false teachers. It is as they minister that they are pushed to dig deeper and grow.

4. *Attractive Reality (4:15a)*—"Instead, speaking *the truth in love*, we will in all things grow up into him who is the Head, that is, Christ" (NIV). Truth is the ultimate reality. Love is the ultimate attraction. The world needs both. When saints are being equipped for ministry, they display the loving truth that attracts the lost to the Lord.

5. *Mutual Vitality (4:16)*—"From him the whole body, joined and held together by *every* supporting ligament, grows and builds itself up in love, as

each part does its work" (NIV). Notice that the beauty of the vibrant body is only visible when every part does its part.

Who would not want to be a part of a church that is perpetually growing in unity, spiritual maturity, doctrinal stability, attractive reality, and mutual vitality? Yet the sad fact is that instead of being the norm, the church Paul described in Eph 4:11–16 is the exception. But that can change. When pastors equip the saints for ministry, the church will grow and flourish.

When Pastors Equip Saints for Ministry, the Church Will Grow

And He Himself gave some to be . . . pastors and teachers, *for the equipping* of the saints for the work of ministry, for the edifying of the body of Christ. (Eph 4:11–12 NKJV, italics added)

The process of perpetual, healthy church growth is impossible if pastors do not equip the saints for the work of the ministry. In the next five chapters we will look at exactly what it means to equip the saints and how to do it.

— What Now? —

Was the church you grew up in good at equipping the saints for the work of the ministry? Why?

— Quote —

Every believer, regardless of background, ability, or status, has a service to perform in the cause of Christ on earth . . . the ministering by all believers, as they have been equipped . . . is intended to accomplish the building up of the church.

—HOMER KENT[2]

Notes

1. Win Arn, *The Pastor's Manual for Effective Ministry* (Monrovia, CA: Church Growth, 1988), 41, 43.

2. Homer Kent, *Ephesians: The Glory of the Church* (Chicago, IL: Moody, 1971), 72.

21

Preparing Saints
to Serve

I was twenty-two years old when I began my first church staff assignment at a dysfunctional church in rural Virginia. The church was the combination of two groups of people who had split off two other churches. They had a nice building, money in the bank, and had gone through four pastors in their first five years of existence.

I was serving as the part-time assistant/associate/youth/children/music pastor when the fourth pastor left, leaving me to be the interim pastor. Out of 120 people who regularly attended worship services, only a few adults and teens were interested in serving. The other people were faithful in attending services and giving, and playing on the softball team, but did little beyond that. For the most part, the people felt that service was what they had hired me and Cathy to do. I was the "minister," and ministers were paid to minister to them and bring in more people to the church.

Six men were quite proud to wear the title deacon (the word translated deacon, *diakonos*, means "servant" or "minister"), but only two of the six did any actual ministry. The other four felt it was their responsibility "to keep the pastor in line," whatever that means. Mostly they just criticized anything and everything the pastor tried to do.

A few years after serving at that church, Cathy and I started a church. We had no building, no money in the bank, and only a handful of people when we started. Yet as I have mentioned, as we focused on preparing the saints for service, our church reached the lost and grew to a few thousand people and several healthy daughter congregations. Beyond that, being the equipper of a church full of people who wanted to be prepared to serve was a thousand times better than trying to please a bunch of immature, inactive, unengaged, carnal, consumer Christians.

Twenty years later, that rural church in Virginia still has the same nice building, still has money in the bank, and still has most of the same 120 people, except those who have died. They change out pastors every few years and will probably keep rolling until all of the members die off. Sadly, they have made no real impact in their community.

Even more sadly, thousands of Christians and churches across America are failing to reach their potential and failing to reach their communities because they violate the clear teaching of Ephesians 4. Pastor, your job is to prepare the saints for service!

> And He personally gave some to be apostles, some prophets, some evangelists, some pastors and teachers, for the training of the saints in the work of ministry, to build up the body of Christ. (Eph 4:11–12)

The responsibility of the pastor(s) is to equip the saints for the work of ministry. In this chapter we want to dig deeper to understand exactly what that means and how to do it. In doing so, we will answer the *what, why,* and *how* of equipping the saints for the ministry.

Why Prepare Saints for Ministry?

Ephesians 4:12–16 offered many good reasons to focus your ministry on equipping the saints for ministry. When equipped and ministering, the saints grow in unity and Christlikeness (4:13). They mature and become doctrinally stable (4:14). They relate to one another and the lost world with love and truth (4:15). Beyond that, Paul also taught that it is only through doing good works that believers will discover the reason for their creation and salvation (2:1–10).

Training the saints to minister not only blesses the individual saints, but also strengthens and grows the church as a whole (4:12). As saints continue to be developed and deployed into ministry, the church continues to experience growth and strength (4:16).

How to Equip the Saints for Ministry

The Lord not only tells pastors that they are responsible to equip the saints, He also tells them how to go about it. A simple study of the word "equip," as used by Paul in Ephesians chapter 4, reveals four tools that are essential for preparing saints for service.

1. Prayer

When we do a study of "equip" (Gk., *kataridzo*), we discover that the first tool the pastor has for equipping the saints is *prayer*. The author of Hebrews concluded his letter with a prayer that God would *equip* his readers with everything they would need to fulfill His will.

> Now may the God of peace, who brought up from the dead our Lord Jesus—the great Shepherd of the sheep—with the blood of the everlasting covenant, *equip you with all that is good to do His will*, working in us what is pleasing in His sight, through Jesus Christ, to whom be glory forever and ever. Amen. (Heb 13:20–21)

Wise pastors recognize that the Holy Spirit is already committed to preparing saints for service; it only makes sense for him to pray that to that end.

No wonder the apostles chose to focus their ministry to prayer and the ministry of the Word (Acts 6:4).

No wonder Paul told Timothy that he was to prioritize prayer (1 Tim 2:1).

No wonder Paul was constantly praying for the churches he gave oversight to (Rom 1:8–10; 15:5–6,13; Eph 1:15–19; 3:14–19; Phil 1:9–11; Col 1:9–12; 1 Thess 1:2–3; 3:11–13; 2 Thess 1:11–12; Phlm 4–6).

No wonder Jesus prayed for disciples (John 17).

No wonder Jethro told Moses to make prayer one of the three things he was to do (Exod 18:19).

Most pastors should spend less time praying that their people get out of the hospital and more time praying that they get into ministry. I suggest that you spend your energy praying that the Lord would "equip [them] with all that is good to do His will, working in [them] what is pleasing in His sight, through Jesus Christ, to whom be glory forever and ever" (Heb 13:21). We discussed this tool in chaps. 8–13.

2. The Word of God

The second tool the pastor has for equipping the saints is the Word of God. Look carefully at the end of this familiar verse.

> All Scripture is inspired by God and is profitable for teaching, for rebuking, for correcting, for training in righteousness, so that the man of God may be complete, *equipped for every good work*. (2 Tim 3:16–17, italics added)

Paul told Timothy that the Word was sufficient to equip him and his men for every good work. No wonder Paul told Timothy to preach the Word (2 Tim 4:2). No wonder Jesus prayed for His disciples that the Father would sanctify them through the truth of the Word of God (John 17:17). No wonder Jethro told Moses to focus part of his energy on "instruct[ing] them about the statutes and laws, and teach[ing] them the way to live and what they must do" (Exod 18:20). We discussed this tool in chaps. 14–19.

3. Intentional Training

The third tool for equipping the saints is intentional investment. Luke records Jesus as using the word *kataridzo* as the result of intentional discipleship training. "A disciple is not above his teacher, but everyone who is *fully trained* will be like his teacher" (Luke 6:40, italics added).

Paul told Timothy to use this tool of intentional investment: "And what you have heard from me in the presence of many witnesses, commit to faithful men who will be able to teach others also" (2 Tim 2:2). We will discuss this tool in more detail in the next chaps. 22–23.

4. Connection with Other Members of the Body of Christ

As you know, the Corinthian church was a disjoined church. One of Paul's primary motivations for writing them the letter 1 Corinthians was to bring them to unity. In his letter he urges them to link together in greater unity. In doing so, he uses the term *kataridzo*.

> I urge you, brothers, in the name of our Lord Jesus Christ, that you all say the same thing, that there be no divisions among you, and that you be *united* with the same understanding and the same conviction. (1 Cor 1:10)

As pastors, we find it difficult to really equip saints for ministry until we begin to place a greater emphasis on healthy holistic small groups. In healthy home groups the saints actively serve each other. Instead of having a professional "minister" serve them, they minister to each other. They pray for one another. They encourage and challenge each other.

Each group can also actively engage with needs in the community. We can adopt a widow, others a single mom, while still others can work at the homeless shelter.

Suggestions for Preparing Saints for Service

Specifically and practically, what does a pastor do to prepare the saints to do ministry? Let me offer six suggestions that should help.

- Teach saints the privilege and responsibility to serve
- Help saints identify how they have been designed to serve
- Identify ministry opportunities available in and through your church
- Intentionally steer people into the ministries where they fit
- Provide specific training for each specific ministry
- Provide ongoing mentoring and coaching

1. Teach Saints the Privilege and Responsibility of Service

Embrace the Bible conviction of every member in the ministry. In order to convince every member in your church to be a minister, you must be convinced yourself. Study the brief outline below as a way of settling the matter in your own mind. Every Christian is:

- created for ministry (Eph 2:10).
- saved for ministry (2 Tim 1:9).
- called into ministry (1 Pet 2:9–10).
- gifted for ministry (1 Pet 4:10).
- authorized for ministry (Matt 28:18–20).
- commissioned into ministry (Matt 20:26–28).
- to be prepared for ministry (Eph 4:11–12).
- accountable for ministry (Col 3:23–24).

Plan an annual sermon series on ministry. If our people do not value service, it is our fault. We have an opportunity every Sunday to open God's Word and communicate truth. The Bible is loaded with passages that highlight the high calling of being a servant. John 13; Phil 2:5–11; and Mark 10:35–45 are classics. The theme of the book of Titus is good works. The word "serve" is used hundreds of times in the Bible.

The first time or two we did a whole sermon series on service we spent several weeks on it. But once it was a part of our DNA that was not necessary. Annually, we would do a one- or two-week series in which the application of the message was for each member to sign up for the place of ministry where they were planning to serve in the next year. There was a ministry fair in the lobby before and after, where people could get their questions answered and new or needy ministries could recruit potential workers.

Have a commissioning of "new ministers" and "new ministry teams." When we launched a new ministry team we tried to make a big deal out of it. We would have them all come forward, and our elders would lay hands on them as we commissioned them to serve. When a new ministry year was starting, we would recognize the leaders of the various ministry teams and have them all come forward so our elders would lay hands on them as we commissioned them to serve in the coming year.

Mention the value of serving and tell about people in your church who are serving whenever it is an appropriate part of your message. The best illustrations for sermons are those that come right out of your congregations. We trained our staff and lay leaders to always be on the lookout for good stories of people who were doing a good job in service.

Show slides of people serving before and after the service, during a worship song, or when you are making announcements.

Require having a place of ministry as a requirement of membership. Even when our attendance was nearly two thousand a week, we found that on any given week we had 70 percent of our members serving somewhere in and through our church. One way we reached this point was by making ministry a membership requirement. What is the point of having nonministering members? If ministry really is a biblical mandate and is important for the health of the Christian and the health of the church, make it a requirement.

2. Help Saints Identify How They Have Been Designed to Serve

Just standing up on Sundays and telling people they need to serve is not equipping and does not work. Every saint is shaped to serve, but not every saint is shaped to serve in the same way. Saints need to be well-placed into ministry roles that best reflect the way God designed them to serve.

Equipping saints for ministry requires that the pastor(s) first get to know the saints and how God has gifted them. Rick Warren popularized the acrostic SHAPE (Spiritual gifts, Heart, Abilities, Personality, and Experiences) to help identify the unique way every saint has been designed to serve God through His church. He writes, "You were shaped to serve God."[1] He also said, "God deliberately shaped and formed you to serve him in a way that makes your ministry unique. He carefully mixed the DNA cocktail that created you."[2]

Spiritual Gifts: God has gifted every Christian to serve Him through His body. Romans 12:3–8 discusses the primary motivational gifts. Other gifts are referred to elsewhere in Scripture. Encourage your people to start experimenting with different ministries, because it is only in doing so that they will discover their spiritual gifts.

Heart: Heart refers to a person's passions. Some of us are passionate about hungry children. Others are heartbroken over unwed moms. Others are really fascinated with the details of the Bible.

Wise pastors steer people into ministries that reflect their passions. In this way, the person stays excited, energized, and motivated even when the going gets more difficult.

Abilities: Abilities are the natural talents that you were born with. Many national studies have proven that the average person possesses from five hundred to seven hundred skills! The wise pastor understands that people need some process of skill identification and help matching their abilities with the right ministry.

Personality: God loves variety. He made introverts and extroverts. He made people who love routine and those who love variety. He made some people who are "thinkers" and others who are "feelers." He made people who work best when given an individual assignment, and some who work better with a team. Effective equippers encourage people to pursue ministries that are in line with their God-given personalities.

Experiences: Every member of your church has a set of life experiences that God has wisely allowed them to experience. These include educational, ministry, vocational, painful, and spiritual experiences.

Your people will be most effective and fulfilled in ministry when they use their spiritual gifts and abilities in the area of their heart's desire in a way that best expresses their personality and experiences. Fruitfulness is the result of a good ministry fit.

There are a number of good inventories you can give your people. Find one and use it. Make it part of your new members class.[3]

3. Identify Ministry Opportunities

Create a list of ministry opportunities that are available in and through your church. Keep it current. Publicize it. Clearly communicate the path a person needs to take to get involved in a particular ministry. Plan an emphasis every six months to facilitate getting people placed in one of those opportunities.

4. Intentionally Steer People into the Ministries Where They Fit

I do not believe in paying a ministry staff person to do ministry. Ministry staff persons are paid to recruit, place, support, and appreciate lay ministers.

We train our paid staff persons how to steer people into the right ministry positions. Every paid staff person are to be constantly on the lookout for places and ways to plug people into the right spots.

We also made it a requirement for church membership to meet with a pastor in a personal interview. Part of that interview involved leading the person to sign up for a specific ministry that they would try out for at least the next six months.

5. Provide Specific Training for Each Specific Ministry

It is wrong to put a person into a ministry position without preparing them to serve effectively. We designed a series of short training seminars to equip people for specific ministries. The training for entry-level ministries such as greeter or parking lot attendant could be done fifteen minutes prior to the first time the person serves. Children's ministry workers needed a session a week before the first time they served, as well as a clear background check. A small-group leader had to complete a half-day training session after doing a six-month on-the-job apprenticeship.

6. Provide Ongoing Mentoring and Coaching

The more intense the ministry, the greater are the odds of burnout. For example, a small-group leader will probably burn out or drop out after three years if they do not receive regular mentoring and coaching. A strong small-group ministry has coaches in place who pray for the group leaders under their care daily, contact them at least every other week, and visit their groups at least every three months.

— What Now? —

As you can see, equipping the saints is not easy. But if a pastor devotes a third of his time to preparing saints for ministry, eventually his church will take off and he will experience the great joy of leading ministers and leaders instead of running himself ragged.

First, make sure you know your shape for service. There are a number of online assessments to help you begin exploring this.

Choose a few people for whom you have spiritual oversight. Make a brief plan for how you will equip them to do the work of ministry.

~ Quote ~

No matter how gifted, talented, and dedicated a pastor may be, the work to be done . . . will always vastly exceed his time and abilities. His purpose in God's plan is not to try to meet all the needs by himself but to equip the people given into his care to meet the needs.

—JOHN MACARTHUR[4]

Notes

1. Rick Warren, *The Purpose-Driven Church* (Grand Rapids, MI: Zondervan, 1995), 365.

2. Ibid., 234–35.

3. Free online assessments

- http://www.churchgrowth.org/analysis/intro.html
- http://mintools.com/spiritual-gifts-test.htm
- http://www.gifttest.org/index.cfm
- http://www.elca.org/evangelism/assessments/spiritgifts.html

4. John MacArthur, *MacArthur New Testament Commentary: Ephesians* (Chicago, IL: Moody, 1986), 155.

22

Multiplying
Your Life

> *Jesus came to save the world, and to that end He died, but
> on His way to the cross He concentrated His life on making
> a few disciples. These men were taught to do the same until
> through the process of reproduction the gospel of the kingdom
> would reach to the ends of the earth.*
>
> —ROBERT COLEMAN[1]

Make Disciples

Change the World

Jesus Christ is beyond a shadow of a doubt, the greatest revolutionary in history. He literally changed the world. Important institutions for the world's good, such as churches, hospitals, orphanages, colleges, universities, mass production of books, and the global literacy movement, can all be traced back to one man—Jesus! Our calendar, legal system, and the best aspects of our culture can be traced back to Jesus. More than two billion people are "Christians" today. Jesus changed the world.

How did a poor carpenter from a forsaken, enslaved nation change the history of the world? He refused to do ministry all by Himself. He prepared for

ministry to continue long after He was gone. He made disciples. Jesus poured
His life into a handful of men who mentored and multiplied others until the
message of Jesus covered the known world.

Jesus left His disciples when He ascended into heaven. Yet the ministry of
Jesus has grown and multiplied many times over because they were multiplying
leaders.

What is world-changing ministry? It is mentoring and multiplying disciples. Think about it. You can begin spiritually multiplying yourself today and
start a dynamic process that could reach beyond your generation and into the
next century. It can reach beyond a handful and eventually touch the world.
Multiplying disciple-making was the global evangelistic strategy of Jesus.

The Example of Jesus

Jesus was the embodiment of what the world needs. Because of His evident love, unconditional grace, amazing words and mighty deeds, huge crowds
chased Him. They were desperately looking for food, and healing, deliverance
and direction, hope, and truth.

> But Jesus withdrew with His disciples to the sea. And a great multitude
> from Galilee followed Him, and from Judea and Jerusalem and Idumea
> and beyond the Jordan; and those from Tyre and Sidon, a great
> multitude, when they heard how many things He was doing, came to
> Him. So He told His disciples that a small boat should be kept ready
> for Him because of the multitude, lest they should crush Him. For He
> healed many, so that as many as had afflictions pressed about Him to
> touch Him. (Mark 3:7–10 NKJV)

Jesus saw large crowds of people with deep and messy needs. He knew that
the crowds of thousands that followed Him represented a mere microcosm of
the millions worldwide who needed Him. How did He meet their needs?

> And He went up on the mountain and called to Him those He Himself
> wanted. And they came to Him. Then He appointed twelve, that they
> might be with Him and that He might send them out to preach. (Mark
> 3:13–14 NKJV)

Instead of working the crowd, Jesus invited a handful of men to join Him
in a three-year mentoring relationship. He withdrew from the many to focus
on a few so they could ultimately reach many more.

What is Christlike ministry?

It is *training a few so you can reach the many*.

The word "disciple" comes from the Greek word *mathetes*, meaning student or learner. The concept of disciple-making was widespread in the Greco-Roman world. Greek philosophers had their own students or disciples. However, the New Testament notion of discipleship is rooted in the Jewish rabbinical model. This might have dated back to the sons of the prophets established by Samuel and popularized by Elijah. Jesus was not the first rabbi to have disciples. John had disciples before Jesus (Matt 11:2; 14:12; Mark 2:18) as did the Pharisees (Matt 22:16).

Rabbis spent years with their disciples, teaching them their way of life, their understanding of Scripture, and how to teach it to others. They often lived with them for extended periods.

The process of discipleship called for the complete shaping of the potential learner. The rabbi would pass on to him everything he had: his character, his knowledge, his values, and his wisdom. The transmission of information was based on a close, trusting relationship. The intense nature of the relationship forced the rabbi to limit the number of disciples he had at one time.

But that is the power of disciple-making. The intense nature of the relationship ensures the quality of the product. When done right, the disciple not only becomes a devoted follower of a rabbi, but becomes a disciple-making rabbi too.

The Last Words of Jesus

The last words and deeds of anyone's life are usually significant as they are an indication of the values and priorities of that person. A few days before Jesus ascended into glory, He gave some final instructions. These words were important because they were His last words of earthly ministry, but they were even more important because of who gave them, Jesus Christ. It is also instructive to see *whom He gave them to*: His followers. Today, we call this statement "the Great Commission."

> And Jesus came and spoke to them, saying, "All authority has been given to Me in heaven and on earth. Go therefore and make disciples of all the nations, baptizing them in the name of the Father and of the Son and of the Holy Spirit, teaching them to observe all things that I have commanded you; and lo, I am with you always, even to the end of the age." Amen. (Matt 28:18–20 NKJV)

A Greek student will tell you the primary imperative of the Great Commission is the imperative verb—"make disciples." The other words, "go," "baptize," and "teach," all modify and explain *how* we are to fulfill the big thing, which is "make disciples." In order to make this evident to English readers, I paraphrase Matt 28:18–20 as follows:

> This is the greatest challenge of your life . . . so take it
> seriously:
> As you are going into the culture,
> MAKE DISCIPLES!!!
> —make disciples of people from every people group by
> baptizing them and staying with them in order to teach them
> to obey everything I have taught you.
> Then you will really experience my presence. (Matt 28:18–20,
> paraphrase mine)

The Marching Orders for Christ Followers

These final words of Jesus in Matthew's Gospel are commonly called the Great Commission. It is a command to Christ's disciples. Obedience is not optional.

No one who is refusing to obey Jesus' orders can call themselves a follower of Jesus. His commission to evangelize the world by mentoring and multiplying disciples was not a suggestion to be considered but a command to be obeyed.

Multiply Your Life and Change the World

The first seventy years of its existence were the most fruitful in the history of the church. Christianity raced across the Roman Empire and penetrated Africa and Asia all the way to India. From a handful hiding in an upper room, the number of Christ followers spread to one million. All of this without digital social networking, mass media, church buildings, and seminaries.

How did this happen?

Disciples made disciples.

Jesus used the power of multiplication.

Leroy Eims, former director of the Navigators, shared an experience he had that drove home the power of multiplication to reach the world.

> Some time ago there was a display at the Museum of Science and Industry in Chicago. It featured a checkerboard with 1 grain of wheat on the first, 2 on the second, 4 on the third, then 8, 16, 32, 64, 128, etc. Somewhere down the board, there were so many grains of wheat on the square that some were spilling over into neighboring squares—so

here the demonstration stopped. Above the checkerboard display was a question:

"At this rate of doubling every square, how much grain would be on the checkerboards by the 64th square?"

To find the answer to this riddle, you punched a button on the console in front of you, and the answer flashed on a little screen above the board:

"Enough to cover the entire subcontinent of India 50 feet deep."[2]

If you want to make a huge impact, implement the power of multiplication. Walter Henrichsen noted, "Multiplication may be costly, and in the initial stages, much slower than addition, but in the long run, it is the most effective way of accomplishing Christ's Great Commission . . . and the only way."[3]

The *slow* process of raising up multiplying leaders is the *fastest* way to fulfill the Great Commission. The world is growing by multiplication, and the church is growing through addition. In order to catch up with and keep pace with the multiplying population of the world, we must multiply multipliers.

I like the way Waylon Moore puts it: "When the church exhales disciples, it inhales converts."[4] He further notes, "Disciple making has no prestige rating, no denominational category; but the results are consistently better than anything I have experienced in thirty years of working with people."[5]

Multiplying leaders is a seemingly small, slow, unappreciated process. But what is exciting to us "ordinary" people is that by using this small process of multiplication we can have a big impact. By using the slow process of multiplying leaders we can reach the most people in the least amount of time. By practicing the principles of multiplying leaders we can make an impact that thrills the heart of Jesus. We must remember that, "We need never fear beginning something quietly and on a small scale. God will cause what is His to grow."[6]

Multiplying by Division. David Yonggi Cho launched a church with six people in 1958. Fifty years later, membership stood at 830,000. How did it happen?

After struggling along for a few years, Cho restructured the church around geographic cell groups. Church members were trained to become home-cell Bible study group leaders. Cell members were encouraged to invite their friends to attend cell meetings to learn about Christianity. Each cell leader was instructed to train an assistant. When cell membership reached a certain number, it would be divided, with about half of its members joining the new cell led by the person who had been the assistant.

The church has a rich history of prayer and multiplication. It has become a model for some of the largest churches in the world.

Multiplying by Twelve. In 1983, Cesar Castellanos and his wife, Claudia, launched a church in Bogata, Columbia, with a small group of eight people. Twenty-five years later, the church has more than 250,000 members. How did it happen?

Cesar got a vision for multiplying his life into twelve disciples. Believing that every Christian can mentor and lead twelve people in the Christian faith, he began to meet weekly with twelve young men. He prayed for them and poured his life into them with the primary focus on training each of them to lead twelve others in a small group. The goal of each of their twelve was to find their own twelve and so on. Over the years the number of leaders in the church has continued to multiply by twelve, going from 12 to 144 to 1728 to 32,288.[7]

In order for this model to work, the members must sell out to the vision and be willing to sacrifice their time. The members of a group of twelve must meet with their leader every week *and* meet with the twelve they are training every week. The model sustains itself because leaders not only pour into others every week, but are also being poured into every week.

Multiply by at Least Two. Maybe multiplying by twelve seems a bit staggering to you. The point is not what number you multiply as much as it is that you do multiply.

Our church multiplied from 12 people meeting as a small group to two thousand meeting in more than a hundred small groups for adults and teens, plus several daughter churches made of as few as six small groups and as many as thirty-five. We multiplied by asking every small-group leader to multiply by two.

This means we asked them to pray in one potential small group leader and spent about a year training that person to launch a new group. In this way, one group became two; two groups became four; four became eight, and so on. Of course not every group multiplied every year, but even if half of them did, we still saw our small group disciple-making ministry grow at a rapid rate.

How to Mentor and Multiply Like Jesus

There is no single method to mentor multiplying disciple makers, but I can give you the primary principles that Jesus used in making His disciples.

1. Build Relationships with Some Potential Disciple-Makers

At His baptism, John the Baptizer pointed to Jesus and said, "Look! The Lamb of God!" (John 1:36). A few hungry young men heard it and became curious about Jesus. He invited them to spend the rest of the day with Him (John 1:37–39). The next thing we know, He has a small posse of young men with whom He is hanging out (John 2:1–2).

When I was a teenager, my youth pastor was Lee Simmons. He poured his life into several young men who eventually became pastors, including me. He had a dream of helping us mature in Christ and in ministry. He demonstrated to us a life of effective ministry. He selected a few people who he believed had ministry potential. (I think a few of us selected him more than he selected us.) He built a relationship with us. He played softball with us, taught us to water ski, and wrestled with us. We were at his house so much that it sometimes annoyed his wife. He influenced us because he built a relationship with us.

Disciple-making begins with relationship building.

2. Pray for a Few Faithful People to Pour Your Life Into

Eventually Jesus had quite a group of young men with whom He had built relationships. His next step was to narrow His focus to twelve guys in whom He would strategically and intentionally pour His life. How did He pick the Twelve?

> During those days He went out to the mountain to pray and spent
> all night in prayer to God. When daylight came, He summoned His
> disciples, and He chose 12 of them—He also named them apostles. (Luke
> 6:12–13)

Jesus commanded us to pray that the Lord of the harvest would send laborers into the harvest (Matt 9:37–38). One way I find potential disciples is to get them together, share the vision of the harvest, and have them join me in praying about the harvest. Several great things happen. First, the harvest gets prayed for. Second, I get to see which ones have a heart for the harvest. Third, they gain a burden for the harvest. Fourth, the Lord directs me as to which ones I am to invite into an intentional disciple-making relationship.

3. Invite Them into an Intentional Disciple-Making Relationship

After knowing His potential disciple-makers for nearly a year, Jesus upped the ante. He issued them a direct invitation into a more intense disciple-making relationship (Mark 1:16–20). As a rabbi, He was inviting them into an apprenticeship with Him. To say yes meant that they would lay aside other interests to be with Him, be with each other, study His teachings, and begin to minister to others.

My favorite method of making disciples is to invite a potential disciple-maker into personal training to lead a small group. At this point they make a six-fold commitment:

- Participate in my small group every week.
- Pray for group members daily.
- Read a chapter each week of a book on leading small groups.[8]
- They meet with me weekly for training. We often do this at lunch or before or after the small-group meeting.
- They start leading various elements of the small-group session—the welcome, the worship time, the Word discussion, or the group prayer time.
- They begin praying for their apprentice and those they invite to join their group when they launch in the next six to twelve months.

4. Pray for Them Every Day

I like to pray for my guys the same prayer Jesus prayed for His guys. It is recorded in John 17. It includes several petitions:

- Unite them (17:11,21–22).
- Fill them with complete joy (17:13).
- Protect them from the evil one (17:15).
- Sanctify them through the Word of truth (17:17).
- Send them out (17:18).

5. Break Them In Slowly before Turning Them Completely Loose

Jesus turned the goal of world evangelization over to His guys and left (Acts 1:8). But this did not happen in a vacuum or come as a shock. He had been breaking them in slowing prior to His departure.

First, He allowed them be alongside Him as He did ministry.

Second, before letting them get their feet wet, He gave them a thorough briefing regarding what to expect (Matthew 10; Luke 10:1–12).

Third, He had a time of debriefing (Luke 10:17–20).

When I am training an apprentice to lead a group, I have to intentionally give more and more of the ministry away. In that way they get the on-the-job training they need to have the confidence necessary to eventually launch and lead their own group.

— What Now? —

Since the Great Commission is mentoring and making disciples, let me ask you, Who are you mentoring right now? Since mentoring and multiplying disciples was the example of Jesus, can you honestly say that you are following His example? Who are your "twelve"? When and how are you pouring your life into them?

Three Final Questions

1. If not you, who?
2. If not here, where?
3. If not now, when?

— Quote —

Jesus spent most of His time with His small group of leaders. He focused his Energy on them, mentoring them, and showing them how to live the life of the Way.

—M. SCOTT BOREN[9]

Notes:

1. Robert Coleman, quoted by Leroy Eims, *The Lost Art of Disciple Making* (Grand Rapids, MI: Zondervan, 1980), 9.

2. Eims, *The Lost Art of Disciple Making*, 9.

3. Walter A. Henrichsen, *Disciples Are Made—Not Born* (Wheaton, IL: Victor, 1979), 143.

4. Waylon B. Moore, *Multiplying Disciples* (Colorado Springs, CO: NavPress, 1981), 5.

5. Ibid., 30.

6. For more on this model, see Joel Comiskey, *Groups of 12* (Houston, TX: Touch, 1999).

7. Moore, *Multiplying Disciples*, 112.

8. We read through three books: Dave Earley, *The 8 Habits of Effective Small Group Leaders* (Houston, TX: Touch, 2001), *The Small Group Leadership Toolkit* (Houston, TX: Touch, 2008), and *Turning Members into Leaders* (Houston, TX: Touch, 2003).

9. M. Scott Boren, *Making Cell Groups Work* (Houston, TX: Touch, 2002), 208.

23

Investing
in Faithful Men

What could happen if we took every ridiculously radical, fully devoted, biblically sound, spiritually hot, missional pastor in America and cloned them thirty times? It would not only wonderfully change America, it would change the world.

Paul, Disciple Maker

Paul had been a rabbinic disciple of Gamaliel, one of the most prominent rabbis of his day (Acts 22:3). As a rabbi-in-training he was to have memorized most, if not all, of the Old Testament. He also learned the interpretations of the great rabbis, as well as those of his teacher Gamaliel. So as a young man, Paul had become a leading young Jewish rabbi (Acts 7:58; 8:1–3).

After his conversion, Paul made disciples. When he needed to escape persecution in Damascus, it was "his disciples" who lowered him over the city wall in a basket (Acts 9:25).

The Scriptures mention more than thirty men and women by name as Paul's fellow laborers. Numerous ones are described as having lived and travelled with Paul during his thirty years of ministry. During this time he would have imparted his extensive knowledge of the Old Testament and the personal revelations he had received from the Lord. They would have also worked alongside Paul as he did pioneer evangelism and church planting.

These thirty or more people became the leaders of the many churches Paul started. Some of them no doubt also went out and started churches.

So even as Paul was busy fulfilling his calling as an apostle to the Gentiles, he also fulfilled the Great Commission by making disciples. He took what the Lord had deposited into him and committed it to faithful men who in turn taught others also. There may have been as many as thirty little "Pauls" doing ministry even after he was imprisoned in Rome.

One of Paul's favorite disciples was a young man named Timothy. Paul later trusted Timothy enough to entrust him to lead the strategic church of Ephesus. It was to the young pastor Timothy that Paul wrote his important letters we now have in our Bibles called 1 Timothy and 2 Timothy.

In 2 Timothy 2, Paul reminded Timothy of the necessity of mentoring multipliers. Read 2 Tim 2:2 carefully. See if you can observe the four generations of spiritual multiplication going in this passage. Because I am nice, I will even get you started by telling you the first generation. Paul wrote this letter, so the first generation is "me"—speaking of Paul.

> And what *you* have heard from *me* in the presence of many witnesses, commit to *faithful men* who will be able to teach *others* also. (2 Tim 2:2, italics added)

The first generation is Paul ("me"). He mentored the young man he wrote this letter to—Timothy ("you"). Timothy was to pass it on to a third generation ("faithful men"). They were to pass it on to a fourth generation ("others"). Paul reminded Timothy that in the midst of all of his many responsibilities as the lead pastor of a significant church, not to forget the main thing—invest in making disciples and mentoring multipliers.

Pastoral leadership is investing in faithful men. God's plan for your life may not be to pastor a megachurch. It may not be for you to become a bestselling author. Maybe nobody but your mom will watch your podcasts.

But without a shadow of a doubt, God's plan is for you to invest everything He has given you into a few faithful men with the purpose being that they would invest it into others. In the rest of this chapter, we will see how to most effectively invest your life in "faithful men."

How to Mentor Multipliers . . .

Recognize the Things that God Has Taught You

Paul told Timothy to take the things he had learned from Paul and pass it on to others. For you to be at the point where you are even considering becoming a pastor, God has obviously been at work in your life. He has saved you, gifted you, used you, and called you. Beyond that, He has taught you.

You have more to give than you realize. I challenge you to start making several lists. Start a list of the things God has brought you through. Write down the big life lessons He has taught you. Identify the top ten things you could teach a young Christian about God. What lessons could you share about living the Christian life? What have you learned about ministry? What have been the top ten most important Scriptures God has used in your life?

Now take the items on your lists and craft a short lesson or even a Bible study about each one. This can become the beginning point of your discipleship ministry. Then as you learn new things, craft new lessons and pass them along as well.

I was just a nineteen-year-old college sophomore when I began intentionally making disciples. I did not know much or have much to give, but I had enough to get started with a few guys who were just a step or two behind me. I knew the what, why, and how of quiet time, prayer, memorizing Scripture, and of leading someone to Jesus. So that's what I passed on to them.

Identify a Few Potential "Faithful Men"

Paul told Timothy to focus his disciple-making ministry on "faithful men." I suggest that you start by considering everyone as a potential candidate for training. Bill Donahue and Russ Robinson suggest, "Rather than looking for leaders, we suggest that you look for people. There's always a greater supply of people than obvious leaders."[1]

Be open to anybody God might bring along your path. God uses unlikely and ordinary people. The founder of the Hebrew nation, Abraham, was a herdsman. Israel's best king, David, had been a shepherd boy. Jesus' disciples were uneducated Galilean fishermen and tax collectors. Remember that God is big enough to use foolish, weak, lowly ones to reveal His glory and power (1 Cor 1:26–29).

Paul told Timothy to focus his efforts on *faithful* men. Effective discipleship, mentoring, and leadership training will take a significant commitment from you. You want your efforts to be as fruitful as possible. Optimal fruitfulness calls for wise selectivity. You want to invest in the people who will go the furthest the fastest.

Jesus did not select everyone to be His disciples. He carefully selected twelve and passed up some others. There are seasons when we cannot be very selective when it comes to seeking potential leaders, but there is often great value in being selective.

Jim Collins, in his book *Good to Great,* details the characteristics of the rare corporations that have made the jump from a run-of-the-mill company to greatness and sustained it. One of the common characteristics is what Collins calls the ability "to get the right people on the bus."[2] Getting the right people on the bus will require less managing and motivating from the leader.

When it comes to selecting potential leaders in whom you will heavily invest your life, it is wise 'to get the right people on your leadership bus." John Maxwell writes, "You must select the right people for your organization. If you select well, the benefits are multiplied and seem nearly endless. If you select poorly, the problems are multiplied and seem endless."[3] Learn to prayerfully look for "the right people" to get on your leadership training bus.

The higher the level of leadership, the more careful we should be in the selection process. For example, as a pastor I am much more selective in choosing paid staff than the volunteer small group apprentices I mentor.

Where to Look for Faithful Men

Look in a current group in which you are involved. These are people with whom you already have a relationship. They already know the other people in the group. They have observed how God has used you to lead the group.

Look for those who already show initiative in serving others.

Look in past groups. Maybe there are some people who were a part of your church in the past, but currently are not. Maybe they got out of your area of ministry for a season. These are people you already have a relationship with who may now be ready to serve as your leadership apprentices.

Look for those who are willing and able to faithfully commit to meeting with you. Training a faithful man takes time. You will meet together consistently. Look for faithful men who have the time to meet with you for training.

Look around your church. There are probably people who attend worship services faithfully but, for whatever reason, have failed to get plugged into a place of service. Look around on Sundays for such people. Invite them to your training group and see where it goes from there.

Look in your family. Sometimes our best ministry is in our own home. The New Testament leaders James and Jude were both half-brothers of Jesus Christ. Currently, some of my top trainees are my eldest sons.

Look at friends. When looking for potential leaders, look at your friends and your friends' friends. Also look at the friends of your children and their parents. The parents of our children's friends have been some of our most fruitful relationships.

Look at new converts. New Christians can make great apprentices for several reasons. They have more contacts with non-Christians and are often more evangelistic minded. They are enthusiastic. They are teachable. And they can be highly spiritually contagious.

Look while on your knees. In Luke's Gospel we see that after more than a year of dynamic ministry, Jesus had several followers. Then He spent the entire night in prayer in order to have the Father's mind on whom to pour His life into in a more concentrated fashion in order to carry out His plan of world evangelization.

> During those days He went out to the mountain to pray and spent all night in prayer to God. When daylight came, He summoned His disciples, and He chose 12 of them—He also named them apostles. (Luke 6:12–13)

Training faithful men is the heart of pastoral ministry. If Jesus needed to pray before He selected His twelve, how much more should you and I?

Meet Regularly with Your Faithful Men

Paul told Timothy to take what he had learned from Paul and "commit" it to faithful men (2 Tim 2:2). The word "commit" means "to transmit; to entrust," and carries the idea of making a deposit in a bank.

God has made a rich deposit of truth into your life. You have a sacred obligation to deposit it carefully into the lives of others. This process does not happen in one short meeting. It happens over months and years as you regularly invest in them.

There is not one standard for how many times a week it takes to make the deposit needed into the life of the faithful man. I met with my first few "disciples" almost every night of the week for months. I met once or twice a week for lunch over a period of three years with a young man who is now a dynamic pastor. He and his wife also came to our house for dinner and Bible study every week for about a year.

I am currently meeting with some young men once a week for dinner and Bible study, plus once a week for prayer, and a few times a month for lunch. The rule of thumb is the more often you meet the better. This is especially true in the early stages.

We are all so busy doing what we think of as "ministry" that we often miss the real ministry that occurs when we simply waste time together. Was not this often the primary method of Jesus? Imagine how many hours He must have spent just walking and talking with His disciples.

Invite Them to Do Ministry Alongside You

Paul invited Timothy to join him on his second missionary journey (Acts 16:3). The young disciple-maker needs to see you in action. They often learn much more from your model than your message.

All of our sons worked alongside Cathy and me as we led a Bible study group for nonchurched high school students. Our group had more than fifty kids showing up every week, with several coming to Christ every month. We also trained new leaders and sent them off with new groups every year. At the time, I really did not see the whole thing as much more than just something I did on Wednesday nights.

When my boys went to college, they all became dynamic group leaders and trainers of group leaders. Andrew had as many as a hundred kids showing up to a group he ran on Friday nights. Daniel had sixty showing up regularly for a prayer group. Luke began training older leaders in his dorm when he was only eighteen.

One day they were all at home for lunch. I asked them how they learned to become such effective leaders and disciple makers. "We just watched you guys and read your books," they said.[4]

Give Them Opportunities to Do Ministry without You

The best and most basic means of developing a potential leader into an effective leader is on-the-job training. This works when the leader delegates areas of responsibility to the potential leader and supervises how they do each of them. For example, the potential leader leads the prayer session of a small-group Bible study as the leader observes and later shares his evaluation with the potential leader. The potential leader learns by doing ministry in a supervised setting.

During his second missionary trip, Paul was chased by a bunch of blood-thirsty Jews out of Thessalonica to Berea. There he started a church, but his pursuers found him and chased him out of town. But the new church of Berea did not suffer for lack of leadership. When Paul got in a boat to Athens, he left Silas and Timothy to run the ministry in his absence (Acts 17:14).

Later, while he was ministering in Ephesus, Paul sent Erastus and Timothy ahead of him to Greece (Acts 19:22). Of course, Timothy later was the pastor in charge at Ephesus.

You will never multiply your ministry if you hang onto your ministry. You need to start turning parts of it over to your disciples so they can get a taste for it, so they can get their nose bloodied a bit, and so they can learn what questions to ask. Realize that after a while their growth will slow down if they are still sitting under you and not serving. They will start growing again, more quickly, once they get to minister on their own.

Remind Them of the Big Picture

Paul reminded Timothy that he was to take what he had learned from Paul and invest it into faithful men, who would be able "to teach others also" (2 Tim 2:2). Paul's deposit into the life of Timothy was for one primary purpose: so he would pass it on by investing in others. Do not lose sight of the goal. The goal is multiplication.

In speaking of the big picture of home Bible study cell groups, Joel Comiskey writes, "Cell reproduction is so central to a cell ministry that the goal of cell leadership is not fulfilled until the new groups are also reproducing. . . . The theme of reproduction must guide cell ministry. The desired end is that each cell grows and multiplies."[5] He also states, "The principle job of the cell leader is to train the next cell leader—not just fill the house with guests."[6]

I find that if you fail to consistently remind your faithful men of the big picture of multiplying their lives into faithful men, they will lose focus and get sidetracked. It is not enough to get them to minister effectively. The task is not completed until they are making disciples who are making disciples.

As I look back over my pastoral ministry I have fond memories of people I led to Christ. I rejoice over couples who I counseled back into marital health. I think of some powerful worship services I led and messages I gave. But the real fruit of my ministry is the faithful men I trained. My greatest joy in my pastorate has been the young men who were saved under my ministry and were trained to the point where they are now starting churches and making disciples as pastors and missionaries.

~ What Now? ~

Start listing the things God has brought you through, the big life lessons He has taught you, the top ten things you could teach a young Christian about God and about living the Christian life. Also list the top ten most important Scriptures God has used in your life. Craft a few short lessons around the items on your list.

Identify several potential "faithful men" whom God has put into your life. Begin to meet regularly with them, preparing them to make their own disciples.

Notes

1. Bill Donahue and Russ Robinson, *Building a Church of Small Groups* (Grand Rapids, MI: Zondervan, 2001), 122–23.

2. Jim Collins, *Good to Great* (New York, NY: Harper Collins, 2001), 41.

3. John C. Maxwell, *Developing the Leaders Around You* (Nashville, TN: Thomas Nelson, 1995), 38.

4. See Dave Earley, *The 8 Habits of Effective Small Group Leaders* (Houston, TX: Touch, 2001), *The Small Group Leadership Toolkit* (Houston, TX: Touch, 2008), and *Turning Members into Leaders* (Houston, TX: Touch, 2003).

5. Joel Comiskey, *Leadership Explosion* (Houston, TX: Touch, 2001), 39.

6. Ibid., 40.

24

Pastoral Leadership Is . . .

Guiding
God's People

Of all of the men in Israel, God selected one of the most unlikely to become the next king. David was the seventh son of Jesse. A shepherd boy, he was to become God's chosen, and ultimately favorite, king. He became a great leader.

You know his story, how as a very young man he defeated the giant, Goliath, and brought Israel a great victory. Then he led his army to one victory after another over the Philistines. In fact he was so successful, paranoid King Saul became murderously jealous and chased David from his home into the wilderness.

Even then, David was still a leader. He gathered a motley crew around him and with those merry men wreaked havoc on God's enemies. Later, when he became king, David took the little ragtag group of tribes called Israel and established them as a legitimate nation focused on worshipping the true God. Under God's direction, he designed a powerful system of worship that brought down the favor of God on Israel.

God put His confidence in David because he was a well-rounded, shepherd-hearted leader. He had everything it took to guide God's people effectively.

> He chose David His servant and took him from the sheepfolds; He brought him from tending ewes to be shepherd over His people Jacob—over Israel, His inheritance. He shepherded them with a pure heart and guided them with his skillful hands. (Ps 78:70–72)

The Fourfold Focus of Effective Biblical Leaders

God put His confidence in David because, even as a young man, David displayed the primary aspects of effective shepherding leadership.

The first necessary aspect of a godly shepherd leader is inward integrity. David had "a pure heart" (Ps 78:72). There is no credibility without integrity. In the first section of this book we discussed these inward integrity characteristics as we addressed cultivating Godly character (chap. 3) and fleeing greed and following purity (chap. 4).

Beyond that, David also had a strong upward focus. God Himself testified of David, "I have found David the son of Jesse, a man after My heart, who will carry out all My will" (Acts 13:22). Being a pastor is serving as a spiritual leader. Your relationship with God is of vital importance. In the second section of this book we discussed the upward intimacy aspect as we addressed prioritizing prayer (chap. 8).

Third, we see that David also evidenced a clear forward outlook. He knew where he was going and "guided" the people (Ps 78:72). We will discuss the forward element of leadership in detail in this chapter.

Last, David was able to lead so effectively because he had an outward mindset. He had a shepherd's heart for people. He knew how to gather followers and cultivate other leaders. We will discuss the people side of leadership in detail in the next chapter.

Maybe you are just beginning to pursue the path to effective, biblical pastoral ministry. Maybe you have already gotten your feet wet. Or, maybe you are a seasoned veteran. Wherever you find yourself in the leadership journey, it is vitally important to remain strong and keep growing in all four areas: (1) *inward*—integrity and godly morality; (2) *upward*—intimacy with God; (3) *forward*—intentionality regarding the future; and (4) *outward*—inspirational ability.

Be encouraged: David was not always a national leader. Before he was ready to lead a nation of people, he led a flock of sheep. Before he was king, he was a shepherd. Before he led others, he learned to lead himself. He grew in his personal integrity, spiritual intimacy, his inspirational ability, and his intentionality.

An effective guide needs to know where they are going *and* how to get there. In the rest of this chapter we will show you how to be a leader who moves forward, and how to use vision, priorities, planning, and action to help your church get where it needs to go.

Vision

The Importance of Vision

A leader with vision sees potential opportunities when others see obstacles. They see the possibilities of the future when others only see problems. They see the future *before* their followers, they see *further* than their followers see, and they see God in and through the whole process and end product.

All of God's great leaders had visionary capacities. For example, the book of Nehemiah shows the power of purpose. The challenge of rebuilding the wall energized the workers (2:17–20), united the people and directed their efforts (3:1–32), kept all of them going in the face of opposition (4:1–23; 6:1–4), and led to great accomplishment—they rebuilt the walls in a jaw-dropping fifty-two days (6:15).

The Description of Vision

Vision is a picture of a preferred future told in the present. It is what *could* and *should* happen. It is a statement of faith as to what God can and will do. Vision is a need-meeting proposal that stretches others to greater sacrifice and impact. It is "a specific, detailed, customized, distinctive, and unique notion of what you are seeking to do to create a particular outcome."[1]

The Keys to Cultivating and Clarifying a Vision

See the need: A great need inspires a great leader. Nehemiah purposed to rebuild the walls after being deeply affected by the need to do so (Neh 1:2–11). Jesus was inspired to reach the multitudes by witnessing the needs of people who were weary and scattered, like sheep with no shepherd (Matt 9:35–38).

See the potential: Some leaders are more motivated by potential than by need. They get excited about what *could be.* They love the notion of doing something no one else has done yet.

Ask probing questions: Ask yourself some probing questions to help you realize two essential aspects of vision—the desire of your heart and the power of God. Below are two probing questions to ask:

1. If I knew I had no obstacles and unlimited resources, what would I love to do?
2. If I knew it was impossible to fail, what do I believe God would have me do?

Listen to God: Vision is born when we take the need and the potential to God in prayer. It is before God's throne that vision is given for meeting the need and realizing the potential. We must learn to listen to the still small voice of God and give everything we have to doing what He says.

Priorities

It is not enough to have a clear vision. Many God-given visions end up unfulfilled as the busyness of life, the plethora of options, and the tyranny of the urgent get the pastor off track. In order to stay on track, you must determine your priorities.

Priorities Are Powerful

The key to a great ending is a prioritized present. Every optimally effective, high-impact spiritual leader makes it a priority to set priorities. They learn to say no to the good in order to say a stronger yes to the best. They choose to concentrate their focus so they can maximize their impact. By narrowing their focus by doing fewer things, they are able to make a greater impact. They choose to prioritize now so they do not have to agonize later.

Are you guilty of living for "the less important"? I seriously doubt that anyone reading this book would die, stand before Jesus, and hear Him say that they had lived a bad life. I also doubt that many of us would hear Him tell us that we maxed out our potential because we lived a life focused on the absolute most important things. Too often we are guilty of living for the less important things. Too often we choose to do a lot of *good* activities, often to the exclusion of the very *best*.

Too many pastors are nice guys saying yes to many good things, but failing to accomplish the important things. The *quality* of your impact ultimately matters much more than the *quantity* of your activities. Some activities are simply more important than others.

Everything *cannot* be a priority. We are not infinite beings. We are very limited. None of us can have it all or do it all. When we try to have it all and do it all, we get overloaded and either become ineffective or break down under the stress.

Everything *should not* be a priority. All things are not created equal. Every activity is not necessarily a good activity. Very few qualify as the *best* activities. Every investment is definitely not a wise investment. We must make tough choices when it comes to selecting priorities. Some activities and investments are *more* important than others. Learn to choose that which is of *greatest* importance.

Let me ask you a few questions to help you with this:

- What are your essentials?
- What are your "nonnegotiables"?
- What are the most important things in your life?
- How much of your time each day is spent on the activities you'd say are of utmost importance?

Some activities and investments are more *lasting* than others. In the Bible there are five investments that are eternal in nature: (1) God (Deut 33:27); (2) people's souls (John 5:28–29); (3) God's Word (Isa 40:8); (4) prayer (Rev 5:6–8); and (5) true fellowship (Mal 3:16). Pastors must focus on eternal investments. Let me ask you, How much of your life is spent on that which will yield an eternal return?

The Pareto Principle. Some activities and investments are more *productive* than others. An Italian economist named Vilfredo Pareto observed that 80 percent of the income in Italy went to 20 percent of the population. Business management thinker Joseph Juran saw a universal application to Pareto's law which he called the Pareto principle. It is also known as the 80/20 rule, the law of the vital few, and the principle of factor sparsity.

The Pareto principle states that, for many events, 80 percent of the effects come from 20 percent of the causes. It is a common rule of thumb in business; e.g., 80 percent of your sales come from 20 percent of your clients.

Pareto's principle applies to churches. Think about it. Twenty percent of the sermon probably yields 80 percent of the benefits to the hearers. In most churches, 20 percent of the church members do 80 percent of the work, and 20 percent of the members give 80 percent of the money. Twenty percent of the members invite 80 percent of the guests, 20 percent of the members take up 80 percent of the pastor's time in counseling, and 20 percent of the members provide 80 percent of the leadership for the church. In most churches, 20 percent of the programs and ministries yield 80 percent of the impact and spiritual fruit, and 20 percent of the members eat 80 percent of the food at a church social.

Priorities are powerful. For example, make a to-do list with ten items. The odds are that of the ten, two of those items are more productive than the other eight combined. The art of prioritizing is learning to choose the top two.

Pests, Procrastinators, Problems, and Producers

When I practice prioritization in my life and ministry I look at every activity through a fourfold lens. I see it as either: a pest, procrastinator, problem, or producer.

- A pest is something that seems urgent but is not important.
- A procrastinator is an activity that is not urgent or important, but it eats up my time.
- A problem is urgent and important, but not much fun.
- A producer is very important, but not very urgent. Good pastoral leaders prioritize producers in their schedule.

The three pastoral tasks that we have been discussing in this book (prayer, practical Bible teaching, and training leaders) *are* the three most important, eternal, and productive pastoral priorities. They rarely feel urgent, but they are of utmost importance. The more time you spend on them, the stronger your ministry will become.

Evaluate, Eliminate, Estimate, and Activate[2]

Good pastoral leaders get in the habit of doing four things with their personal schedule and your church's schedule: (1) *Evaluate:* Pick your top priorities considering importance, eternity, and productivity. (2) *Eliminate:* Determine the activities and investments that really should not be priorities in your life. (3) *Estimate:* Select the activities and investments that best reflect good priorities (they are eternal, important, or productive) for the next three weeks, the next three months, the next three years, and the next thirty years. (4) *Activate:* Stop doing the unimportant, noneternal, and unproductive in your life and plug the most important, eternal, productive priorities into your monthly calendar, weekly schedule, daily to-do list, and annual goal list.

Planning

"Cruise to Nowhere"

In coastal towns in Florida, it is not uncommon to see a sign reading, "Cruise to nowhere." On a "cruise to nowhere" people get on board a cruise ship, leave the pier, go out to sea, and travel in circles for several days. During this time they enjoy several days of resort living as they dine on sumptuous meals and lounge around the pool working on their tan. They enjoy the shows and other ship activities.

"Cruising to nowhere" may be a great vacation, but it makes for a miserable life or a frustrating church ministry. Too many churches are really little more than cruises to nowhere. In order to be fulfilling, our lives, families, businesses, and churches need direction.

Planning puts us on a cruise to somewhere *and* gives us the map to get there. Do not waste your God-given opportunities by cruising to nowhere. Lead your church with purpose and planning.

Planning Is Looking Ahead

"Planning is bringing the future into the present so that you can do something about it now."[3] Because planning is looking ahead, it is foundational to leadership. If we want people to follow us, we must know where we are going and how to get there.

Planning is creating a map for a desired future. Whereas a vision states *where* we want to go and a passion explains *why* we want to go there, planning tells *how to* get there. It is the map.

Leadership is more than steering the ship. It is charting the course. Effective leadership uses the tool of planning to determine the best way to reach the destination.

Planning Is Preparing to Succeed

In his book *Poor Richard's Almanac*, Benjamin Franklin included this insight: "By failing to prepare, you are preparing to fail." Too many pastoral leaders end up in this spot. Unwittingly, they plan to fail because they fail to plan.

Planning Saves Time

Business experts claim that every minute an individual spends planning their goals, activities, and time in advance saves ten minutes of work in the execution of those plans. Read that again. One minute of planning saves ten minutes of doing.

That means that careful advance planning yields a return of ten times, or in other words, a return of 1,000 percent on your investment of mental, emotional, and physical energy. Spending a meaningful period of time reflecting on strategy and goals *before* taking action is almost always a wise course of action for any individual or institution.

Planning Maximizes Your Time

We are all busy. None of us has time to waste. Planning helps use the time we have most effectively.

Three Parts of a Good Plan

Planning is not complicated. A good plan takes into consideration only three major issues:

1. Destination: Where do we want to go? This is the big objective, the primary purpose.

2. Present Location: What is our current situation? What is the gap between the real and the ideal, and why? What are our current strengths and weaknesses, helping and hindering forces, and available resources?

3. Roadmap: How do we intend to reach our hoped-for destination? This is the route that is to be taken. Taking into account strengths and weaknesses, helping and hindering forces, and available resources, the roadmap is like a trip ticket, including the progressive steps of the plan.

Work the Plan

According to some experts, only sixty-seven out of one hundred people set goals for themselves. Of those sixty-seven, only ten have made plans to achieve them. Of those ten, only two take action to make their dreams become realities. That is only two out of a hundred who see their dreams become realities. They are the ones who take action.

It is not enough to plan your work. You must also *work your plan*. The greatest plans in the world will not work if you do not work. Successful spiritual leaders have God-given dreams and carefully laid plans. They also *take action* to see those plans become a reality.

Ninety-Nine Percent Perspiration

Thomas Edison was an American inventor and businessman who developed the phonograph and the long-lasting light bulb. A tireless worker, he eventually racked up 1,093 United States patents in his name.

Edison modeled the power of perspiration. He tried ten thousand times before finally finding the right materials to make the incandescent light bulb. He often said, "Genius is one percent inspiration, and ninety-nine percent perspiration."

Few of us have the intellect to qualify as geniuses, but all of us can be hard workers. Without exception, effective pastors are effective because they work at it. High-impact spiritual leadership does not happen by accident. It occurs as the result of clear vision, wise prioritizing, careful planning, *and* hard work.

"The Common Denominator of Success"

In 1940 at a convention for insurance agents (the NALU—National Association of Life Underwriters) in Philadelphia, Albert Gray delivered what was to become a famous address. His talk, "The Common Denominator of Success," has been turned into a pamphlet that has been circulated around the globe.[4] Gray summarized his findings in one sentence:

> The common denominator of success—the secret of success of every man who has ever been successful—lies in the fact that he formed the habit of doing things that failures don't like to do.

In explaining this statement, he said,

> Perhaps you have wondered why it is that our biggest producers seem to like to do the things that you don't like to do. They don't! And I think this is the most encouraging statement I have ever offered to a group of life insurance salesmen. But if they don't like to do these things, then why do they do them? Because by doing the things they don't like to do, they can accomplish the things they want to accomplish. Successful men are influenced by the desire for pleasing results. Failures are influenced by the desire for pleasing methods and are inclined to be satisfied with such results as can be obtained by doing things they like to do.

As is true in anything else, successful pastors are those who work hard at the things most pastors avoid. They pray and teach their people to pray. They study the Bible hard, preach with clarity, and apply God's Word practically. They equip the saints for ministry and train multiplying leaders. They do all the things we know we should do but usually do not get around to doing.

Effective leaders do what they need to do and learn to enjoy it. They get totally involved in leading the church, become engrossed in it, dig in, and love what they are doing. They do not love it because it is easy or because everything always goes according to plan. They learn to love it because they know they are making a difference in people's lives, an eternal difference.

— What Now? —

Write a simple vision statement for the next five years of your life or your current ministry. Make it concise, clear, specific, measurable, attainable, and personal.

List the top ten things you need to accomplish in the next year. Now pick the two that are the most important and productive.

Put together a simple plan to reach that vision and accomplish those top two priorities.

— Quote —

*Great people are ordinary people who become possessed with
a cause greater than they are.*

—DALE GALLOWAY[5]

Notes

1. George Barna, *Leaders on Leadership* (Ventura, CA: Regal, 1997), 54.

2. Alan Lakein, *How to Get Control of Your Time and Your Life* (New York: New American Library, 1973).

3. Leroy Eims, *Be the Leader You Were Meant to Be* (Colorado Springs, CO: Cook, 1996).

4. Albert Gray, "The Common Denominator of Success," http://www.the intelligentinvestor.com/wp-content/uploads/2011/03/the-common-denominator-of-success.pdf (accessed February 12, 2010).

5. Dale Galloway, *20/20 Vision* (Portland, OR: Scott, 1986), 9.

25

Inspiring
Others

Wise Leaders

David's son, Solomon, watched his dad closely and learned how to become a leader as well. When the time came for him to lead, he built the long anticipated temple, expanded the nation exponentially, and led into peace and prosperity. Later, he recorded a book of wise sayings, which is now in our Bible under the title Proverbs. In this book, Solomon describes ten characteristics of a wise and effective spiritual leader.

Wise Spiritual Leaders

1. Stand on a solid moral foundation (Prov 16:12)
2. Have personal integrity (Prov 17:7; 20:28; 28:16; 31:2–4;)
3. Practice self-control (Prov 20:22)
4. Embrace wisdom (Prov 8:12)
5. Walk with God (Prov 21:1)
6. See the big picture (Prov 25:3)
7. Plan well (Prov 28:2)
8. Practice good people skills (Prov 14:28)
9. Persuade others effectively (Prov 16:10; 16:15)
10. Build a good team (Prov 16:13; 22:11; 20:26; 29:12)

These characteristics can be grouped into the four focuses of leadership that we looked at in the last chapter.

Inward: Stand on a solid moral foundation; have personal integrity; practice self-control; and embrace wisdom (Prov 8:12; 16:12; 17:7; 20:22; 20:28; 28:16; 31:2–4).

Upward: Walk with God (Prov 21:1).

Forward: See the big picture and plan well (Prov 25:3; 28:2).

Outward: Practice good people skills, persuade others effectively, and build a good team (Prov 14:28; 16:10; 16:13; 16:15; 20:26; 22:11; 29:12).

In the last chapter, we observed that an effective guide needs to be forward focused, knowing where they are going and how to get there. But of course that is not enough. The leader must convince others to go with them. In this chapter we will focus on the outward aspects of good pastoral leadership: people skills, persuasion, and team building.

Practice Good People Skills

The mark of a good leader is loyal followers; leadership is nothing without a following. (Prov 14:28 MSG)

Christian leadership is all about people. Without people, there is no one to lead. Goals, plans, and projects are all very important, but only to the extent that they help people. By nature, I am more of a project person than a people person. I learned early on that pastoral leadership effectiveness is closely tied with our ability to get along with people and to influence them. As the Chinese proverb states, "He who thinks he is leading and no one is following, is only taking a walk."

Relational Banking

Relationships can be understood as bank accounts. Realize it or not, you have a relational account with every person within your sphere of influence. Every positive interaction makes a deposit in that account. Every negative dealing with a person makes a withdrawal in your relational account with them.

We influence people most easily when there is a positive balance in the relational account. We struggle to influence people when there is little or no equity in the relationship account.

Leaders who practice good people skills continually place deposits in the relational accounts of others. Then, when they need to call a member to make a change or go to a new level of commitment, the member is willing to follow.

Effective leaders determine to master relational banking. They constantly think of ways to make deposits in the lives of the people around them. They are not only well liked, but they are also easily followed. They understand that effective ministry runs on the train track of healthy relationships and thrives in the atmosphere of positive relational bank accounts.

The Bible supplies the clearest guidelines for how to get along with people. Leaders can improve their people skills immediately by obeying the "one another" commands found in the New Testament.

1. USE GREETINGS TO HELP OTHERS FEEL IMPORTANT

Greet one another with a holy kiss. (Rom 16:16; see also 1 Cor 16:20; 2 Cor 13:12; 1 Pet 5:14)

Let me make one thing perfectly clear: I am not advocating giving everyone you meet a great big smooch on the lips. However, wise leaders use greetings to make others feel important. Relational deposits are made every time we make the other person feel important. Effective leaders must get beyond their comfort zone and positively greet people.

In the first-century church, an appropriate greeting was a kiss. Today, a good greeting may be a handshake or a hug.

Connecting with people is really very simple. But if you are an introvert like I am, it is good to be reminded of the basics. A greeting that makes others feel important involves three aspects: (1) a look—look them in the eye; (2) a word—introduce yourself, and (3) a touch—shake their hand.

There is one other key to a great greeting—remember the power of a name. Jesus taught the value of shepherds knowing their sheep *by name*. The sweetest sound in our ears is often the sound of our own name being called.

2. HONOR OTHERS

Outdo one another in showing honor. (Rom 12:10)

Nothing builds a relationship more than the atmosphere of esteem and honor. Nothing erodes it more than a climate of disrespect. When a leader breathes an atmosphere of respect and regard, followers respond. People respect people who respect them.

Below is a chart that shows the difference between actions that honor others and actions that take advantage of them. See which ones you are already good at and which ones you need to work on.

Actions that Honor Others	Actions that Dishonor Others
Words of appreciation and affirmation	Disapproval, criticism, cuts down
Give credit	Take credit
Take the initiative to clear up misunderstandings	Refuse to act to resolve misunderstandings
Only criticize in private	Criticize in front of others
Ask others for their opinions	Fail to seek the opinions of others
Update people on their status, progress, or anything else that may affect them	Keep people in the dark; withhold information
Impartiality	Favoritism
Give our full attention; active listening	Disinterest
Notice when they need encouragement and give it	Fail to notice

3. SERVE OTHERS

Serve one another through love. (Gal 5:13)

Jesus, of course, is the model servant. His act of leaving heaven, coming to earth, being born as a baby, and dying for us was a stunning example of servant leadership (see Phil 2:5–9). He told His disciples that His purpose in coming was not to be served, but to serve and give His life for others (Mark 10:45). Beyond that, even at the most personally stressful season of His life, hours prior to His arrest and crucifixion, He took a servant's towel and washed His disciples' feet (John 13:1–6). Jesus was a leader who was followed because He was a leader who served His followers.

Servant leadership is an attitude that translates into action. It is a mindset that results in ministry. Servant leadership is humbling yourself to meet the needs of others. It is washing their feet (John 13:14). It is trying to help make them successful.

4. GIVE OTHERS THE FREEDOM TO BE THEMSELVES

Therefore accept one another, just as the Messiah also accepted you, to the glory of God. (Rom 15:7; see also Rom 14:13)

When people sense a spirit of criticism or self-righteousness in a leader, they will either shrink back, close down, or grow defensive. A spirit of criticism will draw the life out of a follower. On the other hand, unconditional acceptance becomes fertile soil to foster deep relationships and grow new leaders.

We respond better to leaders when we sense they like us for who we are. We like it when we do not have to play a role or be something we are not in order to be accepted. We follow more easily when we sense unconditional love and acceptance.

Persuade Others Effectively

A good leader motivates . . . (Prov 16:10 MSG)

Good-tempered leaders invigorate lives; they're like spring rain and sunshine. (Prov 16:15 MSG)

Let me ask you some tough questions:
Do you have followers?
Are people lining up to be discipled by you?
Are you willing to learn to lead in such a way that people cannot help but follow you?

As I have studied the life of Jesus as it relates to leadership, I see several principles He practiced that made Him a leader His disciples would die for.

1. Extend Positive Expectations

Jesus took an average group of men and motivated eleven out of the twelve to become world changers. How did He do it? He used the power of positive expectations. Let me explain.

A study of first-century Hebrew culture reveals rabbis began selecting the best and brightest young men for rabbinical training at an early age. By the age of fourteen or fifteen, only the best of the best were still studying. Most students at that point were learning the family business and starting families of their own. Only those remaining could apply to a well-known rabbi to become one of that rabbi's disciples.[1]

When Jesus came to Peter, Andrew, James, and John and said, "Follow me and I will make you fishers of men" (Matt 4:19 ESV), He was showing great confidence in them when others had not. Can you imagine what it must have been like to have a rabbi say, "Come, follow me"? No wonder they dropped everything to follow Him. He was giving them a second chance. He believed in them. He had positive expectations for their future. He saw them as leaders, and they fulfilled His expectations.

Rats. Dr. Robert Rosenthal of Harvard University discovered that expectations become self-fulfilling.[2] He ran an interesting study with three sets of students and three sets of rats.

He told the students who handled the first group of rats that they would be handling rats that were especially bred for intelligence. He informed his second group of students that they would be handling average rats. Then he shared with his third group of students that they would be handling decidedly below average rats.

For the next six weeks the rats performed experiments involving running a maze. Interestingly, the "smart" rats performed exceptionally, the "average" rats were average and the "slow" rats did poorly.

As you might have guessed by now, there were no genius rats bred for intelligence. They were all average rats out of the same litter. The difference in performance was purely because of the different expectations of their human handlers.

Students. In 1964, Rosenthal tried his experiment with public school teachers and students. The teachers were given the names of children in their school supposedly identified by a new test as being on the verge of blooming intellectually. The children, however, had been chosen randomly.

At the end of the school year, the selected children showed gains in intellectual abilities compared with the other children. Moreover, teachers perceived the children in the "bloomer" group as more appealing, adjusted, and affectionate than the others.

Over the next few years, Dr. Rosenthal was able to review 345 studies showing the power of the Rosenthal effect, or as more commonly known, the "teacher-expectancy effect." Again and again further research has revealed that students perform, on average, twice as well as other students *when* they are expected to do so. It is a kind of self-fulfilling prophecy.

2. Be Open and Transparent

I tend to be more of a project person than a people person. I can default into becoming overly guarded. Several years ago, I read a book that helped me become a better leader. The author, Alan Loy McGinnis, shared two sentences I really needed to hear.

> People with deep and lasting friendships may be introverts, extroverts, young, old, dull, intelligent, homely, good looking; but the one characteristic they always have in common is openness. They have a certain transparency allowing people to see what is in their hearts.[3]

Notice the words "openness" and "transparency." We will never compel people to follow us into spiritual leadership if we do not learn to become open and transparent. We need to move beyond merely sharing facts and opinions and learn to share our true feelings, our struggles, and our delights.

3. Recognize, Compliment, and Praise

In 1936, an unknown YMCA instructor named Dale taught a course on human relations that was so popular he gathered it into book form. When he first published his little book *How to Win Friends and Influence People*, it stayed on the best-seller list for 10 years, a record never since matched. It sold more than 15 million copies globally and sells at a rate of 200,000 a year.

In the book, Carnegie shares one truth he calls "the big secret in dealing with people." It is nothing new or unusual. In fact Jesus used it two thousand years ago. What is Carnegie's big secret? "Be hearty in your approbation and lavish in your praise."[4] The word "approbation" means the act of formally approving, commending, or praising. He discovered that people respond positively when they receive honest and sincere appreciation.

The outstanding American president, Abraham Lincoln, was a very persuasive leader. In leading America through one of the toughest times in its history, he motivated people to make great sacrifices to finish a very bloody war and unify a nation. He keenly observed, "Everybody likes a compliment."

I have yet to meet the person who did not respond positively to positive recognition. Wise leaders take the opportunity to notice when others are behaving positively and recognize it.

Good people will labor tirelessly unnoticed for long periods of time, but eventually they get weary. But when those same workers receive some recognition for what they have done, they will dig down and go on at a higher level.

4. Show Them the Significance

I speak in about thirty-five different churches each year. I was in one the other day where the pastor was complaining about not having enough people who desired to step up and become small-group leaders. He also whined about not having anyone willing to do some necessary Sunday-morning duties such as teaching preschoolers. When he made his Sunday morning announcements, I quickly understood why no one was excited about signing up to serve.

"We need someone to help in the preschool on Sunday mornings," he sighed. Everyone in the congregation dropped their heads and became very busy reading their bulletins. "I know that it is a tough assignment—I certainly would not want to have to do it. But if someone would just suck it up and do it, we would appreciate it." Of course, no one signed up.

Not long after that I was in another church. When it came time for the announcements, a brightly dressed lady in her fifties practically ran up to the microphone. "I am so very honored to stand before you today," she gushed. "I get to tell you about an incredible opportunity. In a few minutes, I will give you a chance to register your interest, but I need to warn you ahead of time, not every one of you can be accepted."

She smiled widely and continued, "A few of you will have the opportunity to invest a few hours each week to change the course of history." At this point I was highly curious what this marvelous opportunity could possibly be.

"The chosen few will get to plant the seed of God's Word deep into the hearts of some future world changers."

Like the rest of the congregation, I was on the edge of my seat.

"Our church has been growing so rapidly in the past few months that we need to add another preschool class on Sundays," she said. "Of course, we won't be able to take all of you, but if you want to help us change the world, one preschooler at a time, please sign the card in your bulletin and bring it to me after the service."

I started to sign the card. Cathy grabbed my arm and stopped me. "We live in another state, Dave. I don't think they want you to commute eight hours each weekend to work in the preschool department of this church."

Jesus motivated His disciples to go out and change the world by pointing out the supreme significance of their task. He described their task as being: global in scope ("all nations," Matt 28:19-20; Luke 24:47; "the ends of the earth," Acts 1:8); regal in nature ("the kingdom of God," Luke 9:1–2,60); eternal in time ("food which endures unto everlasting life" John 6:27 NKJV); impossible in challenge ("without Me you can do nothing," John 15:5 NKJV);

essential in importance ("As the Father has sent me, I am sending you," John 20:21 NIV); and greater in quality ("greater works than these will he do," John 14:12 ESV).

Someone observed that the deepest urge in human nature is the desire to be important. We must learn to *recruit to a vision* and use the power of pointing out significance. I believe that fulfilling the Great Commission by cooperating with Jesus in building His church is the most significant task anyone can do.

The moment you believe that your ministry is not supremely significant you are in trouble as a leader. If your church is not a God-anointed agency of life change, you had better change your church or have the integrity to close it down. If it is what it should be, never be embarrassed to trumpet that reality to the ends of the earth.

Cast the Vision

Never underestimate the power of a God-given vision. It will attract followers and help produce leaders. It compels action or builds morale. It provides a sense of direction. It inspires resolve and encourages sacrifice . . . but only if it is shared and shared well.

As I consult with churches and pastors, I run into one problem over and over—vision. Either the pastor lacks it, or he fails to cast it convincingly. In the previous chapter, we talked about vision and planning. In the rest of this chapter, I'd like to offer several keys to casting vision effectively.

1. See It Clearly Yourself

You cannot share what you do not possess. Vision cannot be achieved until it is conceived and believed. Get with God until you can clearly see the vision God has for your church.

2. State the Vision as Simply and Specifically as Possible

A good vision statement can clarify and direct what you are trying to do. It must be simple enough to be remembered and specific enough to give direction. A purpose statement should be a brief, memorable description in less than two sentences.

In the last chapter we discussed using SMART goals. Learn to motivate your church members through a purpose statement that is SMART—S: specific; M: measurable; A: attainable; R: relevant; T: time-oriented

3. Say It to Your Key People

As you begin to talk about the vision with your key people, they should embrace it. As they begin to own the vision, they become contagious carriers who infect others with the vision.

4. Share the Vision Often

Question: When should the vision be communicated?

Answer: At every opportunity

Vision is only powerful to the extent that it is shared. Too often leaders define their dream but fail to reach it simply because they do not spend enough time sharing their dream with others. The purpose will not accomplish all that it can unless it is shared. It will not attract followers or produce leaders. It cannot compel action or build morale. It will not give a sense of direction. It cannot inspire resolve and encourage sacrifice unless and until it is shared.

A good vision that is shared will always accomplish more than a great vision not shared at all. People need to hear the dream described often enough to be able to recite it back. They need to have the picture painted for them so frequently that they know what it means and where they fit into it. They need to hear it often enough that they can share it with others.

― What Now? ―

Which of the three aspects of the outward side of leadership do you need to work on—people skills, persuasion, or vision casting? What specific steps can you take to grow in that area?

Write a sample vision statement for the ministry in which you are currently involved. Make sure that it is as SMART as possible.

― Quote ―

Let's get one thing straight from the start. If you want to be a leader, vision is not an option; it is part of the standard equipment of a real leader. . . .

—GEORGE BARNA[5]

Notes

1. Rob Bell, *Velvet Elvis* (Grand Rapids MI: Zondervan, 2006), chap. 5.

2. Robert Rosenthal and Lenore Jacobson, "Teachers' Expectancies: Determinants of Pupils' IQ Gains," *Psychological Reports* (1966): 19, 115–18.

3. Alan Loy McGinnis, *The Friendship Factor* (Minneapolis, MN: Augsburg, 1979), 17.

4. Dale Carnegie, *How to Win Friends and Influence People* (New York: Pocket Books, 1964), 40.

5. George Barna, *Leaders on Leadership* (Ventura, CA: Regal, 1997), 48.

Part 5

Shepherding God's Flock

26

Pastoral Leadership Is . . .

Shepherding through Undershepherds

Pity the poor sheep. Sheep are inherently incapable of finding water on their own. They must have someone lead them to clean, calm, lukewarm water. Sheep cannot find food by themselves. They have to be guided to food. They cannot discern between poisonous and nonpoisonous plants. They must be directed to safe plants.

They need a shepherd to lead and feed them. Sheep cannot defend themselves. They cannot outrun an attacker. They cannot outsmart an attacker. Sheep are very gentle and passive. They have no will to fight back when attacked.

They need a shepherd to guard and protect them. Sheep have very oily skin. Because of the natural grease in their wool, dirt sticks to it. They have no ability or dexterity to clean themselves. Without shearing, they quickly become filthy and diseased. They need a shepherd to keep them clean.

Their feet are easily susceptible to foot rot when the soil is too damp. Also, wet grass gives them severe diarrhea, which can actually be lethal to them. They need a shepherd to guide them to fertile, dry pastures.

Sheep are one of the few animals that can be totally lost within a few miles of their home. Most animals have been given by God an instinct to find their way back, but not sheep. If a sheep is taken into unfamiliar territory, it becomes completely lost. It has no sense of direction or orientation. It does not know where it is and it does not know how to get where it is supposed to be. The lost sheep will walk around in endless circles, crying continually in anxious confusion. If they go astray, they are helpless to find food or to find water.

In order to survive and thrive, sheep must have shepherds. It is possible that one reason God created sheep was to give us a portrait of why God's people need pastoral leaders. Without them, God's flock cannot survive or thrive.

This is why God chose a shepherd to serve as Israel's king (1 Chr 11:1–2). This is why Paul told the Ephesian elders to "shepherd the church of God" (Acts 20:28 NKJV). This is why Peter commanded church elders to "shepherd God's flock" (1 Pet 5:2).

> Therefore, as a fellow elder and witness to the sufferings of the Messiah, and also a participant in the glory about to be revealed, I exhort the elders among you: *shepherd God's flock* among you, not overseeing out of compulsion but freely, according to God's [will]; not for the money but eagerly; not lording it over those entrusted to you, but being examples to the flock. And when the chief Shepherd appears, you will receive the unfading crown of glory. (1 Pet 5:1–4, italics added)

This is why, when Jesus saw the disoriented, distressed, dispirited, harassed, helpless, confused, and aimless crowds, He said they were like sheep without a shepherd.

> When He saw the crowds, He felt compassion for them, because they were weary and worn out, *like sheep without a shepherd*. Then He said to His disciples, "The harvest is abundant, but the workers are few. Therefore, pray to the Lord of the harvest to send out workers into His harvest." (Matt 9:36–38, italics added)

But Jesus did not stop at observing the link between lost crowds and their need for shepherds. He also told His disciples to *pray for more workers in the harvest.*

I have read many books on pastoral leadership, and many of them wax eloquent on the beauty of the shepherd-sheep connection. But I think they stop short of explaining how this close connection is to occur when the flock gets large. In this chapter I want to look at not only the science of "shepherdology," but also focus on the wisdom of strategically shepherding the flock by cultivating a system of undershepherds.

Shepherdology 101: Knowing and Instructing the Flock

To shepherd is to tend, feed, nourish, lead, guide, and guard a flock. Good pastors actively care for their flock. They see that they are well fed and well led. They protect them, and they gather them together.

God views His ministry to His flock as *shepherding* (Isa 40:11; Jer 31:10; Ezek 34:11–16). The author of Hebrews called Jesus the Great *Shepherd* of the sheep (Heb 13:20). Jesus is referred to as the Lamb who will *shepherd* the multitude saved during the great tribulation (Rev 7:17).

Jesus contrasted His ministry with that of the Pharisees. In doing so, He gave us insight into the role of a good shepherd.

> I assure you: Anyone who doesn't enter the sheep pen by the door but climbs in some other way, is a thief and a robber. The one who enters by the door is the shepherd of the sheep. The doorkeeper opens it for him, and the sheep hear his voice. He calls his own sheep by name and leads them out. When he has brought all his own outside, he goes ahead of them. The sheep follow him because they recognize his voice. They will never follow a stranger; instead they will run away from him, because they don't recognize the voice of strangers. (John 10:1–5)

Good Shepherds Know Their Sheep

A good shepherd gets to know each of his sheep by name (John 10:3). He works hard to learn their unique personalities and tendencies.

As a pastor, I had the benefit of starting my church from scratch. In that way, I learned a few new families a week. As the church grew, I found that I knew well over eight hundred people by name. Let me tell you how I did it.

I stood at the main door and greeted every new family as they entered. I asked their name, where they lived, and where they worked. After they walked away, I jotted the info on a 3 x 5 card I kept in my pocket. When the service was over, I stood at the door as people left. I made a point of speaking with the new family and using their name in the conversation. I kept the 3 x 5 card on my desk all week and prayed for them.

I called them on Monday evening and in a short, unobtrusive phone call I asked how they had liked the service and if they had any questions. I also offered to come by and visit them briefly to get to know them better and answer more questions if they were interested.

Sometimes I would call them back on Saturday to ask them to be sure and touch base with me in the lobby the next day because I wanted to introduce them to my wife. I also would ask if it was okay if I took a picture of them the next day in the lobby so I could remember their names and faces. Almost everyone agreed. I kept those pictures on my desk and prayed for them all week.

I found that if a family came three weeks in a row, the odds were very high that they would end up becoming a part of our church. I invited the ones who were mostly unchurched to our Christianity 101 class to learn the basics of Christianity and what it meant to follow Christ. If they did have a church background, I invited them to a 201 class to learn about our church.

Between first-time guests, second-time guests, third-time guests, absentees, and others, I tried to make phone contact with twenty families a week through strategic five-minute phone calls. Today, you can also touch base with a lot of people through social media and texting.

I found that it was possible to do a lot of shepherding in mini-bites before and after the weekend worship gatherings. At least until our church reached an average attendance of over six hundred, I tried to speak with every adult who came on the property. I hung out in the lobby before and after the services. I walked around the auditorium talking to people before the service. I stood at the doors when people were leaving. I might just say hi, or I would stop and pray for the person. None of it took very long, but all of it was very important.

The manner in which you get to know your flock is not the issue. The point is, good shepherds know their sheep.

Good Shepherds Instruct Their Flock

Richard Baxter was a noted seventeenth-century English Puritan pastor, church leader, and theologian. His classic book *The Reformed Pastor* is a call for pastors to repent of failing to invest their time to personally instruct and teach their flocks.[1]

Baxter taught doctrine systematically with his assistant in the town of Kidderminster at the rate of fourteen families per week. His intention was to teach the people the basic teachings of Scripture by question and answer in their own homes. His ambition was to cover all the eight hundred families (2,000+ people) in his parish in one year. His clerk would set up the appointments. Then Baxter and his associate pastor would visit three families a day, two full days every week each, in order to get through the whole town every year. In essence, they visited eight families a week, times fifty weeks, times two men.

The benefits of this ministry are obvious. Every family got at least one full hour of specific, personal instruction from a pastor every year. In carrying out this plan, the pastor can really know the state of his flock. The lost could be exposed and converted. Children could be introduced to solid Bible truth from a young age.

I love the fact that Baxter wanted to know the state of his flock and invested in each family personally. I also love the fact that he gave them detailed instructions through a question-answer process.

But I do have a few questions with Baxter's system. Is one hour a year enough to really instruct the flock? Does this system equip the saints to do the ministry? Is he making multiplying, ministering disciples or just students who can give the correct answer?

Shepherdology 201: Shepherding through Undershepherds

As we mentioned in chapter one, Moses was responsible for shepherding a huge flock of as many as a million people. Jethro told him that the idea of the solo, lone-ranger shepherd was ineffective. Instead, he encouraged Moses to focus on three priorities: prayer, practical Bible teaching, and developing layers of leaders. Shepherdology 201 involves that third piece of advice: shepherding through undershepherds. Note what Jethro said:

> But you should select from all the people able men, God-fearing,
> trustworthy, and hating bribes. Place [them] over the people as officials
> of thousands, hundreds, fifties, and tens. (Exod 18:21)

Find and select good men and appoint them as leaders over groups organized by the thousand, by the hundred, by fifty, and by ten—shepherding the flock through layers of undershepherds. While I appreciate Baxter, I found out that Jethro had a better idea.

Learning the Hard Way

When I was a senior at a Christian college, I served as resident assistant in a dorm with seventy-seven young men. I decided to do the sort of shepherding ministry Baxter suggests. I made a plan to meet personally for one hour per semester with each of the young men in my dorm. I figured I could get through all seventy-seven by seeing seven a week for the next eleven weeks.

The first week of the semester I met with seven of the young men one-on-one to ask them ten basic questions. The questions had to do with their testimony of salvation, assurance of salvation, baptism, quiet time, church involvement, sinful habits, ministry to others, and so on.

By the end of the week I was overwhelmed. Two were not saved, so I led them to Christ. Six of the seven needed further discipleship. Two needed some counseling. I had no time. I was scheduled to meet with seven more of the students in my dorm the next week. What should I do?

I quickly revised my strategy and began to work through a system of undershepherds. I had eight prayer leaders in my dorm. I decided to meet with them all together for an hour and a half as a group each week *and* to meet with each one separately for an hour every other week. They in turn were to do the same thing with eight other young men, meeting with them in groups of eight for one hour a week as a small group *and* also meeting with each guy in their group for one hour individually every two weeks. In this way every student received both a small-group experience weekly *and* one-on-one instruction every other week.

A Church with Layers of Shepherd Leaders

Later as a pastor, our church grew from 11 adults and a baby to the size of Baxter's parish with 800 active families numbering 2,000 people. Starting when our church only had only a few hundred people, I realized that I would burn out if I tried to shepherd everyone by myself. I selected a few good men and we began to use a form of the Jethro system. I developed them to shepherd people through a weekly home Bible study group. They in turn developed other men to shepherd people through a weekly home Bible study group. As our church grew, our group system of shepherding leaders grew. We went from 5 shepherding leaders to 25 to 125.

Our home groups were not usually "the front door" to our church. Our weekend worship gatherings were the place most guests first visited. Our home groups were very effective at "closing the back door." Very few of the people who joined our church ever left.

We worked a system of group leaders to shepherd our flock. I met with our 5 other main elder/pastors each week as a group for an hour and a half *and* individually for an hour (1 x 5 = 5 families being shepherded). This took me six and a half hours a week, plus some preparation time for our weekly meetings.

The 5 other pastors each met with 5 directors for an hour and a half and individually for an hour every week (1 x 5 x 5 = 25 families being shepherded). This took them six and a half hours a week, plus preparation time for the weekly meeting.

The 25 directors each oversaw 5 home Bible study group leaders (1 x 5 x 5 x 5 = 125 families being shepherded). The directors visited a different group every week and met with their group leaders individually every other week.

The 125 group leaders met with 5 to 8 families each week for a group Bible study for an hour and a half every week (1 x 5 x 5 x 5 x 5+ = 725+ families being shepherded). They also tried to visit each of their families every other month and call them every other week.

In Baxter's plan, only 2 men did the shepherding ministry. In our plan, 155 men did shepherding ministry.

In Baxter's plan, no new shepherding leaders were developed. In our plan, we went from 1 shepherding leader to 5 more shepherding leaders to 25 more shepherding leaders, to 125 additional shepherding leaders, for a total of 155. We also sent out many of our leaders to plant new churches.

The typical family in Baxter's church received one hour of personal pastoral instruction each year. In our church, the typical family received fifty to seventy-five hours of small group study, *plus* six or more hours of personal instruction each year.

Also, I found that after a certain point in their development, people grow more by doing the teaching than by being taught. In Baxter's plan, only 2 men did the teaching. In our plan, 155 men did the teaching.

Setting the P.A.C.E.

When we talk about shepherding the flock of God and consider employing lay persons to invest in others as spiritual shepherds, what are we asking them to do? We found that the key to shepherding was simplifying the shepherding role into four responsibilities. You could call these responsibilities "setting the PACE: (1) Prayer, (2) Availability, (3) Contact, and (4) Example."[2]

Prayer: A shepherd prays for those he is shepherding. Through our shepherding system, every member of our church was prayed for every day. In our system, I prayed for the other pastor/elders and their families each day. The pastor/elders prayed for the five ministry directors they oversaw and their families each day. The ministry directors prayed for the five small-group leaders they shepherded and their families every day. The small group leaders prayed for their small group members and their families every day.

Availability: As your church gets larger, it becomes impossible and unhealthy to be available to everyone all the time. Jethro told Moses that this solo-shepherding was not good for him or his people. By using a strategic system of shepherding, the person doing the shepherding is primarily responsible for being available to the five families he oversees and also helps with the families those under him oversee. So if a church member had a crisis, their small-group leader would be available to support him or her *and* the director over their small-group leader would also help.

Contact: As a church gets larger, people tend to slip through the cracks. They miss a few weeks. No one contacts them, and the next thing you know they have not been in church in months, and their spiritual life is headed in the wrong direction.

Our desire as a church was that no one was allowed to fall between the cracks. Our goal was that every member in our church was contacted every two weeks. By having a system of shepherding, this is not overwhelming. The shepherds only have to reach out to five families every two weeks.

Example: It is much easier to follow Jesus if you have a good example of what that means in daily life. Yet, no one is a perfect example. Everyone knows they are not perfect. Often people do not step up to minister to others because they feel that they are not good enough. We found it helpful to our shepherds if we asked them not to be perfect followers of Jesus, but rather to be progressing followers of Jesus.

⚊ What Now? ⚊

Create a system of shepherding. Develop several layers of shepherding leaders. Start where you are. Begin setting the PACE for a few people. Encourage them to do the same with some other people. Keep it up. You will be amazed at how quickly it can grow.

⚊ Quote ⚊

Do the math and you'll see that Jethro's recommended span of care was five to ten people per leader. One person could shepherd ten people. Someone else could care for the leaders of five or ten units. Another could oversee leaders at the "thousands" level.

—BILL DONAHUE AND RUSS ROBINSON[3]

Notes

1. Richard Baxter, *The Reformed Pastor* (Edinburgh, UK: Banner of Truth, 1981).

2. See Melvin Steinbron, *Can the Pastor Do It Alone? A Model for Preparing Lay People for Lay Pastoring* (Ventura, CA: Regal, 1987).

3. Bill Donahue and Russ Robinson, *Building a Church of Small Groups* (Grand Rapids, MI: Zondervan, 2001), 48.

27

Counseling
the Flock

A shepherd is primarily a guide. He guides the flock by directing them to green pastures every morning and by leading back to the safety of the pen at night. He also gives guidance to an individual sheep who is wandering. He might use his staff to hook it and pull it back into the flock. If it is young or injured, he might carry it close to him for a time until it is ready to walk on its own.

A pastoral shepherd also is a guide. He leads the church in the right paths through godly vision, planning, prioritization, and action (see chap. 24). But he also gives guidance to individuals. When they are in need of direction, he counsels them. When wandering, he rebukes and corrects them. When they are hurting, he comforts and carries them close for a time.

The Goal of Counseling Is Change

Paul told the Colossian church that the goal of his ministry was to "present everyone mature in Christ" (Col 1:28). This implies that everyone is not already mature in Christ. The role of the pastor is to help them mature in areas where they need to grow. Often, the means of helping them to make the necessary changes in order to become more mature in Christ is counsel.

When counseling a Christian brother or sister, it is important to note that the goal is not merely to help him or her feel better. It is to help that person change. Ultimately, they will feel better *only* as they make changes and more closely align their lives with the Scriptures.

The change can occur spiritually as the counselee gets to know God better, socially as they love others more effectively, and/or intrapersonally as they better understand and apply who they are in Christ. The change sought should help them rationally to renew their mind in Christ so they see life, God, others, and themselves from an eternal perspective. It can aid them emotionally so they learn to manage their moods biblically. Ultimately, the change sought produces greater Christlikeness in their lives.

The Guidebook for Counseling Is the Bible

The Bible gives us all we need for life and godliness. The Bible provides real answers for real people with real problems.

> All Scripture is inspired by God and is profitable for teaching, for rebuking, for correcting, for training in righteousness, so that the man of God may be complete, equipped for every good work. (2 Tim 3:16–17)

The Bible is able to show people the path of righteousness (teaching), reveal to them where they got off the path (rebuking), show them how to get back on the path (correcting), and the way to stay on the path (training). It is the tool for making people mature and complete in Christ and for equipping them to serve others.

Henry Brandt has been called the "father of modern Christian counseling." Even though he is a trained psychologist, his primary tool in counseling is the Bible. He states, "The only tool that I really use in my own practice with people is the Bible." He continues, "As far as I'm concerned, I've found that the scriptures have been quite adequate for me in helping other people."[1] He advises counselors to use the Word of God like a scalpel to cut quickly through to the core of the person's problems (Heb 4:12). The Word is also a mirror that exposes the person's root problems and where they need to make changes (Jas 1:22–25).

Brandt states that it is not enough to have the Bible on your desk, or in your lap, or to even have verses written in a notebook. He states that the effective counselor has internalized the Word. He states, "If you're going be an effective counselor using the Bible, it's not just owning a Bible, but using it, and becoming familiar enough with it so that you have it in your head."[2] He advises using the Word as a lamp to guide the counselor as to how to best help people (Ps 119:105).

The Ultimate Counselor Is the Holy Spirit

When you need to counsel someone else, you do not have to go it alone. God has given you a marvelous resource—the Holy Spirit.

Billy Graham has noted, "Man has two great spiritual needs. One is forgiveness. The other is for goodness. . . . We need this two-sided gift God has offered us: first, the work of God the Son for us; second, the work of God the Spirit in us."[3]

Since the day of Pentecost in about AD 30, the Holy Spirit has been primary in God's work on planet earth. After a person is saved, the Holy Spirit is the most important person in their spiritual life. The Holy Spirit is their Spiritual Life-changer (Gal 5:22–23) and their Spiritual Gift-giver (1 Cor 12:4–11). Beyond that He is described as their Guide (Rom 8:14; 1 Thess 5:19), and Power-giver (Eph 3:16). Most importantly, He is their Counselor.

> And I will ask the Father, and He will give you another Counselor to be with you forever. . . . But the Counselor, the Holy Spirit—the Father will send Him in My name—will teach you all things and remind you of everything I have told you. (John 14:16,26)

When we counsel others, the Holy Spirit wants to use us to aid in the process that He is already working in the counselee's life. True Christian counseling is the work of the Holy Spirit. The Holy Spirit has to be the one convicting the person of the need to change and convincing them that the Bible reveals the right path to take.

Effective counseling cannot be done without the Holy Spirit. Therefore, the role of the counselor is simply to cooperate with the Holy Spirit as He works.

Beyond working in the counselee's life, the Holy Spirit also works in the counselor's life—giving them the spiritual guidance and spiritual power necessary to speak powerfully into the person's life. I suggest that as you listen to counselees share their struggle, you prayerfully petition the Holy Spirit to guide you to the right words to say, the right Scriptures to read, and the right prayers to pray.

The Power Behind Counseling Is Prayer

Prayer is a huge, yet often untapped, resource for the Christian counselor. The role of prayer in counseling takes several forms. First, the counselor should ask God for wisdom. This conversation or set of conversations could be used of God to radically change this person's life and future. As you recognize that God already wants to work in the counselee's life, it should encourage you to ask God for the wisdom you need to do your part (Jas 1:5).

It is not only important that the counselor pray for himself or herself to have the wisdom they need, they should also use prayer as a means of involving change in the life of the counselee. Pastor James told his scattered flock that praying for each other brought healing, wholeness, and deliverance to the needy person (Jas 5:14–16).

The Role of the Counselor Should Match the Need of the Person Being Helped

And we earnestly beseech you, brethren, admonish (warn and seriously advise) those who are out of line [the loafers, the disorderly, and the unruly]; encourage the timid and fainthearted, help and give your support to the weak souls, [and] be very patient with everybody [always keeping your temper]. (1 Thess 5:14 AMP)

In Paul's counsel to the Thessalonians, he reveals the diverse forms counseling may take. The sinful person needs to be warned and corrected. The struggling person should receive encouragement and challenge. The weak ones need support and comfort. Everyone needs patience.

Comfort the suffering spiritual friend. The goal of the comforter is to support the weak and help them gain a biblical view of suffering. Robert Kelleman suggests that such comfort involves listening to their story of suffering, communicating that *it's normal to hurt*, weeping with those who weep (Rom 12:15), and empathizing with the agony of living in a fallen world. Comforting includes stretching the sufferer to see the heavenly, eternal story, communicating that *it's possible to hope*, and encouraging people to find God in the midst of their suffering by looking at life with spiritual eyes (Gen 50:20).[4]

Warn and correct the sinful friend. The goal of the corrector is to help the counselee have a changed view of sin and disobedience. This new view of sin and disobedience should lead to a biblical response such as confession, restoration, reconciliation, and forgiveness. The corrector should confront the sinning brother or sister lovingly and humbly and then empower them to battle against besetting sins. Spiritual correction includes *helping* them own the fact that "it's horrible to sin, but wonderful to be forgiven." It involves empowering people to live out Christ's resurrection power to be victorious over the world, the flesh, and the Devil.

Encourage and challenge the struggling friend. One of Satan's favorite tools to render Christians ineffective is discouragement. Life is hard and unfair, people disappoint us, and the world is corrupt. The struggling Christian friend needs to be encouraged to see things from God's perspective and embrace eternal values.

Counsel and guide the confused. The person you are trying to help may need advice regarding handling their money, making a career decision, parenting their children, dealing with in-laws, or managing with stress.

The Foundation for Counseling Is Listening

Too frequently we view counseling as us talking. But in order to counsel effectively we must both talk *and* listen. Until the other person feels understood, they may not make the effort to listen and take the steps needed to change.

> Post this at all the intersections, dear friends: Lead with your ears, follow up with your tongue, and let anger straggle along in the rear. (Jas 1:19 MSG)

The counselee might not agree with what you shared, but initially this might not be as important as them walking away from their conversation with you feeling that you at least listened to what they had to say. Entry-level counsel is simply listening to the person share and praying for them.

It is very hard to be a good counselor if you are not fully attending to what the counselee is saying and feeling. Much of the time when people are speaking to us, our heads become filled with our own personal thoughts and agendas. We are so busy thinking how we are going to respond that we do not really hear what they are saying or note what they mean behind the words.

To listen well you must *look at them* while they are talking. You should try to fully engage with the words and the emotions they are expressing. You should also listen without thinking about how you are going to respond.

None of these things can be easily accomplished when you are listening to your own inner thoughts instead of fully focusing on the other person. You may not always be able to stop such thoughts from occurring, but you can learn to put them aside for the moment and focus your attention on the other person.

Get rid of the notion that you already know all you need to know about your counselee. Otherwise you will not discover what you do need to know. You probably know a lot less about them than you think you do. Open your own mind and look for the reasons behind the behavior, and you will take a big step toward connecting with their heart and giving them the right direction.

When people speak, they always reveal their deepest thoughts, ambitions, and concerns. Most of the time, neither the speaker nor the listener pick up on these subtle, underlying issues, but they are always there. Good counselors attend to these background, unspoken emotions and concerns. By noticing them and empathizing with them (either verbally or nonverbally) the other person feels heard.

The Atmosphere for Counseling Is the Body of Christ

I earned my undergraduate degree in biblical pastoral counseling. The key passage of Scripture we used in my program was one of Paul's admonitions to the church in Rome.

> Personally I am satisfied about you, my brethren, that you yourselves are rich in goodness, amply filled with all [spiritual] knowledge and *competent to admonish and counsel* and instruct one another also. (Rom 15:14 AMP, italics added)

As a young pastor, I felt competent to counsel because of my degree in biblical pastoral counseling and because I had invested a great deal of time studying the Scriptures related to people's common problems. So, I spent hours upon hours a week counseling people.

After a few years of doing so much counseling, I was getting burned out. I happened to be re-reading Rom 15:14 and realized something I had forgotten. Paul wrote Rom 15:14 to the saints who lived in Rome (Rom 1:1). He is stating that every mature Christian who has been equipped with the Word of God is "competent to counsel" others in the body of Christ. The counseling of those in the body of Christ was to be done by the body of Christ, not just the pastors and not just the trained counselors.

Paul's exhortation to the Thessalonians to adapt their approach to fit the need of the person was written to all the "brethren" in Thessalonica (1 Thess 5:14), not just the pastors and not just the trained counselors. Biblically, counsel is not the exclusive domain of the highly trained, or highly gifted, highly educated specialists. It can be done by the body of Christ.

Obviously there are some situations and issues that are beyond the expertise of the average Christian and require the help of someone who is a trained counselor.[5] But we miss the message of the Scriptures if we relegate all counseling to the experts. Clearly, in most cases, the body of Christ has the ability to minister effectively by encouraging and edifying one another (1 Thess 5:11).

Larry Crabb is a well-known clinic psychologist and serves as Professor and Distinguished Scholar in Residence at Colorado Christian University. He is a recognized authority on counseling and the Christian life. Crabb, after years of doing clinic counseling and training biblical counselors, writes in his book *Connecting,*

> We have made a terrible mistake! For most of this century we have wrongly defined soul wounds as psychological disorders and delegated their treatment to trained specialists. Damaged psyches aren't the problem. The problem is disconnected souls. What we need is connection! What we need is a healing community![6]

Crabb, the psychologist and biblical counselor, sees the healing value of community as an essential system of pastoral care. He sees community as the missing ingredient in healing soul wounds. Crabb's view indicates that a functional small-group ministry is an essential effective pastoral care system.

The Vehicle for Encouragement Is the Small Group

Solomon, the world's wisest man, pointed out the numerous benefits of interdependence. Greater accomplishment, help, warmth, and support are more accessible to those in community that to those outside of it.

> It's better to have a partner than go it alone. Share the work, share the wealth. And if one falls down, the other helps, But if there's no one to help, tough! . . . By yourself you're unprotected. With a friend you can face the worst. Can you round up a third? A three-stranded rope isn't easily snapped. (Eccl 4:9–12 MSG)

When I realized that the New Testament points out the ability of mature Christians to counsel and encourage each other effectively through most situations, I began to notice something: The people in our church family who were living in community and connectivity through regular involvement in a healthy small group were *not* the people with whom I was spending most of my time counseling. The people who came in for counseling were mostly people who were not involved in small groups.

So the next few years we focused most of our equipping ministries toward giving our small-group leaders better training. We taught them to listen. We gave them insights into the common counseling issues and how to walk people through them scripturally. We taught them to pray for others more effectively.

We showed how to engage the other members of the group more effectively in ministering to each other.

We also focused a great deal of energy on getting everyone in our church involved in a small-group. We began to let people know that pastoral care starts with small group involvement. I took myself off the pedestal as the trained professional counselor and elevated the power of community in small groups.

A funny thing happened. Even though our church grew, our pastoral counseling load declined. Many issues were headed off before they became serious problems as the body ministered to itself through the connected community of healthy small groups.

The reality is that most people dealing with most issues need some spiritual friends more than they need intense therapy. A healthy small group has the power to create community and connectedness. True connectedness to others in the body of Christ produces health and healing. People are helped through stressful, painful situations by participating in life with others as they get to really know them, feel their hurts, share their joys, and encourage their hearts.

⚊ What Now? ⚊

Have you ever enjoyed the benefits of good Christian community? Are you currently linked to others in a small group that gathers regularly? If not, why not, and what will you do about it?

How can you shift your church to take better advantage of the power of the body of Christ to encourage, support, strengthen, and heal itself? How can you better equip your small-group leaders to provide basic Christian counseling by obeying 1 Thess 5:11,14?

⚊ Quotes ⚊

No Christian can grow strong and stand the pressures of this life unless he is surrounded by a small group of people who minister to him and build him up in the faith.

—CHARLES COLSON[7]

God chose to embed in us a distinct kind of DNA. God created us all with a "communal gene," an inborn, intentional, inescapable part of what it means to be human. . . . This relational DNA or "community gene" helps explain

*why churches need small groups. People don't come to church
simply to satisfy spiritual needs. They come internally wired
with a desire for connection. . . . Their hunger for togetherness
is an inescapable mark of humanity.*

— BILL DONAHUE AND RUSS ROBINSON[8]

Notes

1. Henry Brandt, "Applying God's Word in Counseling," *Biblical Counseling Insights*, http://biblicalcounselinginsights.com/blog/2010/04/applying-gods-word-in-counseling/#more-932 (accessed July 4, 2011).

2. Ibid.

3. Billy Graham, *The Holy Spirit: Activating God's Power in Your Life* (Nashville, TN: Thomas Nelson, 2000), xi.

4. Robert Kelleman, "How to Care Like Christ," www.rpmministries.org (accessed February 12, 2009).

5. Often an equipped lay person can help another person with ordinary struggles with anger, anxiety, bitterness, boundaries, burnout, conflict resolution, discouragement, fear, financial bondage, grief, guidance, self-esteem, singleness issues, worry, and providing accountability for ordinary lust or anger issues. However, it is usually wise to turn to professional Christian counselors when the other person is facing issues of addictions (alcohol, drug, gambling, and sex addictions), overcoming severe sexual or physical abuse, bipolar disorder, cutting, eating disorders, suicidal thoughts, panic attacks, obsessive compulsive disorder, hoarding, gender identity issues, phobias, and traumatic stress disorder.

6. Lawrence Crabb, *Connecting* (Nashville, TN: Word, 1997), 6.

7. Charles Colson, *Kingdoms in Conflict* (Grand Rapids, MI: Zondervan, 1987), 47.

8. Bill Donahue and Russ Robinson, *Building a Church of Small Groups* (Grand Rapids, MI: Zondervan, 2001), 24.

28

Resolving
Conflict

Be at peace with one another. (Mark 9:50)
Live in harmony with one another. (Rom 12:16 NIV)
Blessed are the peacemakers,
for they will be called children of God. (Matt 5:9 NIV)

A few years ago, I surveyed a group of twenty-five successful, veteran pastors who were leading a variety of healthy churches. I asked a few simple questions. One of the questions was, "Please list the three things you did not learn in seminary, but wish you had." I was surprised that there was one response given by all of them: *Learning to resolve conflict effectively.*

Most pastors leave a church because of unresolved conflict. One seasoned church consultant told me that he discovered that, regardless of the size of the church, once a pastor has seven cases of unresolved conflict, the stress of the pastorate increases to the level that he feels the need to leave.

Biblical pastoral leadership requires getting along with others and helping others get along with each other. Effective pastoral leadership is often about resolving conflict and making peace.

The Truth about Conflict

Conflict Is Inevitable

If two people are around each other very long, conflict will result. We are all different. We have unique personalities, tastes, habits, preferences, experiences, passions, and ways of looking at and navigating life. These distinctions create differences. Beyond that, most of us live at a very fast pace which naturally creates friction. Plus we live in a fallen world and have fallen natures. The world throws us stressful situations and painful circumstances. We are not always at our best all the time. As a result, conflicts arise. Someone feels misunderstood, wronged, denied, or unappreciated.

As relationships start, they are usually built upon three factors. First, there are the things we have in common. Second, there are the things about us that are different, yet complementary. Third, there are the things that are different, but *not* complementary. The third factor causes friction.

No matter how deeply a man and woman love each other, no matter how long two friends have known each other, no matter how mature two Christians are in spiritual matters, they will eventually have conflict in that third area. It is unrealistic to expect otherwise.

Conflict That Goes Unresolved Devastates Relationships

Conflict in and of itself is not a problem. It is neutral—neither bad nor good. The badness or goodness of conflict all depends on how we respond to it. If we fail to make peace effectively, our relationships will suffer.

Unresolved conflict is the ugly white elephant and lethal cancer in too many of our failed relationships. Unhandled conflict will eventually erode the joy, rob the peace, and shred the commitments from our relationships.

Conflict Is an Assignment, Not an Accident

Ken Sande is the founder of Peacemaker Ministries. He joined with a group of pastors, lawyers, and business people who wanted to encourage and assist Christians to respond to conflict biblically. As part of the peacemaker's pledge, he states that "conflict is an assignment, not an accident."[1]

Our sovereign God might not necessarily create conflicts, but He often allows them to arise in our relationships for our good and His ultimate glory. Therefore, we need to realize that conflict is always an opportunity.

Conflict can either be very destructive or very beneficial, depending on how it is handled. Every conflict we experience has great potential. When handled well, conflict can make us better people, give us stronger relationships, and glorify God.

Jesus applauded peacemakers. In His teachings on true happiness He said that peacemaking is an opportunity for us to discover ourselves and our place in God's family, experience deeper personal satisfaction, and reflect the image of God.

Blessed are the peacemakers, for they will be called children of God. (Matt 5:9 NIV)

Jesus also prayed for peacemakers. In the agonizing prayer He offered to His Father just hours before dying on the cross, Jesus prayed that His followers would become peacemakers and thereby experience true unity.

I pray not only for these, but also for those who believe in Me through their message. May they all be one. (John 17:20–21)

Conflict is a necessary part of close relationships. It is always an opportunity to grow and to glorify God. Learn to view it as an assignment, not an accident.

Conflict Does Not Resolve Itself

The path of least resistance is not the solution to relational conflicts. Some, when faced with conflict, try avoiding it entirely. Pretending that conflict does not exist, however, does not solve the situation and will ultimately only make matters worse.

Others acknowledge conflict exists, but refuse to take action. This only accelerates and compounds problems (Gen 16:1–6; 1 Sam 2:22–25).

Still others try to escape conflict by ending the relationship, quitting the job, filing for divorce, or changing churches (Gen 16:6–8). Their world gets smaller and smaller as they bail out of every relationship when it starts getting difficult.

Conflict Cannot Be Ignored

Conflict must be courageously addressed. Jesus made it clear. You cannot have a bad relationship with people and maintain a good relationship with God. Your horizontal, human relationships impact your vertical, spiritual relationship with God. Jesus told His followers that attempts at making peace would need to be taken *before* they could freely and fully worship God. In fact, He even said that their vertical worship of God was to be immediately halted until attempts were made to resolve a personal conflict with someone else. Only then could they return to worship God.

So if you are offering your gift on the altar, and there you remember that your brother has something against you, leave your gift there in front of the altar. First go and be reconciled with your brother, and then come and offer your gift. (Matt 5:23–24)

Jesus taught us that there comes a point when action must be taken whether we are the offender or the offended. If we are the offender, we are to interrupt our worship in order to go and make things right. In the same way, if we are the offended because someone has significantly hurt us, we are obligated to go to them privately, share with them how they have hurt us, and seek resolution to this conflict.

If your brother sins against you, go and rebuke him in private. If he listens to you, you have won your brother. (Matt 18:15)

Putting these two passages together, it becomes clear that conflict must not be ignored. Whether we are the offender (Matt 5:23–34) or the offended (Matt 18:15) we are to take the initiative to make peace. Ideally, both parties are to meet in the middle as they run to each other to make things right.

Conflict Must Be Handled Wisely

Conflict is inevitable, so the issue is not *if* you will have conflicts in your relationships—you will. The issue is *how* you will handle the conflicts when they arise. People with good relationships handle conflict wisely. People with poor relationships do not. Successful relationships are the result of making peace without leaving scars. Good relationships result from learning to fight fair.

Let's think in terms of marriages. All couples fight. Good couples fight clean. Bad couples fight dirty. Research indicates that "being in love" is a very poor indicator of marital happiness and success. Far more important to the successful survival of a marriage is how well couples handle disagreements.

Unwise Ways to Handle Conflict

After more than twenty years of studying conflict, John Gottman has found a reliable way to track a relational breakdown based on how the people handle conflict. He has observed four escalating stages of dealing with conflict which he calls "the Four Horsemen of the Apocalypse."[2] They mark disastrous ways of interacting. I have found that these are true not only in marriage, but in all relationships.

1. Criticism

There is a difference between a legitimate complaint and an unnecessary criticism. A complaint can serve as a positive step toward resolving a conflict, but criticism only makes the conflict worse. A complaint is objective and attacks a problem, while a criticism is subjective and attacks the other person. A complaint focuses on the other person's behavior, while a criticism focuses on their personality.

According to relationship experts Les and Leslie Parrot, "As a general rule, criticism entails blaming, making a personal attack or an accusation, while a complaint is a negative comment about something you wish were otherwise. Complaints usually begin with the word *I* and criticisms with the word *You*."

2. Contempt

Unresolved issues fester and turn toxic. They are like a spreading cancer as mild irritation becomes outright contempt. One member of the relationship insults and psychologically abuses the other. Everything good in the relationship is overwhelmed by the contemptible acid of name-calling, hostile humor, and mockery.

3. Defensiveness

Conflicts are resolved when people take responsibility for their part of the problem. When criticism and contempt enter the scene, defensiveness arises. Walls are erected to protect, rather than bridges built to connect.

4. Stonewalling

Worn down by attacks, one member in the relationship will shut down and stop responding. The very act of nonresponse conveys arrogant disapproval, distance, and distrust.

Once these four negative responses to conflict become normal, the relationship becomes very fragile at best. The best scenario is to never start down this ugly path, but rather learn to handle conflict wisely and make peace.

Wise Ways to Handle Conflict

Overlook

Most things probably aren't worth fighting about. Les and Leslie Parrot tell married couples that 90 percent of the issues they bicker about can be overlooked.[3] The Bible lauds the wisdom of learning to overlook small irritations.

> Good sense makes a man restrain his anger, and it is his glory to overlook
> a transgression or an offense. (Prov 19:11 AMP)

A fool's displeasure is known at once, but whoever ignores an insult is sensible. (Prov 12:16)

If you are going to get upset about something, make sure it is worth getting upset about—because if you choose to get upset over it, you must act responsibly to resolve it. So pick your battles wisely.

To start a conflict is to release a flood; stop the dispute before it breaks out. (Prov 17:14)

Often the solution is to choose to be the bigger person and to love without conditions. Sometimes it is a matter of choosing to extend the same undeserved forgiveness to the other person that the Lord has extended to you.

Above all, keep your love for one another at full strength, since love covers a multitude of sins. (1 Pet 4:8)

Regarding overlooking an offense, Ken Sande writes,

As a general rule, an offense should be overlooked if you can answer "no" to all of the following questions. If you answer "yes" to any of these questions, an offense is too serious to overlook.
- Is the offense seriously dishonoring God?
- Has it permanently damaged a relationship?
- Is it seriously hurting other people?
- Is it seriously hurting the offender himself?[4]

Get the Log Out of Your Eye

Jesus warned us against trying to resolve conflict without first examining ourselves and taking responsibility for our part in the problem.

Why do you look at the speck in your brother's eye but don't notice the log in your own eye? Or how can you say to your brother, "Let me take the speck out of your eye," and look, there's a log in your eye? Hypocrite! First take the log out of your eye, and then you will see clearly to take the speck out of your brother's eye. (Matt 7:3–5)

Regarding "logs" Ken Sande writes,

There are generally two kinds of "logs" you need to look for when dealing with conflict. First, you need to ask whether you have had a critical, negative, or overly sensitive attitude that has led to unnecessary conflict . . . The second kind of log you must deal with is actual sinful words and actions. Because you are often blind to your own sins, you may need an honest friend or advisor who will help you to take an objective look at yourself and face up to your contribution to a conflict.[5]

We must resist blaming others for a conflict, but rather take responsibility for our own contribution to conflicts. We should confess our sins to those we have wronged. We must ask God to help us change any attitudes and habits that lead to conflict. We must take the initiative to repair any harm we have caused.

Make Peace

Some things just cannot be overlooked. The hurt is too real and the offense too damaging. At this point, as we have seen earlier in this chapter, the wise person will courageously take action to resolve the conflict and make peace (Matt 5:23–24; 18:15).

When you feel a conflict arising, it is wise to ask yourself if it really is worth fighting over. If it is, define the issue clearly and share your feelings directly. Be careful to make an objective complaint instead of a personal criticism.

Later in Matthew's Gospel, Jesus provided three important aspects of making peace.

> If your brother wrongs you, go and show him his fault, between you and him privately. If he listens to you, you have won back your brother. (Matt 18:15 AMP)

Take action. "If your brother wrongs you, go." Approach the other person; do not avoid them. It seems easier to do nothing but pout. But Jesus said that letting your resentment fester is unacceptable.

Keep it private. ". . . between you and him privately." Conflict should be dealt with privately if possible. Some people will not go to the ones who offend them to try to make peace. Instead, they go to someone else who is not a part of the conflict and tell how the other person has hurt them. This is wrong on many levels. First, it only deepens resentment toward the offender.

Second, it slanders the offender to the third party and gives them a negative view of the offender. It also puts them in a difficult position, especially if they are the offender's friend or family member.

Third, if the offender finds out that they have been talked about behind their back, it will make it more difficult to make peace with them.

Fourth, God's command to "make peace" is being disobeyed.

Fifth, the problem is still not resolved.

Be sensitive. No one wants to be called out in front of someone else. Approach the other person as you would want to be approached.

Seek restoration. "Show him his fault." We must not pretend that conflict doesn't exist or talk about others behind their backs. Instead, we are to go to the other person privately in an attempt to seek reconciliation. Regarding restoration, Ken Sande offers nine things to remember when facing conflict.

- Pray for humility and wisdom.
- Plan our words carefully (think of how you would want to be confronted).
- Anticipate likely reactions and plan appropriate responses (rehearsals can be very helpful).
- Choose the right time and place (talk in person whenever possible).
- Assume the best about the other person until you have facts to prove otherwise (Prov 11:27).
- Listen carefully (Prov 18:13).
- Speak only to build others up (Eph 4:29).
- Ask for feedback from the other person.
- Recognize your limits (only God can change people; see Rom 12:18; 2 Tim 2:24–26).[6]

Train Your People to Resolve Conflict

Cathy and I started a church with ten other people. One of the most amazing things about our church was that all ten of us were still serving together fourteen years later. One of the primary reasons for this was that we tried to practice the principles discussed in this chapter.

A second astounding aspect of our church was that in the first twenty years of our existence, we did not have a split or even a splinter. Of course, a random person here and there got their feelings hurt and left. Because we tried to teach our people to handle conflict biblically, there was never a big division. What is also interesting is that when a family left, they often returned a few years later because the other situations they found were not what they thought they would be.

— What Now? —

Instead of accepting premature compromise or allowing relationships to wither, we must actively pursue genuine peace and reconciliation. This includes forgiving others as God, for Christ's sake, has forgiven us. It also involves seeking just and mutually beneficial solutions to our differences.

Notes

1. Ken Sande, "The Peacemakers Pledge," http://www.peacemaker.net/site/c.aqKFLTOBIpH/b.958159/k.A440/Peacemakers_Pledge.htm (accessed June 1, 2011). The Peacemaker website gives many helpful tips for conflict resolution. For more details, I suggest that you read Ken Sande's *The Peacemaker* (Grand Rapids, MI: Baker, 2004).

2. John M. Gottman and Nan Silver, *The Seven Principles for Making Marriages Work* (New York: Three Rivers, 1999), 25–46.

3. See Les and Leslie Parrott, *Saving Your Marriage Before It Starts: Seven Questions to Ask Before (and After) You Marry* (Grand Rapids, MI: Zondervan, 2009), 132.

4. Ken Sande, "The Four G's," http://www.peacemaker.net/site/c.aqKFLTOBIpH/b.958149/k.303A/The_Four_Gs.htm (accessed June 1, 2011).

5. Ibid.

6. Ibid.

29

Pastoral Leadership Is . . .

Celebrating
the Ordinances

A s pastors, we have been given a sacred stewardship of preaching the gospel
(2 Tim 1:10–11). The word "gospel" simply means "good news." When
the Bible speaks of the gospel, it is speaking of truly the best news ever given:
*God's son, Jesus the Christ, died for our sins, was buried, and rose again so we
can be forgiven and experience an eternal relationship with God* (see 1 Cor
15:1–4).

The gospel is the power of God unto salvation (Rom 1:16). The gospel
is what must be preached so people can believe and call upon the Lord to be
saved (Rom 10:13–16). Preaching the gospel produces spiritual children (1 Cor
4:15) and spiritual fruit (Col 1:6). The gospel is eternal (Rev 14:6). The gospel
is a message so powerful and a treasure so valuable that it is worth it to endure
great opposition and suffering in order to share (Eph 6:19–20; 1 Thess 2:2;
2 Tim 1:8; Phlm 13).

Obviously, the wise pastor looks for the best ways to preach the gospel.
One of the best ways is through celebration of the two church ordinances:
Baptism and the Lord's Table. An ordinance means that these practices were
ordained, or set apart, as significant and sacred by the Lord. Both are symbolic reminders and clear object lessons of the gospel. An ordinance is a church
ceremony to be observed to honor Jesus, preach the gospel, and to build our
commitment to Him.

Preach the Gospel by Celebrating the Lord's Table

In 1 Corinthians 11, Paul gives us the most extensive teaching in the Bible on the subject of celebrating the Lord's Table. The section of verses 23–26 is so significant that the pastor should commit it to memory.

> For I received from the Lord what I also passed on to you: on the night when He was betrayed, the Lord Jesus took bread, gave thanks, broke it, and said, "This is My body, which is for you. Do this in remembrance of Me." In the same way [He] also [took] the cup, after supper, and said, "This cup is the new covenant in My blood. Do this, as often as you drink it, in remembrance of Me." For as often as you eat this bread and drink the cup, you proclaim the Lord's death until He comes. (1 Cor 11:23–26)

The Lord's Table was established by Jesus as part of the Last Supper. Paul opens this section by setting the context and showing us the importance of celebrating the Lord's Table as he writes, "For I received from the Lord what I also passed on to you: *on the night when He was betrayed*" (v. 23, italics added). Jesus instituted the ordinance of the Lord's Table on the night of the Last Supper. As He was observing the Passover with His disciples, Jesus took bread and a cup and used them to create an ongoing object lesson about the significance of His death and resurrection for our sins.

The Lord's Table or Lord's Supper is the name given it in the Bible. In his lengthy discussion of the protocol surrounding observing an ordinance with a bread and cup, Paul refers to it as "the Lord's Table" or "the Lord's Supper" (1 Cor 10:21; 11:20). Traditionally, it has taken on other names. Many call it "Communion." Some call it "the Eucharist," which is a word that means "thanksgiving." Catholics call it "Mass." The Bible only calls it "the Lord's Table" or "the Lord's Supper."

The Lord's Table is a sacred reminder of Jesus' sacrifice, not a re-sacrifice of Jesus. Paul quotes Jesus as saying, "This is My body, which is for you. Do this in remembrance of Me" (1 Cor 11:24). Peter states that "Christ died for sins *once*" (1 Pet 3:18 NIV). The Bible is very clear that the death of Jesus on the cross was sufficient. On the cross, Jesus Himself cried, "It is finished!" His death was God's masterpiece of reconciliation. It cannot be added to by our good works, and it does not need to be repeated by a priest holding a piece of bread in the air.

The Lord's Table is symbolic, not literal. Some teach that during the ceremony the bread and cup literally *become* the body and blood of Jesus. I think that is why they will not allow anyone but a priest to even touch the cup. Others teach that Jesus does not become the bread and cup, but He is somehow *uniquely present* in and around them. Others teach that Jesus is somehow *spiritually present* in the bread and the cup.

This all sounds nice and mystical, but it does not make sense. At the Last Supper, Jesus was not turning the bread into His literal body, but He was using it in a purely symbolic fashion. Remember what Paul said, "For as often as you eat this bread and drink the cup, you proclaim the Lord's death until He comes" (1 Cor 11:26).

Notice that He says, "eat *this* bread and drink *the cup*." Notice that He does not say, "eat this *body* and drink the *blood*." Clearly, He was trying to teach them a lesson and was using the bread and cup as object lessons.

Celebrating the Lord's Table is an opportunity to examine ourselves to be sure that nothing is hindering our communion with Christ and His body. In His discussion of the protocol surrounding the celebration of the Lord's Table, Paul issues a strong warning.

> Therefore, whoever eats the bread or drinks the cup of the Lord in an unworthy way will be guilty of sin against the body and blood of the Lord. So a man should examine himself; in this way he should eat of the bread and drink of the cup. (1 Cor 11:27–28)

Celebrating the Lord's Table is a chance to take the time to deeply examine oneself. It is a serious time to confess every sin and turn from them. It is a wonderful opportunity and excuse to get really clean and right before God.

The frequency of celebrating the Lord's Table is not specifically demanded by Scripture, but its perpetuity is. We know the early church initially met daily (Acts 2:46) and eventually placed its primary meeting on the first day of the week—Sunday (1 Cor 16:2). Nowhere in the Bible does it say we have to celebrate the Lord's Table daily, weekly, monthly, or whatever. That is not the point. The point is that we do it with regularity, but also that it does not become a mindless, meaningless routine.

Celebrating the Lord's Table is a powerful act of remembering what the Lord did for us on the cross. Paul wrote, "This cup is the new covenant in My blood. Do this, as often as you drink it, in *remembrance* of Me" (1 Cor 11:25, italics added). The celebration of the Lord's Table is an opportunity to *remember* Jesus and what He has done for us through His death and resurrection. The concept of "remember" means to go in one's mind and recapture the reality and significance of the event as best one can. When the church celebrates the Lord's Table, we are powerfully reminded of the Lord's death. We should actively remember it in song, in words, in prayers, in the bread and cup, and in pictures.

Celebrating the Lord's Table is a proclamation of His death, resurrection and return. Paul wrote, "For as often as you eat this bread and drink the cup, you proclaim the Lord's death *until He comes.*" We do serve a *risen* savior and a *living* God. We are to live each day in active anticipation of His return.

Celebrating the Lord's Table challenges us to look *inward* and deal with our sin. It is a call to look *outward* as to our responsibility to proclaim the gospel to others. But it is also a reminder that we must be living each day looking *forward* and *upward* with our eyes on eternity, actively anticipating the fact that Jesus is coming again.

Leading the church in celebrating the Lord's Table is a wonderful privilege and solemn responsibility of the pastoral leader. When it comes to the actual process of how to celebrate the Lord's Table, there is no one right way to do it. However you choose to do it, do it with a sense of honor and joyous seriousness.

In the early church and in house churches today, it may simply be a matter of the pastor shifting people's attention from enjoying a fellowship meal to remembering Jesus. This could be done with a few statements and a recalling of the Scriptures, primarily (1 Cor 11:23–28). The bread could be distributed with a short season of examination. Afterward, the cup could be passed around with a time of thanks.

Many churches pass trays of little crackers of bread and little plastic or glass cups of juice around the auditorium. Some have people come forward to a table and serve themselves. Others ask people to get up and go to a couple in the aisle of the auditorium who are holding the cup and bread.

You may choose to celebrate the Lord's Table in connection with instruction about the Passover. You may occasionally choose to precede the Lord's Table with a time of foot washing.

It is wise to make the celebration of the Lord's Table the central part of the service. Every song that is sung, Scripture that is read, and word that is said points to Jesus. You can use banners, unique lighting, video clips, dramatic presentations, and even concerts to get people's attention focused squarely on the cross. You can celebrate it in connection with a strong evangelistic message and invitation or with long, solemn seasons of confession. You can celebrate linked with joyous music and Jewish dance. As I said before, there is no one prescribed method for doing it. However you choose to do it, everyone involved should have a strong sense of serious respect linked with grateful joy.

Preach the Gospel through Baptism

Believer's baptism is a picture of the gospel. The first church ordinance is the Lord's Table, and the second church ordinance is baptism. Like the Lord's Table, baptism by immersion clearly symbolizes the gospel by picturing the death, burial, and resurrection of Jesus for our sins. Believer's baptism is a public confession of faith in Jesus Christ and the expression of desire to fully follow Him.

Baptism is a very important part of church life. In the passage of Scripture we call the Great Commission, Jesus commanded the church to baptize those who desired to become His followers.

> Therefore go and make disciples of all nations, *baptizing them* in the name of the Father and of the Son and of the Holy Spirit. (Matt 28:19 NIV, italics added)

At the close of the first sermon ever given to the first church gathering in history, Peter commanded those who wanted to become Christ followers to be baptized. And three thousand were.

> When the people heard this, they were cut to the heart and said to Peter and the other apostles, "Brothers, what shall we do?" Peter replied, "Repent and *be baptized*, every one of you, in the name of Jesus Christ for the forgiveness of your sins. . . . Those who accepted his message *were baptized*, and about three thousand were added to their number that day. (Acts 2:37–41, italics added)

Baptism is a confession of allegiance to Jesus before others. Jesus said that if we want Him to acknowledge us, we need to acknowledge Him before others (Luke 12:8). What is the clearest way to acknowledge Jesus? One answer is public baptism.

Paul equated willingness to identify publicly with Jesus as the indication of salvation (Rom 10:9). When baptized, the person being baptized is making a public confession of Jesus as Lord.

Of course, baptism alone does not save a person from sin. Baptism is an outward sign of an inward commitment. Without the commitment, the sign has no meaning. Just as a wedding ring is an outward symbol of an inner commitment to be faithful to another in marriage, baptism is an outward symbol of an inner commitment to follow Lord Jesus. Without the commitment to the mate, the wedding ring is just a piece of metal. Without the commitment to Jesus, baptism is just getting wet.

Baptism is a ceremony of identification. Believer's baptism is a ceremony of identification through immersion in water. It identifies the one being baptized in two ways. First, baptism shows *identification with the church.*

> Those who accepted his message were baptized, and about three
> thousand were *added to their number* that day. (Acts 2:41 NIV, italics
> added)

The group of 120 followers praying in the upper room (Acts 1:13–15) became a church of 3,120 on the day of Pentecost (Acts 2:47). Three thousand people were added to the church that day because they were baptized. From that point, they were identified with the church. This is why most churches require baptism as a prerequisite to membership.

Second, baptism shows *identification with Jesus* in His death, burial, and resurrection for our sins.

> We were therefore buried with him through baptism into death in order
> that, just as Christ was raised from the dead through the glory of the
> Father, we too may live a new life. (Rom 6:4 NIV)

Baptism by immersion pictures the death, burial, and resurrection of Jesus. When someone is immersed, they are laid down in the water, or in other words, they are buried in the water. Resurrection is pictured as they are brought up out of the water. Every time someone is baptized, they symbolize the death, burial, and resurrection of Jesus that paid for sin. Baptism also reminds us that when we get saved, we, in a sense, die to the type of life we were living prior to salvation and have been born again to a new life with Jesus as Lord.

Baptism means immersion. The word translated in our English Bible as "baptize" is the Greek word *baptizo*, which means to "immerse" or "dip."

Recently, Cathy and I were in Greece visiting the cities of Paul's second missionary journey. The first church on European soil was begun in the city of Philippi. The oldest church building discovered in Europe is in the agora of ancient Philippi. Our guide showed us that the baptistry of this ancient building dedicated entirely for church use was not an elevated bowl, but a fairly large pool. There were several steps leading down into the water and steps leading up out of the water. This means that if you were an early church Christian in Philippi, you were baptized by immersion.

The baptisms in the Bible were by immersion. The first baptism we see in the New Testament is the baptism of Jesus. Matthew writes, "As soon as Jesus was baptized, *he went up out of the water*" (Matt 3:16 NIV, italics added). Why did Jesus have to come *up out of the water* when He got baptized? Obviously,

He came up out of the water because He had been immersed down into the water.

Later we read of John the Baptizer's ministry. Note where he baptized: "John also was baptizing in Aenon near Salim, because there was plenty of water there" (John 3:23). Why did John need plenty of deep water? The answer is, he needed plenty of water because he was immersing the people he baptized.

In Acts 8, we have the beautiful story of the Ethiopian eunuch becoming a follower of Jesus. He was in the desert riding in a chariot talking with Philip and decided he was ready to become a follower of Jesus. We read that "both Philip and the eunuch *went down into the water*, and he baptized him. . . . They *came up out of the water*" (Acts 8:38–39, italics added). Obviously, the man was baptized by immersion. Biblical baptism is by immersion in water. You have to be buried in the water to show your identification with the death, burial, and resurrection for sins. If you were not immersed, you have not been biblically baptized.

Baptism should occur after a person trusts in Christ as Savior. The scriptural accounts of people being baptized always show that they believed before they were baptized. For example, when the people of Samaria believed, they responded by being baptized. "But when they believed Philip, as he proclaimed the good news about the kingdom of God and the name of Jesus Christ, both men and women were baptized" (Acts 8:12). Belief preceded baptism.

When Saul of Tarsus was converted, his next step was to be baptized. The Scriptures tell us, "At once something like scales fell from his eyes, and he regained his sight. Then he got up and was baptized" (Acts 9:18). When the Lord opened the heart of Lydia and those in her household, they were baptized, marking them as believers in the Lord (Acts 16:14–15). When Crispus and other people of Corinth believed, they responded by being baptized immediately: "Crispus, the leader of the synagogue, believed the Lord, along with his whole household; and many of the Corinthians, when they heard, believed and were baptized" (Acts 18:8).

Leading the church in celebrating baptism is a wonderful privilege and solemn responsibility of the pastoral leader. One of the great privileges of being a pastor is baptizing people who have trusted Jesus as Savior and called upon Him as Lord. Most use a simple baptismal formula that gives conciseness and clarity to the baptism experience.

When the person comes down into the water, most pastors will introduce the person to the audience. They then ask the baptism candidate, "Have you trusted Jesus Christ as your personal Lord and Savior?"

After the person's favorable response, the pastor says the person's name and states, "Upon your profession of faith I baptize you in the name of the Father, Son, and Holy Spirit. . . ." As he says these words, he is lowering them backward into the water. Then he continues, "Buried in the likeness of His death . . ." When they are fully immersed, he brings them up out of the water while he says, "Raised to walk in newness of life."

When a church baptizes, it should be a joyous celebration. If heaven is rejoicing (Luke 15:7,10), why should not we? I have found it helpful to have the persons being baptized write a short testimony that will be read by someone at the microphone as they enter the baptismal tank to be immersed. You can also video their testimony and show it when they enter the water.

It is meaningful to have those who participated in the person coming to Christ be mentioned in the testimony, or invite them to join you on the platform, or even come in the water if you are baptizing in a pool, a river, or a Jacuzzi. This serves as a great reminder to the church of its obligation to continually preach the gospel.

— What Now? —

If you have never led a church in celebrating the Lord's Table, I suggest you commit 1 Cor 11:23–26 to memory. If you have never led a church in baptism, I suggest that you memorize the baptismal formula given in the immediately preceding section above ("Leading the church . . .").

If you are currently leading a church, use some of the ideas given and think of ways to more creatively and effectively celebrate the Lord Table and baptism.

30

Pastoral Leadership Is . . .

Doing Premarital Counseling and Weddings

Christian marriage is a sacred and significant occasion that demands and deserves serious and joyous preparation and celebration. The wise pastor will use this opportunity to help disciple the new couple, to strengthen their relationship with him and the church, and to provide a testimony to their friends and family. In order to do so, there are several aspects necessary for capitalizing on the wedding opportunity.

Pastoral Procedures Regarding Weddings

1. Determine the Eligibility of the Couple to Be Married

When a pastor is asked to officiate at the wedding, he should set up an appointment to meet with the couple prior to agreeing to perform the wedding in order to review the eligibility of the couple to be married.

Share the gospel. A surprising number of nonchurched persons would like to be married in a church building and/or by a pastor. Sitting down to discuss the wedding gives the pastor a great opportunity to share the gospel.

Discuss divorce and remarriage. In America, 50 percent of marriages end in divorce. If your church reaches nonchurched people, you will find that a surprising number of the people who want to use your facilities for their wedding and/or would like one of your pastors to perform their wedding have been divorced.

If it has not already, your church should adopt a clear policy on divorce and remarriage. The policy should clearly state what constitutes acceptable grounds for divorce and when it is acceptable for a divorced person to be remarried. Once adopted, this policy should be consistently followed.

Discuss the significance of purity and living together. A surprising number of persons who would like to be married in a church building and/or by a pastor are already living together. If the couple does not have children, you may ask them to live separately prior to marriage. Our church fortunately had a few widows with homes large enough and who viewed it as a ministry to take in an engaged young lady until the wedding.

When the couple has lived together a long time and there are children involved, a pastor might perform a private wedding in the church chapel or offices right away. A large public wedding ceremony for family and friends can be held later on.

Discuss financial viability. The couple seeking marriage should be able to stand on their own financially. If they do not have jobs and are living with their parents, they should wait to get married until they are ready "to leave father and mother and become one."

Discuss the importance of premarital counseling. For the couple, the next step after the eligibility meeting is premarital counseling. The pastor should use the eligibility meeting to excite and enlist the couple for premarital counseling.

2. Prepare the Couple for Marriage

Research shows that premarital counseling reduces the risk of divorce by up to 30 percent. A recent study reviewed twenty-three studies on the effectiveness of premarital counseling and found that the average couple who participates in premarital counseling reports a 30-percent stronger marriage than other couples.[1] *Make it a policy that you will not marry any couple that has not first been prepared through a time of premarital counseling.*

The premarital counseling should focus on the biblical basics of marriage, an explanation of the covenantal nature of Christian marriage, and how to put God first in a marriage. It should also include appreciating the differences between each other, showing love and respect to each other, and love banking. There should be information about romance and sex within marriage, affair-proofing the marriage, listening, and conflict resolution. The couple should also learn how to fight fair, budget, and how to handle finances. Before being married, a couple should discuss children and extended family issues. They should also discuss expectations, hobbies, marital roles, church involvement, and the significance of the components of the wedding ceremony.

Because of the necessary amount of information to be covered, I suggest you make use of some of the numerous books, workbooks, CDs, DVDs, and seminars available.[2] It is time efficient to put several engaged couples in the same class and cover the information together over a series of weeks. You can also enlist the help of a qualified counselor.

When my church was smaller, I did most of the premarital counseling. I had done a series of Bible-based sermons on marriage and had a packet of those messages put together. As part of their premarital counseling, each week the couple would listen to one of the messages before seeing me.

As our church grew, the number of people wanting to be married became overwhelming. We trained one of our other pastors to lead a class for engaged couples. We required that everyone wanting to use our facilities to be married or wanting to be married by one of our pastors had to successfully complete the class.

Some churches enlist and equip older couples to mentor the engaged couples through the premarital process and on through the first few years of marriage. Our church developed an entire section of small groups focused on various seasons of marriage. There were groups for engaged couples, newlyweds, couples with a new baby, blended families, and empty nesters.

It is wise to have a deacon, elder, church staff member, or pastor whose primary ministry responsibility is the health and well-being of your church's marriages. A wise pastor will use the occasion of a wedding and especially premarital counseling as a golden opportunity to mobilize his church to disciple couples at a level they would not have reached otherwise.

3. Plan the Wedding Ceremony

Your church should have a clear policy regarding all that is involved in having a wedding at your church. It should be written and readily available to the couple. It should include cost, appropriate fees for custodial care, media tech, wedding coordinator, premarital counseling materials, and pastoral fees. There should be a statement about the use of alcohol during the reception and any wedding reception restrictions. There should be information about the scheduling of the facilities, requisite meetings with the pastor performing the ceremony, and contact information regarding the wedding coordinator.

I highly suggest that you require any couple who wants to get married in your church's facilities to hire a church-approved wedding coordinator.

In essence, the couple pays the wedding coordinator a small fee to help them through the process and prepare them for a great wedding. The wedding coordinator is the couple's liaison to the church policy, staff, schedule, and facilities.

The church wedding coordinator is familiar with all of the facilities available to the wedding party and the church's wedding provisions (candelabras, kneeling bench, etc.). The wedding coordinator should be able to offer the bride lists of recommended photographers, caterers, and florists. She is aware of the church's policies concerning the use of such things as candles, appropriate music, photography, and the cleanup that is expected. She helps the couple prepare a detailed description of the mechanics involved in a wedding ceremony, such as where to stand, when to turn, how to usher, and so on.

4. Prepare to Rehearse the Ceremony

Before the wedding rehearsal, the pastor should *meet with the couple to review the rehearsal*. Require the couple to bring to this meeting a clear, detailed written description of the wedding ceremony as discussed by them and the church's wedding coordinator. During the meeting with the couple, the pastor will talk through each component of the ceremony.

After the meeting with the couple, the pastor should prepare his notes on his role in the wedding. Personalize your comments and message to fit this couple and this context.

5. Rehearse the Ceremony

When everyone who will participate in the wedding ceremony arrives, they should be handed a printed order of the wedding ceremony including instructions for each member. When they are all assembled, the pastor should stand, welcome everyone, and lead in prayer.

Have each person go around and very briefly introduce themselves by telling the relationship they have with the couple and their role in the ceremony.

Assemble everyone on the platform standing as they will be at the *end* of the wedding ceremony. Next, practice the recessional.

Then completely walk through the service, briefly practicing each component. Be sure the wedding coordinator notes any changes that come up.

Then quickly go through the ceremony again. This time incorporate any changes or details that surfaced during the first time through.

Regather the group. Stress the importance of being on time for the wedding. Close in prayer and give out directions to the rehearsal dinner.

6. Officiate at the Ceremony

Be there early. Touch base with the wedding coordinator to be sure everything is going as planned. Find the groom. Pray with him and encourage him as a soon-to-be husband.

As you lead the ceremony, realize that in the eyes of some of the guests, this may be one of their few introductions to Christianity and the church. Represent Jesus well. Lead the ceremony with joy and confidence.

Sample Wedding Ceremony

No particular wedding ceremony outline is given in the Bible, so we can choose to create a Christian wedding that reflects our individual tastes and creativity. There are several traditional components of a Christian wedding ceremony; however, it is not necessary to incorporate all of them in your wedding. Every bride likes to add to and rearrange these elements to fit her personality. However it is done, it should reflect worship, joy, celebration, respect, dignity, and love.

Prelude

As the guests arrive, they are seated by ushers on the side of either the bride or the groom. Last to be seated are honored guests such as the bride and groom's grandparent's, the groom's parents, and the bride's mother. Often the mothers of the bride and groom are ushered in and light the unity candles. They are then seated, the bride's mother last.

The pastor, groom, and his best man enter the front of the auditorium and await the bridal party. The bridesmaids are often ushered to the platform one at a time by the groomsmen. A flower girl and ring bearer also enter.

Last, the bride and her father enter. As they enter, the pastor may announce that all rise for the bride.

Welcome, Greeting, and Prayer

After the bride has arrived at the front, the pastor welcomes the audience.

You may be seated.

*Family and friends, we are gathered together here in the presence of
God, and in the company of these witnesses, to join together
_____ and _____ in Holy Matrimony.
Marriage is indeed an honorable estate. It is commended by God and*

to be honored by all men. Therefore, it is not by any to be entered into unadvisedly or lightly, but reverently in the fear of God. Let us therefore remember that God has established and sanctified marriage for the welfare and happiness of mankind. Marriage was instituted by God in the garden when He saw that it was "not good that man should be alone." God gave marriage its final crown of glory when He led the apostle Paul to liken it unto the mystical union that exists between Christ and His Church, in which Christ is called the Bridegroom, and His Church the Bride.

Of all the pictures given in the Bible of salvation, none is clearer than the picture painted by a marriage. In fact, we who know Christ will participate in that great event called The Marriage Supper of the Lamb. At this occasion, those who have trusted Christ on this earth will be wed to our Bridegroom, Jesus Christ. In Bible times, the groom needed to pay a price in order to receive the hand of his bride in marriage. In like manner, the Lord Jesus Christ shed His blood on the cross to pay the price for our sin. He died that we might live. He died that we might be wed to Him.

Several months ago, _____ asked _____ to be his bride. _____ could accept the invitation by committing her life to _____. In the same way, Christ has offered each of us the opportunity to be a part of His bride. The invitation is also accepted by committing our lives to Him.

Nothing would please _____ and _____ more than if you would commit (or recommit) your life to the Heavenly Bridegroom Jesus Christ today as a result of being at this wedding.

Let us pray . . .

Pastoral Charge to the Couple

_____ and _____, I charge you both as you stand in the presence of God to remember that Christian marriage is a sacred three-fold covenant. Today the two of your are covenanting with God to make an unconditional commitment of yourselves to each other and to God in the establishment of a God-honoring, Christian home. If you keep the commitments made today, God will bless your lives and new family.

Giving of the Bride

The pastor asks, *"Who gives this woman to be married to this man?"*
Her father replies, *"Her mother and I."*
Her father gives the bride a kiss and is seated. The bride and groom stand facing the pastor.

Scripture Reading:

Devotion to the Couple:

Exchange of Vows

The pastor to the bride and groom:

Since it is your desire to take each other as husband and wife, will you please indicate this desire by: (1) joining your hands and (2) repeating in this presence the marriage vow. And if married here today, let this be a renewal of those vows you made in the past.

To the groom:

Please repeat after me the vow that you are taking before God, these witnesses, and to your bride.

I, _____ take you, _____,/ to be my lawful, wedded wife,/ to have and to hold/ from this day forward,/ for better, for worse,/ for richer, for poorer,/ in sickness and in health,/ to love and to cherish,/ till death do us part/ and commit myself completely unto you.

To the bride:

Please repeat after me the vow that you are taking before God, these witnesses, and to your groom.

I, _____, take you, _____, to be my lawful, wedded husband, / to have and to hold/ from this day forward,/ for better, for worse,/ for richer, for poorer,/ in sickness and in health,/ to love and to cherish,/ till death do us part/ and commit myself completely unto you.

Ring Ceremony

Pastor to the couple:

What token do you bring as a pledge that you will faithfully perform your vows?

_____ *and* _____ *say, "Our rings."* Best man takes the rings from the ring bearer's pillow. Gives ring to Groom, who gives it to Pastor.

Pastor holds the ring and says the following:

The ring has long been the symbol of the sealing of important contracts. In the earlier history of man, the king wore a ring upon which was pressed the seal of the kingdom. With this ring he stamped the treaties of his land. But in more recent generations, the ring has been used to seal the marriage contracts. The wedding ring is an outward, visible sign of an inward and spiritual bond that unites two hearts in ongoing love. The circle of the ring reminds us of the constant nature of your loves, the circle having neither beginning nor end.

Pastor to the groom:

_____, *take this ring and place it upon the third finger of* _____ *left hand. As you do, you will give it to her because you love her, and she will wear it to show the world her love for you.*

Groom will repeat the vow as he holds the ring on her left index finger.

Pastor to the groom:

_____, *please repeat after me.*

With this ring,/ I thee wed,/ with all my worldly goods,/ I thee endow./ I pledge my love,/ and my loyalty forever./ To the glory of God.

Pastor to the bride:

_____, *take this ring and place it upon the third finger of* _____ *left hand. As you do, you will give it to him because you love him, and he will wear it to show the world his love for you.*

Bride will repeat the vow as she holds the ring on his left index finger.

Pastor to the bride:

_____, *please repeat after me.*

With this ring,/ I thee wed,/ with all my worldly goods/ I thee endow./ I pledge my love,/ and my loyalty forever./ To the glory of God.

Prayer of Confirmation

Bride and groom face each other and hold hands as the pastor places his hands on both of their hands and prays.

The Lighting of the Unity Candle

The two outside candles have been lighted to represent your lives up to this moment. They are two distinct lights, each capable of going its separate way. To bring joy and radiance into your home, there must be the merging of these two flames into one. From this time onward, may your thoughts be for each other rather than for your individual selves. May your plans be mutual, your joys and sorrows shared.

Each of you take a candle and together light the center one, thus having the center candle represent the union of your two lives into one flesh. As this center light cannot be divided, let not your marriage be divided, but instead be the united testimony of a Christian home, as Christ gives you light.

Pronouncement of Husband and Wife

By the authority committed unto me as a pastor of _____ Church, and for as much as _____ and _____ have consented together today in holy wedlock, have witnessed the same before God and before this company of witnesses, and have established the same by joining hands, exchanging vows, and the giving and receiving of a ring, I now pronounce you "husband and wife" according to the ordinance of God and the law of the state of _____.

You may now kiss the bride.

Let me be the first to introduce to you Mr. and Mrs. _____.

⁓ What Now? ⁓

If you have not already, you and/or your church should adopt a clear policy on divorce and remarriage.

If you have not already, you and/or your church should create a premarital counseling course.

If you have not already, you and/or your church should draft a policy regarding all that is involved in having a wedding at your church.

If you have not already, you should write a devotional that you can give to a couple during their wedding ceremony.

Notes

1. "Premarital Counseling Builds Better Union," *WebMD Health News*, http://women.webmd.com/news/20030404/premarital-counseling-builds-better-union (accessed July 4, 2011).

2. Because I was struggling to find a marriage book that covered all the areas from a biblical foundation, I wrote one: Dave Earley, *14 Secrets to a Better Marriage: Powerful Principles from the Bible* (Uhrichsville, OH: Barbour, 2011).

31
Conducting Funerals

If you surveyed ten pastors and asked them which they enjoyed more, nine out of ten would tell you they like conducting funerals better than performing weddings. This is because memorial services offer prime ministry opportunities.

The wise pastor can use the death of a loved one as a strategic time to bring genuine comfort to the family and encourage the church to do the same. He and his church can also enhance his relationship with them and with their non-churched friends and family members as well.

Most people today give very little thought to death and eternity. A funeral or memorial service is a golden opportunity to speak to people's hearts about these ultimate issues and to preach the gospel.

Pastoral Procedures Regarding Funerals

1. Contact the Family

From the moment you are notified of the death of one of your church members or one of their family members, you must immediately call the family. Express your sympathy and listen attentively. If they ask you to conduct the funeral ceremony, set a time when you can come by for a brief visit.

2. Mobilize the Church

Your church should have a plan for responding to a funeral. Flowers should be sent. Meals should be organized for the closest survivors. A meal can be offered for the family after the service memorial. The pastor need not do all of these things, but he should see that they get done. It is wise to have one person who is trained and ready to run point on these things.

3. Help the Family Understand the Grieving Process

Try to get all of the close family members in the same room at the same time. If not in one of their homes, you can do this an hour before the first viewing begins.

Introduce yourself to everyone in the family. Again offer your sympathy. Lead in prayer. Then briefly discuss the process of grieving. I usually say something like this:

> *Losing someone we love produces genuine pain and grief. While we have tears of joy, we also have tears of sorrow. Those who've walked this road know that grieving takes several forms and progresses through several stages. Going through these stages does not mean you are crazy; it means you are human. You will experience them. The closer you were to [the deceased] the more you will experience these stages. The goal is to experience the emotions and then move on. God will help you if you turn to Him.*
>
> *The first stage is shock, numbness, and/or denial. At this stage we have these types of thoughts: "I can't believe it." "It seems like a bad dream." "I feel numb." "It has not really sunk in yet."*
>
> *The second stage is often resentment and/or anger. Not everyone experiences anger as they grieve, but many do. It is not uncommon to find yourself overcome with a wave of anger. The anger can be projected in numerous directions: sickness, death, doctors, hospitals, funeral homes, your own siblings, and even God. The issue is not that we feel angry, but what we do with the anger—putting it into perspective and not staying angry.*
>
> *The third stage is loss, loneliness, sorrow, emptiness, and pain. After a loved one dies, we find ourselves wrestling with the reality that they are no longer physically here. This sense of loss may be most keenly felt on holidays, birthdays, and other occasions that the deceased would normally have attended. We hurt because a part of our lives is missing.*
>
> *The fourth stage is acceptance. You will have arrived at acceptance when you not only say, but deeply feel, these truths: (1) the loved one is*

gone; (2) they are with God; (3) being with God is a much, much better place; (4) my life must go on. I can honor the deceased by learning from this experience and living a much better life than before.

4. Ask the Family to Share Favorite Memories

I have found that the best moments surrounding the loss of a loved one are when the family members come together to share their favorite memories of the deceased. I tell them ahead of time to be ready and that I will use some of their memories in my memorial service message. After a few minutes of sharing memories, laughing, and crying together, the family really opens up to each other, to me, and to God. Much productive ministry occurs during this time.

5. Gather Information

At some point prior to the memorial service, you will need to gather helpful information. Often the funeral home will do much of this work for you. Below is a listing of the type of information you want to ask for.

- Name and contact information of the funeral home handling the arrangements
- Dates, times, and location of visiting hours
- Time and location of funeral service
- Time and location of gravesite service
- Information about the deceased
- Full name
- Preferred or nickname
- Date of birth
- Birthplace
- Date of death
- Location and cause of death
- Occupation
- Name of spouse
- Names of surviving siblings, children, grandchildren
- Education
- Church affiliation/involvement
- Community service
- Hobbies/interests
- Favorite Scripture

6. Plan the Memorial Service

Planning for the memorial service can be made during your visit with the family. Most families have not thought about it much, so do not be afraid to give clear direction and suggestions. Generally the service follows a simple outline such as the one given below:

- Song
- Opening comments
- Reading of pertinent information or from the obituary
- Prayer
- Scripture
- Message: Keep it brief, personal, and biblical. Be genuine and warm, but serious. Include the deceased's salvation testimony (if appropriate). The first half of the message can focus on the person who died. The second half can focus on the Word of God and the promises of God. Be certain to include the gospel. This may be the only opportunity some of those in the audience have to hear it. If the saint who is deceased was older, it is very powerful to bring a message on heaven.
- Invitation: As you speak, you can tell when God is opening people's hearts. Give them an opportunity to respond even if it is through looking you in the eye and nodding or raising their hand.
- Closing remarks. Include information about gravesite service and dinner when appropriate.

7. Other Observations and Advice

When the service is for a follower of Jesus, it should be treated as both a celebration of life and a graduation of the deceased. It should be upbeat and triumphant.

When the service is for a person who was not a follower of Jesus, the pastor should not act like it is. On the other hand, there is a possibility that they trusted Christ with their dying breaths. Therefore, be careful about preaching them into hell. The pastor should speak sincerely about the brevity of life, the certainty of death, and the need for a savior.

Prior to the funeral service, check in with the funeral home director so they know you are present.

Dress appropriately. In our culture, that usually means a dark suit and tie.

At the end of your message, personally greet and console the family members seated in the front row. Then stand by the side of the casket as the funeral director dismisses people from the back to the front to pay their final respects.

After everyone has paid their final respects, you will often be expected to stay in the room as the funeral director prepares the body for the closing of the casket.

Then you will wait there as the funeral director gathers the pall bearers. At this point, you will lead the casket to the hearse.

Then you will go to your car and wait to proceed behind the hearse in the caravan to the gravesite. At the gravesite, the funeral director will wait until everyone arrives. He or she will then expect you to lead the pall bearers as the casket is carried from the hearse to the grave.

After everyone is gathered near the tent, you will give a very brief gravesite service. This includes a Scripture reading, pertinent comments, and a prayer of committal of the soul to God and of the body to the earth. Afterward you can again console family members and assure them of your availability.

It may be extremely beneficial to visit the family a few days after the service. Also, consider mailing them an encouraging note, letter, or booklet.

Sample Funeral Sermons

"To Die Is Gain"

"For to me, to live is Christ, and to die is gain." (Phil 1:21)

At the time of the writing of these words, the apostle Paul was in prison. He was probably in his sixties and was facing a probable death sentence. Instead of bemoaning his difficult situation, he wrote a letter to the church at Philippi in order to encourage them. In essence his message is, "Don't worry about me; I am in a win-win situation. To live is Christ and to die is gain."

1. *"To Die Is Gain"*

"To die"—this refers to *physical* death. It references the separation of the soul from the body. The Bible does not measure death by the moment a heart stops beating, but rather by the moment a soul leaves the body. The Bible also mentions *spiritual* death, which describes the separation of the soul from God.

Because our world is stained by sin, death is inevitable for all of us. "And as it is appointed for men to die once, but after this the judgment" (Heb 9:27). Death is an appointment we all must keep. It cannot be avoided or rescheduled.

The Bible clearly teaches that death can be gain or loss.

A. DEATH CAN BE LOSS

> For what will it profit a man if he gains the whole world, and loses his own
> soul? Or what will a man give in exchange for his soul? (Mark 8:36–37)

For the person whose soul is never reconciled to God, death is loss. The
person who refuses a relationship with God in this life will definitely not
receive the joys of one in the next. Heaven, eternity, rewards, reunions with
loved ones, and seeing Jesus are things the lost person will lose out on after
death. The separation their soul experienced from God in earthly life is merely
finalized in death. For the person who does not know Christ, death is loss. No
wonder the program for the funeral service of famous atheist Robert Ingersoll
carried this solemn instruction, "There will be no singing."

B. DEATH CAN BE GAIN

In Paul's case, death was gain. For Paul, the separation of the soul from the
body meant union with Jesus.

> So we are always confident, knowing that while we are at home in the
> body we are absent from the Lord, for we walk by faith, not by sight—
> yet we are confident and satisfied to be out of the body and at home with
> the Lord. (2 Cor 5:6–8)

"Today we are celebrating in that for _____ death is gain. This is the
graduation service, the promotion party, the home-going of our friend. The
psalmist wrote, 'Precious in the sight of the lord is the death of his saints or his
children.' Because of that, we rejoice. _____ is now fully in the presence
of Jesus.

"We do sense the presence of Jesus here today giving us hope and comfort.
But that presence is limited. _____ is in that place where the presence of
Jesus is unlimited, unrestricted and unhindered—heaven."

> In thy presence is fullness of joy. (Ps 16:11)

> And God will wipe away every tear from their eyes; there shall be no
> more death, nor sorrow, nor crying. There shall be no more pain, for the
> former things have passed away. (Rev 21:4)

2. "To Live Is Christ"

"Paul could say, death was gain, because for him, life was Christ. We
can also say that of _____, to die is gain because for _____ life was
centered on Christ."

"Several years ago _____ came to a vital understanding of the facts of the gospel. He accepted the truths that: (1) there is a God; (2) we are accountable to God; (3) we have failed to live up to God's standard, we have sinned; (4) sin separates us from God; (5) the only truly sinless person who ever lives was God's son, Jesus Christ; He is the only one who didn't deserve death; (6) yet, He died for us an innocent sacrifice for our sins; (7) _____ put his trust in Jesus Christ as Lord and Savior.

"_____'s life was wonderfully changed. Christ was given center-stage. _____ began to live for Christ—no longer for self or business, or even family, but for Christ. Because of living for Christ, Christ helped _____ be a better spouse, parent, friend, and employee.

"So today we celebrate life. We celebrate the wonderful life that _____ experienced while with us here on earth. We also celebrate the joyous life that _____ is now experiencing in heaven."

"To Everything There Is a Season"

To everything there is a season, a time for every purpose under heaven:
A time to be born, and a time to die; a time to plant, and a time to pluck
what is planted; . . . a time to weep, and a time to laugh; a time to mourn,
and a time to dance. (Eccl 3:1 NKJV)

"Today is not just an ordinary day for us. Today marks one of those special times and seasons of life. Our confident hope is that for _____ today marks:

1. A Time of True Living and Great Rejoicing

A. TRUE LIVING

"I tell you the truth, whoever hears my word and believes him who sent me has eternal life and will not be condemned; he has crossed over from death to life." (John 5:24 NIV)

"For the Christian a funeral does not mark the end of life, but the graduation to real life. _____ loved God. As a result _____ is not in this casket. Their body is, but they aren't. They have gone on, "crossed over," graduated. They have been promoted to a place called paradise and are more alive than they have ever been.

"God loved (the deceased) and on (day and time of death) God called _____ home. Today they are more alive than ever. They are experiencing life on a far higher, deeper, sweeter level."

B. GREAT REJOICING

"_____ does not want us to feel any sorrow for them today. They are experiencing more joy than they have ever tasted. They are in the presence of Jesus."

> You will show me the path of life, In your presence is fullness of joy.
> (Ps 16:11 NKJV)

"The last few months (the deceased) experienced pain. We need to stop and rejoice today because in heaven _____ is feeling no pain. After a long, hard journey down here on earth, they are home with God and many other loved ones in heaven. They are rejoicing."

> And God will wipe away every tear from their eyes; there shall be no more death, nor sorrow, nor crying. There shall be no more pain, for the former things have passed away. (Rev 21:4 NKJV)

2. A Time of Remembering

"Many of the tears that have been shed the past few days and the next few days are tears of love. They are physical reminders of good memories. It is good to allow your eyes to express what your heart is feeling. As we remember _____ we do so with many good memories.

"Today _____ is warmly remembered as . . ." (This is where you share the appropriate highlights of the favorite memories shared with you by the family members.)

3. A Time for Giving and Receiving Divine Comfort

> Praise be to the God and Father of our Lord Jesus Christ, the Father of compassion and the God of all comfort, who comforts us in all our troubles, so that we can comfort those in any trouble with the comfort we ourselves have received from God. (2 Cor 1:3–4 NIV)

A. GOD COMFORTS US . . .

> Jesus said, "Come to me, all you who are weary and burdened, and I will give you rest [comfort for your souls]." (Matt 11:28)

God is there with a peace that surpasses understanding, but He won't force it on you. You don't get it unless you come to Him and ask for it.

B. . . . SO WE CAN COMFORT OTHERS.

It is sad, but true, that sometimes the only time families come together is at funerals. Sometimes the only time we hug one another is at a funeral home.

Yes, this is a good time and a good place to comfort each other, but let's not let it be the only time and the only place.

4. A Time for Examining

And as it is appointed for man to die once, and after this the judgment. (Heb 9:27 NKJV)

Today, we come face to face with:

A. THE REALITY OF DEATH.

B. THE CERTAINTY OF DEATH.

C. THE INEVITABILITY OF JUDGMENT.

Each of us will give an account of himself to God. (Rom 14:12 NIV)

Although the exam will be comprehensive, the focus will be on two issues:

1. AM I IN THE FAITH?

Examine yourselves to see whether you are in the faith; test yourselves. (2 Cor 13:5 NIV)

Trust in Jesus as Savior (John 3:16) and call upon Him as Lord (Rom 10:13).

2. AM I LIVING WITH ETERNITY IN VIEW?

If _____ could stand here before you and speak today they would say to us, "Please get ready. Heaven is better than I imagined. Don't miss it. I want you to join me here soon. Get ready!"

D. THE NECESSITY OF SALVATION BY GRACE THROUGH FAITH IN JESUS.

- A: Admit you are a sinner and need God.
- B: Believe in Jesus Christ. Believe that Jesus lived a sinless life, died for you, rose again.
- C: Call upon Him to save you; commit your life to Him.
- D: Determine to spend the rest of your life doing what He says.

⁓ What Now? ⁓

If you have not already, you and/or your church should adopt a clear plan for responding to a funeral.

Write out a sample funeral message for the following situations:

- Death of a faithful Christian
- Death of a baby
- Death of a person who was probably not saved

⁓ Quotes ⁓

You represent the love of Christ at a crisis moment. And your loving concern may be just the thing to lead a friend or survivor into Christ's kingdom.

—STAN TOLER[1]

The funeral service poignantly, and pathetically, tenderly and sometimes tragically, cries out for a man of God. Where is he? Does he have any word from the Lord? Oh, for the man of God who can offer help and comfort in this sad hour!

—W. A CRISWELL[2]

Notes

1. Stan Toler, *Stan Toler's Practical Guide to Pastoral Ministry* (Indianapolis, IN: Wesleyan, 2006), 114.

2. W. A. Criswell, *Criswell's Guidebook for Pastors* (Nashville, TN: B&H, 1980), 295.

Appendix: Ordination

The Bible and Ordination

1. Moses ordained Joshua to assume the role of Israel's leader.

   The LORD replied to Moses, "Take Joshua son of Nun, a man
   who has the Spirit in him, and lay your hands on him. Have him
   stand before Eleazar the priest and the whole community, and
   commission him in their sight. Confer some of your authority
   on him so that the entire Israelite community will obey
   [him]. . . ." Moses did as the LORD commanded him. He took
   Joshua, had him stand before Eleazar the priest and the entire
   community, laid his hands on him, and commissioned him, as
   the LORD had spoken through Moses. (Num 27:18–23)

2. The apostles ordained spiritual leaders to assume the role of tending
   to the widows.

   They had them stand before the apostles, who prayed and laid
   their hands on them. (Acts 6:6)

3. Barnabas and Saul were ordained and sent out on a church-planting
   journey from the church of Antioch.

   In the local church at Antioch there were prophets and teachers:
   Barnabas . . . and Saul. As they were ministering to the Lord
   and fasting, the Holy Spirit said, "Set apart for Me Barnabas and
   Saul for the work that I have called them to." Then, after they

had fasted, prayed, and laid hands on them, they sent them off. (Acts 13:1–3)

4. Paul reminded Timothy that he had been ordained by Paul and a council of elders.

> Do not neglect the gift that is in you; it was given to you through prophecy, with the laying on of hands by the council of elders. (1 Tim 4:14)

> Therefore, I remind you to keep ablaze the gift of God that is in you through the laying on of my hands. (2 Tim 1:6)

5. Paul warned Timothy not to be hasty in ordaining others.

> Don't be too quick to lay hands on anyone, and don't share in the sins of others. Keep yourself pure. (1 Tim 5:22)

The Meaning of Ordination

Ordination is an important event in the life of the church leader. The essential ceremony consists of the laying of hands of the ordaining pastor(s) upon the head of the one being ordained, with prayer for the gifts of the Holy Spirit and of grace required for the carrying out of the ministry.

Ordination is understood as signifying three important aspects:

1. Consecration, commissioning, or setting apart for the service of God (Num 27:19).
2. Transmission of a divine gift (Deut 4:9; 1 Tim 4:14; 2 Tim 1:6).
3. Identification as the one being ordained is identified with the authority of the one(s) laying their hands on them (Num 27:20; 1 Tim 5:22).

Ordination is an act performed by a local church as the church's official recognition and confirmation of God's call in the life of a person who is pursuing vocational ministry. It takes note that God is present by the Holy Spirit in the actual act of the ordination prayer, accompanied by the laying on of hands.

Ordination carries with it society's legal and social recognition that a person has a unique function as a church leader. As such, the United States government allows a tax-free housing allowance to be given to a pastor by his church.

Ordination recognizes that the ordained person is authorized to lead certain functions in the church. Depending upon the church, these functions may include the preaching and teaching the Word, presiding at the ordinances, and/ or performing weddings and funerals.

Usually, the person being ordained is a member of the local church that ordains him. Generally, it is recommended that the candidate have at least one year of ministry experience in the leadership of the church so that the congregation can adequately ascertain the candidate's character, calling, giftedness, and effectiveness in the ministry. Often, the process of licensure to the gospel ministry is a precursor to ordination.

The Process of Ordination

1. The ordaining church works with the candidate in calling a council of ordained men to examine the candidate. The candidate prepares a document to give to the council prior to the examination. The document includes five sections:
   - Testimony of the candidate's salvation
   - Testimony of the candidate's call into vocational ministry
   - Testimony of the candidate's spiritual gifts and evidence of fruitfulness in ministry
   - A brief study of the qualifications for church leadership as described in 1 Timothy 3 and Titus 1 and the candidate's status compared with each
   - The candidate's doctrinal statement, including Scripture references to document the candidate's beliefs[1]

2. The ordination council holds an examination of the candidate and his mate and makes the appropriate recommendations to the candidate and the church. If approved, an ordination service is planned.

3. Have an ordination service.
   - Presentation of findings of council
   - A charge to the candidate from one of the members of the council
   - A charge to the church from one of the members of the council
   - Laying on of hands for prayer by the council
   - Gifting the candidate with a new Bible or set of commentaries by the church

Note

1. An example of a doctrinal statement is *The Baptist Faith and Message*, http:// www.sbc.net/bfm/bfm2000.asp (accessed July 4, 2011).

Scripture Index